# MORAL EDUCATION

# Moral Education

A STUDY IN THE
THEORY AND APPLICATION OF THE
SOCIOLOGY OF EDUCATION

## By Emile Durkheim

FOREWORD BY PAUL FAUCONNET

TRANSLATED BY EVERETT K. WILSON AND HERMAN SCHNURER

EDITED, WITH A NEW INTRODUCTION, BY EVERETT K. WILSON

 The Free Press
A Division of Macmillan Publishing Co., Inc.
NEW YORK

COLLIER MACMILLAN PUBLISHERS
LONDON

This edition translated from L'éducation morale,
published by Librarie Félix Alcan, 1925

THE FREE PRESS
A Division of Macmillan Publishing Co., Inc.
866 Third Avenue, New York, N.Y. 10022

Collier Macmillan Canada, Ltd.
Library of Congress Catalog Card Number: 59–6815

Printed in the United States of America
FIRST FREE PRESS PAPERBACK EDITION 1973

Hardbound printing number
3 4 5 6 7 8 9 10
Paperback printing number
7 8 9 10

ISBN: 978-0-0290-8320-8

# ᮃᯱ  FOREWORD

THIS COURSE ON MORAL EDUCATION WAS THE FIRST IN THE
science of education that Durkheim offered at the Sorbonne
in 1902–3. He had for some time sketched it out in his
teaching at Bordeaux. He repeated it later, e.g., in 1906–7,
without change or editing. The course consisted of twenty
lectures. We present here only eighteen; the first two dealt
with methods of teaching. The introductory lecture was
published in January, 1903, in the *Revue de métaphysique
et de morale* and reproduced in the small volume *Éducation
et sociologie*, published in 1922.[1]

Durkheim wrote out his lectures *in extenso*. The reader
will find here a textual reproduction of his manuscript. Our
corrections are purely matters of form or are substantively
insignificant, and we have felt it unnecessary to indicate them.
In any case, they do not affect the thought.

We ask the reader to indulge the inevitable shortcomings
of the book. Almost invariably, the beginning of a lecture
overlaps the past pages of the preceding lecture: Durkheim
repeated himself in order to tie things up better, or to
develop further what he had not had time to handle the
preceding week. To correct this defect it would have been
necessary to undertake extensive and inevitably arbitrary

---

1. The recently published American edition was translated, with an introduction, by Sherwood D. Fox (Glencoe, Ill.: The Free Press, 1956).

changes. We concluded that purely literary compunctions ought not prevail over the regard due the original text. Moreover, the two successive treatments often differ in some interesting details.

The first part of the course, which Durkheim left more complete, deals with what is called moral theory—theory of duty, of the good, of autonomy. One part of these lectures went into a communication on "The Determination of Moral Behavior," inserted in the *Bulletin de la société française de philosophie*, in 1906, and reprinted in the volume entitled *Philosophie et sociologie* (1924).[2] The same questions would have been taken up again in the introduction of *La morale*, on which Durkheim was working during the last months of his life, and of which Marcel Mauss has given a fragment in the *Revue philosophique*, LXXXIX (1920), 79. Doubtless Durkheim's thinking had changed on certain points between 1902 and 1917.

The second part of the course, paralleling the first, should comprise three sections—one on the spirit of discipline, the second on sacrifice and altruism, and the third on autonomy of the will—each of them studied this time from a specifically pedagogical point of view. The last of these three sections is missing here. Education in autonomy is a matter of moral instruction in the elementary school, a subject to which Durkheim had many times—notably in 1907–8—devoted a whole year's course. The manuscript for this course is not so organized as to permit publication.

The lectures do not correspond exactly with the chapters and often in the course of one lecture a transition to the following subject is effected. The plan of the work is given in the table of contents.

PAUL FAUCONNET
*Lecturer at the Sorbonne*

---

2. This volume is available in an English translation by D. F. Pocock (Glencoe, Ill.: The Free Press, 1953).

# ◄§ PREFACE

PROFESSOR FAUCONNET'S FOREWORD WOULD SERVE VERY WELL
to get this essay under way were it not for three circumstances that differentiate this from the edition of 1925.[1]
First, that was in French and this is in English. Thus, the
translator must follow ancient precedent by stressing the
non-equivalence of key terms and the plausibility of the decisions made in rendering difficult terms. Second, in the
French edition, M. Fauconnet's editorial decision was *stet*;
our decision has been the very opposite. Third, the French
edition went to an audience quite familiar with Durkheim's
work. Beyond the small fraternity of sociologists, one cannot
assume familiarity for a United States audience.

Problems of translation stemmed chiefly from two sources.
First, Durkheim's conception of society involves him in the
use of terms that have mystical, even supernatural, conno-
tations for English and American readers. Society, as he
states toward the end of the last chapter, is not bound in
time and space, since it is "first of all a complex of ideas
and sentiments, of ways of seeing and feeling, a certain
intellectual and moral framework distinctive of the entire
group. . . . society is above all a [shared] consciousness,
[and] it is therefore this collective consciousness that must
be imparted to the child." And so we are confronted with
words like *conscience, esprit, représentations collectives,* and

---

1. *L'éducation morale* (Paris: Libraire Félix Alcan, 1925).

*âme,* all of which refer in one way or another to the knowledge, beliefs, and values shared by members of the group. Such terms have been rendered in each case as the context required. Durkheim was expressing some important ideas half a century ago—powerful and influential ideas, congenial to much current thinking in sociology and social psychology, if not to education. But the translator must take care lest the language repel the reader or obscure Durkheim's intended meaning.

A second problem of translation results from the very significance of Durkheim's ideas. Precisely because they are still relevant, still fruitful, there is the danger of over-modernizing him. We have tried not to put current terminology in his mouth except where his meaning might otherwise be unclear.

Hence, we could not follow M. Fauconnet's decision for Durkheim's French audience of 1925. What he did, in effect, was to hand a set of classroom lectures to the printer. We have had to translate and edit with a different audience in mind. Our concern has been to convey Durkheim's ideas; and to eliminate everything that might impede this communication. The translation is free. We have omitted redundant phrases here and there. Conscious of the danger of reading the present into the past we have, nonetheless, occasionally used current terminology—e.g., rendering *role* as "function"—where Durkheim's intent seemed to justify it. We have italicized where it served to clarify the author's meaning. We have substituted the word "chapter" for "lecture" throughout. In short, we have done whatever seemed necessary to bridge some fifty years and two languages in order to bring Durkheim's ideas on moral education to an English-reading audience.

Ann Arbor, Michigan                    E.K.W.
Yellow Springs, Ohio                 H.S.

## ✍ EDITOR'S INTRODUCTION

I SHALL USE THESE INTRODUCTORY PAGES TO SEVERAL ENDS: TO highlight for the reader Durkheim's idea of morality and his view of the school as the appropriate setting for moral education; to comment on Durkheim's influence on contemporary social thought, noting the possibility that morality may be founded in the predictability of others' responses. Finally, there is the matter of the priority of the group in matters of the good—as well as those of the true and the beautiful— Durkheim's alleged "sociologism." These do not exhaust the issues. Rather, they provide various ways of thinking about this work.

A conventional introduction would sketch pivotal points in Durkheim's life. His 59 years (1858–1917) followed almost immediately the 68 years of Auguste Comte's life, so providing symbolic continuity in the development of French social thought. We might follow him from Épinal in eastern France to l'École Normale Supérieure in Paris, note the influence of Émile Boutroux (the notion of emergent levels of reality) and of Fustel de Coulanges, recall his appointment at Bordeaux for a few years, and his return to Paris where he taught, wrote, founded *l'Année Sociologique,* and worked for the ministry of education. But there is no point in repeating biographical details recounted elsewhere.¹ Here, I should like to fix on the major themes in *Moral Education*, and on related issues bearing on Durkheim's social theory.

In our times, and despite the profound moral problems posed by war, poverty, and race, morality remains a niggling word implying an obsequious and unpalatable primness. For Durkheim, however, morality was crucial, from both a theoretical and a practical point of view. Theoretically, any enduring system of human relationships must be seen as intrinsically moral, involving obligatory elements that coerce conduct and which, since they represent shared conceptions of the good, provide the basis for social unity. From a practical standpoint, a sound secular morality was for Durkheim the condition of national health—or even survival.

" 'Our first obligation at this time is to create a moral consensus.' Thus Durkheim concludes his thesis which began with the assertion 'that science can help us determine the way in which we ought to orient our conduct.' "² The critical times inspired a real anxiety in Durkheim, and he did not think the intellectual exempt from the obligation to apply his special knowledge. "Voir pour prévoir; prévoir pour pouvoir." Durkheim accepted the Comtean injunction. In both *The Division of Labor*³ and *The Rules of Sociological Method*,⁴ he asserts that the ultimate justification for basic research lies in its practical uses. The art-for-art's-sake argument would have been altogether inconsistent with a theory that views man as preeminently a social creation, endowed with society's gifts of

1. See especially the excellent sketch in Part I of Harry Alpert, *Émile Durkheim and His Sociology* (New York: Columbia University Press, 1939), and the more recent paperbacks by Robert Bierstedt and George Simpson cited below.

2. Georges Gurvitch, "La morale de Durkheim," in *Essais de sociologie* (Paris: Libraire du Recueil Sirey, 1939), p. 279.

3. Émile Durkheim, *The Division of Labor in Society*, trans. George Simpson (Glencoe, Ill.: Free Press, 1949).

4. Émile Durkheim, *The Rules of Sociological Method*, trans. Sarah A. Solovay and John H. Mueller, ed. George E. G. Catlin (Glencoe, Ill.: Free Press, 1950).

mind and literacy, and both responsive and responsible to this single source of his humanity. His objective was the moral integration that he saw as necessary for the well-being of French society—or, for that matter, of any society. This unity he would build on a secular morality, founded in reason rather than revealed religion. And the seedbed for germinating this morality was, he contended, the public school.

Part I of this work, therefore, presents a theory of morality that grew out of years of inquiry and reflection. It lays the foundation for practical prescriptions addressed to the teacher in Part II. The theoretical discussion is so central not only to this work, but to the whole pattern of Durkheim's thought, that it deserves special emphasis.

## The Nature
## of Morality

Durkheim begins, as is his wont, with definitions. What is meant by morality as we see it in practice? Certainly it involves consistency, regularity of conduct: What is moral today must be moral tomorrow. It also invariably involves some sense of authority: We are constrained to act in certain ways; we feel a resistance to strictly idiosyncratic impulses. Now, these two features of morality—regularity of conduct and authority—are, in fact, aspects of a single thing: discipline. (The union of different or apparently antithetical aspects of reality in a single conception is a familiar tactic with Durkheim. He uses the reverse procedure, too. A single concept, such as suicide, is subdivided or qualified so as to provide an exhaustive and exclusive classification of the phenomena under inquiry.) Thus, the first element of morality is discipline, compounded by regularity of conduct and authority.

But discipline is not to be viewed as sheer constraint, for at least two reasons. In the first place, it predetermines appropriate modes of response, without which order and organized life would be unthinkable. It emancipates us from the need to contrive each solution *de novo*. Second, it responds to the individual's need for restraint, enabling him to reach, successively, determinate goals. Without such limits, he would suffer the inevitable frustration and disillusionment entailed by limitless aspiration. (Here we see reflected a central theme of Durkheim's classic study, *Suicide*.)

Morality means an impersonal orientation of activity. Self-serving action is never regarded as moral. But if behavior properly deemed moral is not oriented toward the self, what object is its proper focus? Since others cannot legitimately demand gratification which, if directed toward ourselves, would be amoral, the object of moral behavior must be something beyond the person, or beyond any number of individuals *qua* individuals. What is left, then, as the object of moral behavior is the group, or society. "To act morally is to act in terms of the collective interest . . . the domain of the moral begins where the domain of the social begins."⁵ Thus, we arrive at the second element of morality: attachment to, or identification with, the group.

Once again, both these elements of morality are aspects of a single thing: society. Discipline is society seen as the father, as commanding us, as prompting us to do our duty. Attachment to the group implies society as mother, the image of the good, attracting us.

Finally, as in all good academic enumerations, there remains a third element. The third essential of morality is autonomy. If strictly self-centered conduct must be regarded as amoral, that which denies the agent's autonomy is equally so; for controlled behavior is not good behavior. Yet Durkheim has strongly emphasized the coercive character of the first two elements of morality—discipline and commitment to the group. How does he resolve this dilemma? Reliable knowledge

---

5. Émile Durkheim, *L'éducation morale* (Paris: Libraire Félix Alcan, 1925), p. 68.

is the answer. The difference between self-determination and submission lies in the ability to predict accurately the consequences of alternative courses of action. Autonomy entails a personal decision in full knowledge of the inexorable consequences of different courses of action. Thus, an understanding of the laws of morality promotes autonomy. A comparable situation is this: On a cold and blustery day, a man has the option of donning his Bermuda shorts and T-shirt or his overcoat and muffler. He *freely* chooses in accordance with the laws of health, which point to differing consequences for different choices. Fundamental to the notion of autonomy is the imperative need for a science of morality.[6]

These are the major theses in Durkheim's theoretical discussion of moral education. They are aspects of a conception of education that differs dramatically from that which apparently prevails among Americans. For us, education is much more child-centered, an individual matter, an enterprise dedicated, as the stock phrase puts it, to the maximum development of the individual personality.[7] The adaptation of curriculum, personnel, and facilities to the needs of the individual child—this is the great good in the pantheon of pedagogical virtues.

It is at least plausible that this emphasis on the individual child, in American education, draws support from: (1) a short history in which the self-reliance and self-determination of frontier life became celebrated elements of the American way; (2) a tradition in Protestant theology that minimized the community and emphasized a personal responsibility, both for success and salvation—if these are to be differently construed; (3) the virtual monopoly of psychology, among the

6. This expression of a need for a science of morality points to the core of Durkheim's conception of society and the nature of sociology. In 1893, he wrote as the first sentence of his preface to *Division of Labor*: "This book is pre-eminently an attempt to treat the facts of the moral life according to the methods of the positive sciences." *Op. cit.,* p. 32.

7. See, for a contrast, Urie Bronfenbrenner's comparison with education in the U.S.S.R., *Two Worlds of Childhood: U.S. and U.S.S.R.* (New York: Russell Sage Foundation, 1970).

social sciences, over matters of educational theory and practice. The great preoccupation with testing, beginning with World War I, led to instruments promoting a fix on the individual. With few exceptions, the contributions in learning theory and perception bore on individual processes. In the United States, Willard Waller was, for many years, almost the only observer who expressed the view that something might be gained by looking at a school system *as a social system*—as a system of interdependent and interlocking roles.[8]

If we have erred on the side of excessive individualism, Durkheim stands ready to rectify the imbalance. For him, education is above all a social means to a social end—the means by which a society guarantees its own survival. The teacher is society's agent, the critical link in cultural transmission. It is his task to create a social, a moral, being. Through him, society creates man in its image. "That," says Durkheim, "is the task and the glory of education. It is not merely a matter of allowing an individual to develop in accordance with his nature, disclosing whatever hidden capacities lie there only waiting to be revealed. *Education creates a new being.*[9] (Elle crée dans l'homme un être nouveau.)

## The School
## as Setting for
## Moral Education

For us in the United States, the school has become increasingly important in unanticipated ways. Although the figure is

---

8. Of course, one could scarcely accuse John Dewey of neglecting the social aspects of education. But the reference here is to research on and within the school or classroom as a social system. Dewey's insights leaped from the philosophic to the applied level. The intervening level, that of social analysis and empirical research, was left pretty much virgin territory. Certainly Willard Waller's work stood out in splendid isolation. See his *The Sociology of Teaching* (New York: John Wiley and Co., 1932).

9. Émile Durkheim, *Education et sociologie* (Paris: Félix Alcan, 1922), p. 51.

inelegant, one might suggest that the school is used as an institutional trash can, taking on a host of residual activities either relinquished or not yet pre-empted by other agencies—such as driver-training, entertainment, babysitting, domestic and industrial arts, guidance and therapy, and the like. For Durkheim, the school had a crucial and clearly specified function: to create a new being, shaped according to the needs of society. While this might seem restrictive and repressive to child-centered educators, Durkheim argues that the very reverse is true. Only by imposing limits can the child be liberated from the inevitable frustrations of incessant striving. Only as the child is systematically exposed to his country's cultural heritage can he achieve a sense of identity and personal fulfillment. Only as he is conscious of his implication in a society to which he is bound by duty and desire can he become a moral being. In short, excessive individualism in education can lead to personal defeat and social chaos. Moral education is the specific against such maladies.

The exclusion of clerical influence from the French public schools is quite understandable to people whose constitution specifies a separation of church and state. But a proposal for systematic instruction in a secular morality stripped of all supernatural elements doubtless would be pushing things too far. Yet, just such a secular morality is what Durkheim is proposing and what, in effect, was becoming an integral part of the public school program in France.

Why is the school the proper setting for moral education? Durkheim eliminates the church because a sound morality must be founded in reason, not revelation. The family is out since the indulgent warmth of kinship ties is incompatible with the sterner demands of morality. If the family, small and intimate as it has become, can provide emotional support and tension release, it is not the setting for cultivating the abstract idea of duty. On the other hand, moral education cannot be deferred until adulthood, nor can it be entrusted to adult agencies whose demands are excessive for a young child. So the task of moral education devolves upon the school. Ways of accomplishing the task are discussed in Part II. Although some of these lectures date back to 1903, any reader interested in the problems of education will find many provocative ideas. While the argument is often better than the evidence, Durkheim is always perceptive, the issues are topical and relevant, and the discussion is profitable. For example, it would be enormously useful were teachers to discuss seriously Durkheim's suggestions on school discipline and punishment or the part to be played by biology and other sciences in moral education. Consider these assertions:

Punishment does not give discipline its authority; but it prevents discipline from losing its authority.

Severity of treatment is justified only to the extent that it is necessary to make disapproval of the act utterly unequivocal.

For the child . . . punishment is only the palpable symbol through which an inner state is represented: it is a notation, a language through which either the general social conscience or that of the school teacher expresses the feeling inspired by the deviant behavior.

The true sanction . . . is blame.

Thus, we have a principle on which we can rely for determining what punishment in the school ought to be. Since to punish is to reproach, the best punishment is that which puts the blame . . . in the most expressive but least costly way possible.[10]

Or again, think of the implications for education of such statements as these:

To forestall simplistic thinking [he has alleged that the French are peculiarly vulnerable to the simplistic reductionism of Descartes' philosophy] . . . we must convey the need for experimentation, for observation, and the necessity of getting out of ourselves and submitting to the teachings of experience, if we really want to know and to understand.

The biological sciences are especially useful in making the child under-

---

10. Translated from *L'éducation morale*, pp. 213–232, *passim*.

stand the complexity of things . . . the cell is a perfect demonstration
of [such complexity]. . . . That small living mass is of course made up
of inorganic elements—atoms of hydrogen, oxygen, nitrogen, and carbon . . . which, in combination and association, suddenly manifest new
properties characterizing life. Here is one thing that will make the
child understand . . . that in one sense a whole is not identical with
the sum of its parts. This can lead him on the road to understanding
that society is not simply the sum of individuals who compose it.[11]

Thus, we find in Part II prescriptions for pedagogical practice in the service of sharpening children's moral sensibilities.

Despite the often redundant stress in our curricula on problems of American democracy, civics, and American history—
matters germane to Durkheim's thesis—there is little evidence
that he has had any impact on education in the United States.
This is not the case in other spheres. And it is worthwhile to
set this study in context by considering other facets of social
thought where Durkheim's influence has been marked.

## Influence on
## Contemporary
## Social Thought

Durkheim's influence persists, but in attenuated fashion.
Ten years ago, in trying to trace his impact on empirical research in the United States (inquiries into suicide, anomie,
division of labor, social integration, and the like), I found 60
studies, three-fourths of them published in the just preceding
decade.[12] Thus, the use of Durkheim's ideas seemed vastly to
accelerate between 1950 and 1960. Since then, my impression
is that his *acknowledged* influence has declined. For example,
over the past five years, the official journal of the American
Sociological Association has carried only one article clearly

---

11. From this translation, pp. 263–264.
12. Everett K. Wilson, "L'influence de Durkheim aux États-Unis: Re-
cherches empiriques sur le suicide," *Revue Française de Sociologie*, Vol. 4,
No. 1 (January–March 1963), pp. 3–11.

directed at a Durkheimian thesis,[13] and among hundreds of citations, only twenty-five refer to him.

If it is indeed the case that Durkheim is not so prominent today, I would guess that it is so because his ideas have been both assimilated (unfortunately and erroneously so, Douglas would contend[14]) and displaced. The socially uniting effect of the division of labor, the influence of population density on specialization, the link between religion, education, marital status and suicide rates, concepts such as anomie and social integration (and even such murky terms as collective representation, or mechanical and organic solidarity) have crept into the lingo of the social sciences, becoming so commonplace that their borrowers honor the author by using them without attribution. But Durkheim also has been displaced by other men and interests. Marx is being rediscovered as a sociologist. Spencer ("Who now reads Spencer?" Talcott Parsons asked in 1937) is enjoying a revival with the quickened interest in evolution.[15] And he has been displaced by new theoretical, ideological, and methodological interests. In social theory, functionalism has been under attack, yielding by error or default to conflict theory, or critical sociology. And Durkheim has been identified—correctly, I think, although George Simpson would disagree[16]—with functionalism. As to ideology,

13. Theodore D. Kemper, "The Division of Labor: A Post-Durkheimian Analytical View, ASR, Vol. 37, No. 6 (December 1972). Of course, his influence appears in many other places. For example, a very useful paperback by Stephen Cole, The Sociological Method (Chicago: Markham, 1972), begins with Durkheim's study of suicide as an example of the sociological perspective.

14. Jack D. Douglas, The Social Meanings of Suicide (Princeton, N.J.: Princeton University Press, 1967).

15. See, for example, the stimulating work by J. D. Y. Peel, Herbert Spencer: The Evolution of a Sociologist (New York: Basic Books, 1971).

16. Simpson writes testily: "to portray him [Durkheim] as the father of the arid 'functionalism' found in the works of Talcott Parsons and Robert K. Merton is a disservice and a flight from moral philosophy. This functionalism emphasizes but a single aspect of Durkheim's thought, and, in my opinion, not the most important one." Émile Durkheim: Selections from His Work with an Introduction and Commentaries by George Simpson (New York: Thomas Y. Crowell, 1963), p. ix.

Durkheim has been stigmatized as offering static, cross-sectional social theories that have the effect of blessing whatever is (while failing to explain, much less appreciate, social change). Here, too, there are dissenters, for the very competent intellectual historian Anthony Giddens asserts that Durkheim was preoccupied not with the problem of order, but with the problem of the changing nature of order.[17] As to methodology, professional concern with such matters as the assessment of measurement error, factor analysis, Markov chains, or harmonic series models tends to drive social and moral philosophy into the background. And so Durkheim fades to the wings.

This is not to say that he is dead or doing poorly. In addition to the works of Giddens and Simpson, there are others who attest to his vitality. Nisbet has collected some essays on Durkheim.[18] Robert Bierstedt has brought together selections from his chief works.[19] And, recently, Ernest Wallwork has produced a careful study of Durkheim that bears directly on *Moral Education*.[20] For Wallwork contends that Durkheim was, first of all, a moral philosopher and that his sociology derived from his moral posture. This is an intriguing suggestion for the sociology of science: the influence of moral (or religious) commitments for ideas and achievement in different vocations. One recalls the suggestion that sons of ministers were disproportionately represented in the development of sociology in the United States. Certainly it is clear, as Durkheim says here, that the realm of the moral is the realm of the social. For above all else, morality defines the good, true,

---

17. See his *Capitalism and Modern Social Theory: An Analysis of The Writings of Marx, Durkheim and Weber* (Cambridge: Cambridge University Press, 1971).
18. *Émile Durkheim* (Englewood Cliffs, N.J.: Prentice-Hall, 1965).
19. Robert Bierstedt, *Émile Durkheim: A Biography Interwoven with the Writings of the French Sociologist and Philosopher* (N.Y.: Dell, 1966).
20. *Durkheim: Morality and Milieu* (Cambridge, Mass.: Harvard University Press, 1972).

and beautiful in human relationships. It is not surprising, then, that there is some affinity between a clerical tradition and sociological analysis.

But to say that persistent patterns of human relationships are necessarily evaluated by the actors as good and informed with a sense of the obligatory—in other words, to say that the moral is an inevitable aspect of the social—is a far cry from asserting, as Durkheim does, that there can be a *science* of morality. Catlin derides Durkheim's attempt to build such a science. "There is . . . nothing to be said for Durkheim's attempt to have the best of both worlds [that of the *is* and the *ought*: the scientifically demonstrable and the ideal to be sought] and to survey the realm of values with a tape measure."[21] But the assertion is too glib. Weber appears to make a similar assertion: ". . . the validity of a practical imperative *as a norm* and the truth-value of an empirical proposition are absolutely heterogeneous in character."[22] But we must agree, as Durkheim and Weber would, that given a valued end, objective analysis can enable us to (1) select from among various means that which leads with least cost to its achievement, (2) estimate the consequences of pursuing that goal, and (3) as between that goal and another, determine which is more compatible with some other, more remote end.

Now there is something here that is consistent with Durkheim's third element of morality: autonomy. Beyond the imperatives of law and the attractions of the ideal (the givens in a concrete social setting), there is the matter of means–ends linkages. The means are not automatically given to fulfill requirements or achieve ideals. The personal self-determination, or autonomy, without which the person would be utterly subservient and his required behavior amoral, if not

---

21. In his introduction to Durkheim's *The Rules of Sociological Method* (Chicago, Ill.: University of Chicago Press, 1938), p. xxxi.

22. Max Weber, *The Methodology of the Social Sciences* (Glencoe, Ill.: Free Press, 1949), p. 12.

immoral, is brought into play in the choice of correct means. Morality means not only that I *must* but that I *want* to; and not only that I want to, but that my *reason* (science) tells me that certain actions are the best available means to a desired end. Duty and desire—each in its way—are external to the person. We are required, we are drawn by the strength and benefactions of the group. But autonomy, the third element of morality, represents personal choice in the light of reason. But is not reason—or rationality—itself constraining, damping out choice and spontaneity? Durkheim answers, No, and for much the same reason that Weber refuses to equate freedom with the irrational or unpredictable.

The characteristic of "incalculability" . . . is the privilege of—the insane. On the other hand, we associate the highest measure of an empirical "feeling of freedom" with those actions which we are conscious of performing rationally, in which we pursue a clearly perceived end by "means" which are the most adequate in accordance with the extent of our knowledge, i.e., in accordance with empirical *rules*.[23]

The first two elements of morality seem to point to ends, the third to the choice of means for their achievement. After the attack on Pearl Harbor, we know it is our duty to defend our country; and we know it is good to do so. But the means by which such ends are to be served depend on our reasoned assessment of collective needs and our particular capacities. Whenever, through reason or experiment, we can assess alternate means, the application of science to moral issues becomes feasible. And, if we conceive the possibility that a given end may be transformed into one of several means to a more distant goal, then the application of reason to all but the most remote end is feasible. Thus, all but the ultimate moral issue may be approached scientifically.

23. *The Methodology of the Social Sciences* (Glencoe, Ill.: Free Press, 1949), pp. 124–125.

*The Moral
Defined by
the Recurrent and
Predictable*

At various points in his writings, Durkheim contends that patterns of behavior persisting over fair periods of time must be assumed to have some useful consequences for some part of the social system in which they appear. Thus, the persistence of both religious and criminal behaviors have moral elements.

...it is an essential postulate of sociology that a human institution cannot rest upon an error and a lie ... if it were not founded in the nature of things, it would have encountered in the facts a resistance over which it could never have triumphed ... in reality, then, there are no religions which are false.[24]

Or again,

Crime is, then, necessary; it is bound up with the fundamental conditions of all social life, and by that very fact it is useful [good? moral?] because these conditions of which it is a part are themselves indispensable to the normal evolution of morality and law.[25]

The link between regularly recurring behaviors and positive moral evaluations is worth pondering.[26] Durkheim provides a distinctively sociological explanation. Recurrent violations of the law provide the occasions, through legal proceedings, for recurrent affirmation of common values. The courtroom is the secular counterpart of the cathedral. The weekday trial and the Sunday mass promote similar (moral) ends.

---

24. *The Elementary Forms of the Religious Life* (Glencoe, Ill.: Free Press, 1947), pp. 2, 3.
25. *The Rules of Sociological Method* (Chicago, Ill.: University of Chicago Press, 1938).
26. This proposition is empirically supported in an inquiry by Professor Philip W. Blumstein, in his study of "Subjective Probability and Normative Evaluations," *Social Forces*, Vol. 51, No. 1 (September 1973).

Or, at a more abstract level, persistent patterns of behavior (including criminal conduct) are linked with the nature of the social structure. For example, persisting levels of white collar crime are tied to the distribution of power, enabling the privileged to preserve and enhance their advantage. And, of course, if the rich, the well born, and the able define the moral—by invoking the ideology of social Darwinism, let us say—then a certain morality is sustained by a stable level of white collar crime. But, as Durkheim implies, inequities supported by a prevailing power structure and opposed, say, by an antithetical stress on equality of opportunity, may lead "to the normal evolution of morality and law." One requires both thesis and antithesis in the dialectical evolution of morality.

Consistent with his insistence that social facts can only be explained by other social facts, Durkheim does not entertain another possibility. We might suppose that positive moral evaluations lead to regularly recurring behaviors: Learning what the elders define as good (and the associated sanctions), we proceed to act that way. But consider the possibility that it is not their intrinsic goodness, or the indoctrinated appraisal of acts as good, but their *regularity* that leads to a positive evaluation. As the previous quotation from Weber indicates, a world of random events is an insane world. And we know what happened to Pavlov's animal when the stimulus–response sequence was unpredictably disrupted. So it is plausible that some underlying association with health, in a basic neurological way, may account for the positive moral judgment attached to highly probable behaviors. And certainly, such recurrences are linked with a sense of control. Perhaps, deep in our glands, we have a feeling of impotence in the face of unanticipated consequences. It is only with a high probability of covariance that we have some control over our fates. Thus, we evaluate the likely, positively.

Should this be the case, we can understand why the customary equals the moral, and why established ways, however evil they may be, resist change. We might better understand why false consciousness persists—why the deprived and disadvantaged can prefer existing conditions when change might, by objective calculation, improve their lot.

This might seem to out-Homans Homans—a reduction of social explanation to the neurological level. This is a superficial conclusion. If morality and custom in the group, integrity and habit in the individual are grounded in neurological inertia, this is something we may take as a constant. The task of sociology is not to explain the fact of social patterns. These are evident always and everywhere. The questions arise from the *differences* in patterns. What is common to all men may well be grounded in biophysical attributes. What *differs* among men does so in accord with social circumstance.

## The Social Creation of Morality

From one perspective, Durkheim looks like a cultural anthropologist, for the shared meanings so primal in his social analysis ("collective representations" or the "collective conscience") are indeed the core of culture. From another perspective, he is pure sociologist, following the ratio of civil to criminal sanctions (restitutive to retributive) over time as an index of the changing nature of the social order: the shift from a social identity based on likenesses to one based on the interlocking of complementary specialties.

But, from a third perspective, he is social psychologist, finding in group characteristics the explanations for individual conduct—as, for example, suicide. (He would disagree, of course, that suicide as he studies it is individual conduct. He studies suicide rates, and rates are not individual but collective measures. But an aggregation of individual acts still lacks the interactional binder of group life.)

It was as a social psychologist that Durkheim aroused most critical response. For, it was alleged, he hypostatized the group giving it a reality independent of the persons who composed it, temporally and causally prior to the individual, and exercising an uninfluenced influence on the individual.

The accusation has a touch of hyperbole and reminds one of the endless controversy over Marx's alleged one-way causal sequence, from material substructure to social and psychological superstructure. But it *is* clear that for Durkheim *homo sapiens* derived from *homo gregarius*. In the beginning was not the word, but social intercourse. With Marx he would agree: It is not men's consciousness that determines the conditions of social existence, but quite the reverse. Social reality is out there, a refractory reality emerging from the combination of parts—that is to say, of persons. The person then reflects and reacts to this emergent reality. (In Marx's terms, we have here the irony of history. Men create a social reality that then turns back on them engendering, in the bourgeois epoch, unanticipated consequences: a deepening gulf between classes, repression, alienation.)

This social psychological perspective was reflected by scholars working with Durkheim in producing the *Année sociologique*—and others less directly associated with him. The nature of group life shapes the way men think, feel, remember—and what they deem moral. Thus, Maurice Halbwachs, in *Les cadres sociaux de la mémoire*,[27] stresses the social determination of that which is to be remembered, the way such memories are to be evoked and celebrated, and the integrative effect of group memorials. Lévy-Bruhl studied modes of thought under these assumptions: The problems men judge significant, the mode of solving them, the range of tolerable solutions—these differ according to social context.[28] And ten years before this, the social origins of categories of thought

27. Paris, Presses Universitaires de France, 1952 (first edition, 1925).
28. *Mental Process in Primitive Groups, Primitive Mentality,* and *The Soul of the Primitive* (Paris: Alcan, 1923, 1925, and 1927, respectively).

was a central interest in Durkheim's study of religion. Others, influenced by Durkheimian views, analyzed psychic traits—cognition, emotion, and volition—as products of group life.[29] The same orientation informs this essay on moral education. The duty imposed by the group, the affection generated by one's fellows, the use of reason with which the group endows us, and the group's social mechanism (education) through which duty, affection, and reason are generated—these constitute the social seedbed of morality. This is what has led critics to label Durkheim as a social realist and to the dubbing of his school of thought as "sociologism."[30] Durkheim's social realism, or "sociologism," has been an issue for 75 years. Entailing the assertion of generally shared meanings, emerging from people's dealings with one another (but differing from any individual cognition or conviction), external to each and coercing each, this perspective has run into heavy sailing. There is, for example, the muddiness of those transcendent meanings called collective representations which we apprehend only indirectly, through various indices. The stress on shared meanings, or consensus, as the condition of social life leads to the neglect of omnipresent conflict. To fix on the functional utility of all persisting behaviors (and the ideas underlying them) is to emphasize conditions of social stability and to neglect social change. Finally, Durkheim attends little to those processes through which people work out the rules to govern their transactions. In the following statement, he stresses the last six words; the first dozen also require attention.

Whenever certain elements combine and thereby produce, by the fact of their combination, new phenomena, it is plain that these phe-

---

29. For example, Charles Blondel, in his Introduction à la psychologie collective (Paris, 1928) asserts that what men feel, the conditions under which feeling is evoked, and the mode of expressing feelings are group products.

30. See Pitirim A. Sorokin, Contemporary Social Theories (New York: Harper, 1928), and Emile Benoît-Smullyan, "The Sociologism of Émile Durkheim and His School," in Harry Elmer Barnes, ed., An Introduction to the History of Sociology (Chicago, Ill.: University of Chicago Press, 1948).

nomena reside not in the original elements but in the totality formed by their union.[31]

The attack is carried forward in various ways. A contemporary foe, Mr. George Homans, raises the question: What is there in social life beyond the hedonistic exchange of two or more parties? He answers: not much. At any rate, this is where we start, with the elemental acts of two or more persons, illuminated with propositions drawn from behavioral psychology and economics. The ethnomethodologists, like the Skinnerians, hope to explain social conduct and social creations without invoking the milieu of meaning conveyed through tradition and imposed through custom, varying from place to place and time to time. They will not accept culture —as Durkheim is held to have accepted it—as a given, but as a continuous creation which must be observed and interpreted first hand. Morality is seen as a process rather than a fixed and given attribute.

Doubtless there is a tail and a trunk and a tusk. One suspects, though, that there may also be an elephant. Personal experience, theory, and research lead to the conviction of supra-individual sources of moral life. Despite Mr. Catlin's carpings, there is something persuasive about George Herbert Mead's notion of the "generalized other." Solomon Asch (before him, Muzafer Sherif and after him, Robert Rosenthal) has offered empirical evidence of group influence on individuals' beliefs and behavior.[32] A current stress in the explanation of delinquency, labelling theory, underlines the way in which deviants are created by the responses of others. Carefully constructed probability polls reveal climates of opinion

---

31. *The Rules of Sociological Method* (Chicago, Ill.: University of Chicago Press, 1938), p. xlvii.

32. Both Sherif and Asch provide research evidence as to how perception of a physical object—pinpoint of light and length of line—are influenced by others' judgment. Rosenthal's work illustrates how the false perception of an object—such as the student seen as exceptionally able—leads to actions that create an exceptionally able student.

(collective representations). And current research makes plausible the notion of a world of covert or subliminal stimuli constituting an influential milieu—influential since each of us shapes his behavior by internalizing the significant aspects of his environment.[33] The illustrations could be multiplied. No social scientist acts as though the elephant were a fiction.

\*    \*    \*

This is not, obviously, to suggest that all's right on the French front. But it is to assert that Durkheim offers us the legacy of a powerful mind, a legacy that, to date, has stimulated more fruitful research than that of any other sociologist —Marx, Weber, Simmel, Pareto, to say nothing of lesser mortals.

This work is probably his least well known, despite its being the best illustration of Durkheim's applied sociology. There is much that is wrong in this essay. Child psychology has advanced considerably beyond the state in which James Sully left it, and neither anthropologist nor sociologist will be content with much of Durkheim's evidence and some of his argument. Yet, despite the dross, the gold in Durkheim sparkles through, in those perceptive and provocative propositions that demonstrate their generative power by the response they produce in us.

EVERETT K. WILSON
Chapel Hill, North Carolina

---

33. See, for example, "Covert Behavior in Interpersonal Interaction," by Leonard S. Cottrell, Jr., *Proceedings of the American Philosophical Society*, Vol. 115, No. 6 (December 1971).

# CONTENTS

# Part II: How to Develop
# the Elements of Morality in the Child

# MORAL EDUCATION

# CHAPTER ONE

# ✍ INTRODUCTION:

# SECULAR MORALITY

I PROPOSE TO TALK ABOUT MORAL EDUCATION AS AN EDU-
cator; therefore, I ought to give you my conception of education at the very outset. I have previously suggested that we
are not dealing with a science.[1] A science of education is
not impossible; but education itself is not that science. This
distinction is necessary lest we judge education by standards
applicable only to strictly scientific research. Scientific inquiry must proceed most deliberately; it does not have to
meet deadlines. Education is not justified in being patient
to the same extent; it must supply answers to vital needs
that brook no delay. When a change in the environment
demands appropriate action of us, our hand is forced. All
that the educator can and should do is to combine as conscientiously as possible all the data that science puts at his
disposal, at a given moment, as a guide to action. No one
can ask more of him.

---

1. As Paul Fauconnet points out in his preface, this refers to the first
two lectures in this series. The first of these was published in 1903 in the
*Revue de metaphysique et de morale*. In 1922, it was reproduced in *Education et sociologie*, recently translated and published by The Free Press.

However, if education is not a science, neither is it an art. Art, indeed, is made up of habit, practice, and organized skills. Pedagogy is not the art of teaching; it is the *savoir faire* of the educator, the practical experience of the teacher.

What we have here are two clearly differentiated things: one may be a good teacher, yet not very clever at educational theory. Conversely, the educational theorist may be completely lacking in practical skill. It would have been unwise to entrust a class to Montaigne or to Rousseau; and the repeated failures of Pestalozzi prove that he was not a very good teacher. Education is therefore intermediate between art and science. It is not art, for it is not a system of organized practices but of ideas bearing on these practices. It is a body of theories. By that token it is close to science. However, scientific theory has only one goal—the expression of reality; whereas educational theories have the immediate aim of guiding conduct. While these theories do not constitute action in themselves, they are a preparation for it, and they are very close to it. Their *raison d'être* is in action. It is this dual nature that I have been trying to express in referring to education as a practical theory. The uses that may be expected of it are determined by this ambivalent nature. It is not action itself and thus cannot replace action. But it can provide *insight* into action. It is therefore useful to the extent that thought is useful to professional experience.

If educational theory goes beyond its proper limits, if it pretends to supplant experience, to promulgate ready-made formulae that are then applied mechanically, it degenerates into dead matter. If, on the other hand, experience disregards pedagogical thinking, it in turn degenerates into blind routine or else is at the mercy of ill-informed or unsystematic thinking. Educational theory essentially is the most methodical and best-documented thinking available, put at the service of teaching.

These preliminaries over, I can now go on to the problem

of moral education. To treat this question methodically, we must look at the conditions under which it is posed today. It is within the framework of our traditional, national educational system that the crisis to which I have alluded before has reached particularly serious proportions. Let us examine it a little more closely.

The question is not only intrinsically interesting to all teachers. It is especially urgent today. Anything that reduces the effectiveness of moral education, whatever disrupts patterns of relationships, threatens public morality at its very roots. The last twenty years in France have seen a great educational revolution, which was latent and half-realized before then. We decided to give our children in our state-supported schools a purely secular moral education. It is essential to understand that this means an education that is not derived from revealed religion, but that rests exclusively on ideas, sentiments, and practices accountable to reason only—in short, a purely rationalistic education.

Such a change could not take place without disturbing traditional ideas, disrupting old habits, entailing sweeping organizational changes, and without posing, in turn, new problems with which we must come to grips.

I know that I am now touching on questions that have the unfortunate effect of arousing passionate argument. But we must broach these questions resolutely. We cannot speak of moral education without being very clear as to the conditions under which we are educating. Otherwise we will bog down in vague and meaningless generalities. In this book, our aim is not to formulate moral education for man in general; but for men of our time in this country.

It is in our public schools that the majority of our children are being formed.[3] These schools must be the guardians par

---

2. Again, this refers to the preceding lecture, which was omitted from the 1925 volume.

3. The reference here is to the elementary school system.

excellence of our national character. They are the heart of our general education system. We must, therefore, focus our attention on them, and consequently on moral education as it is understood and practiced in them and as it should be understood and practiced. As a matter of fact, I am quite sure that if we bring to our discussion of these questions just a modicum of the scientific attitude, it will not be hard to treat them without arousing passions and without giving offense to legitimate feelings.

In the first place, a rational moral education is entirely possible; this is implied in the postulate that is at the basis of science. I refer to the rationalist postulate, which may be stated thus: there is nothing in reality that one is justified in considering as fundamentally beyond the scope of human reason. When I call this principle a postulate, I am in fact using a very improper expression. That principle had the character of a postulate when mind first undertook to master reality—if indeed one can say that this intellectual quest ever had a beginning. When science began to organize itself, it necessarily had to postulate that it, itself, was possible and that things could be expressed in scientific language—or, in other words, rational language, for the two terms are synonymous. However, something that, at the time, was only an anticipation of the mind, a tentative conjecture, found itself progressively demonstrated by all the results of science. It proved that facts should be connected with each other in accordance with rational relationships, by discovering the existence of such relationships.

There are of course many things—in fact, an infinity of things—of which we are still ignorant. Nothing guarantees that all of them will ever be discovered, that a moment will come when science will have finished its task and will have expressed adequately the totality of things. Rather, everything leads us to think that scientific progress will never end. But the rationalist principle does not imply that science can in fact exhaust the real. It only denies that one has the right to look at any part of reality or any category of facts as invincibly irreducible to scientific thought—in other words, as irrational in its essence.

Rationalism does not at all suppose that science can ever reach the limits of knowledge. If it is understood in this fashion, we might say that this principle is demonstrated by the history of science itself. The manner in which it has progressed shows that it is impossible to mark a point beyond which scientific explanation will become impossible. All the limits within which people have tried to contain it have only served as challenges for science to surpass them. Whenever people thought that science had reached its ultimate limit, it resumed, after varying periods of time, its forward march and penetrated regions thought to be forbidden to it. Once physics and chemistry were established, it was thought that science had to stop there. The biological world seemed to depend upon mysterious principles, which escaped the grasp of scientific thought. Yet biological sciences presently came into their own. Next, the founding of psychology demonstrated the applicability of reason to mental phenomena. Nothing, then, authorizes us to suppose that it is different with moral phenomena. Such an exception, which would be unique, is contrary to all reasonable inferences. There is no ineluctable reason for supposing that this last barrier, which people still try to oppose to the progress of reason, is more insurmountable than the others. The fact is, we are witnessing the establishing of a science that is still in its beginnings, but that undertakes to treat the phenomena of moral life as natural phenomena—in other words, as rational phenomena. Now, if morality is rational, if it sets in motion only ideas and sentiments deriving from reason, why should it be necessary to implant it in minds and characters by recourse to methods beyond the scope of reason?

Not only does a purely rational education seem logically

possible; it seems to be determined by our entire historical development. If our education had suddenly taken on this character several years ago, one might well doubt whether so sudden a transformation were really implied in the nature of things. In reality, however, this transformation is the result of a gradual development, whose origins go back, so to speak, to the very beginnings of history. The secularizing of education has been in process for centuries.

It has been said that primitive peoples had no morality. That was an historical error. There is no people without its morality. However, the morality of undeveloped societies is not ours. What characterizes them is that they are essentially religious. By that, I mean that the most numerous and important duties are not the duties of man toward other men, but of man toward his gods. The principal obligations are not to respect one's neighbor, to help him, to assist him; but to accomplish meticulously prescribed rites, to give to the Gods what is their due, and even, if need be, to sacrifice one's self to their glory. Human morality in those circumstances is reduced to a small number of principles, whose violation is repressed less severely. These peoples are only on the threshold of morality. Even in Greece, murder occupied a much lower place in the scale of crimes than serious acts of impiety. Under these conditions, moral education could only be essentially religious, as was morality itself. Only religious notions could serve as the basis for an education that, before everything, had as its chief aim to teach man the manner in which he ought to behave toward religious beings.

But gradually things change. Gradually, human duties are multiplied, become more precise, and pass to the first rank of importance; while others, on the contrary, tend to become attenuated. One might say that Christianity itself has contributed most to the acceleration of this result. An essentially human religion since its God dies for the salvation of humanity, Christianity teaches that the principal duty of man toward God is to love his neighbor. Although there are religious duties—rites addressed only to divinity—the place they occupy and the importance attributed to them continue to diminish.

Essential sin is no longer detached from its human context. True sin now tends to merge with moral transgression. No doubt God continues to play an important part in morality. It is He who assures respect for it and represses its violation. Offenses against it are offenses against Him. But He is now reduced to the role of guardian. Moral discipline wasn't instituted *for his benefit,* but *for the benefit of men.* He only intervenes to make it effective. Thenceforth our duties become independent, in large measure, of the religious notions that guarantee them but do not form their foundation.

With Protestantism, the autonomy of morality is still more accentuated by the fact that ritual itself diminishes. The moral functions of divinity become its sole *raison d'être.* It is the only argument brought forward to demonstrate its existence. Spiritualistic philosophy continues the work of Protestantism. But among the philosophers who believe today in the necessity of supernatural sanctions, there are none who do not admit that morality could be constructed quite independent of any theological conception. Thus, the bond that originally united and even merged the two systems has become looser and looser. It is, therefore, certain that when we broke that bond definitively we were following in the mainstream of history. If ever a revolution has been a long time in the making, this is it.

If the enterprise is possible and necessary, if sooner or later it had to be undertaken, and even if there were no reason to believe that it was long in the making, it still remains a difficult process. It is well to realize it, for only if we do not delude ourselves concerning these difficulties will it be possible to triumph over them. Gratified as we may be with what has been achieved, we ought to realize that advances would have been more pronounced and coherent had people not begun by believing that everything was going to be all too simple and easy. Above all, the task was conceived as a purely negative operation. It seemed that to secularize education all that was needed was to take out of it every supernatural element. A simple stripping operation was supposed to have the effect of disengaging rational morality from adventitious and parasitical elements that cloaked it and prevented it from realizing itself. It was enough, so they said, to teach the old morality of our fathers, while avoiding recourse to any religious notion. In reality, the task was much more complex. It was not enough to proceed by simple elimination to reach the proposed goal. On the contrary, a profound transformation was necessary.

Of course, if religious symbols were simply overlaid upon moral reality, there would indeed be nothing to do but lift them off, thus finding in a state of purity and isolation a self-sufficient rational morality. But the fact is that these two systems of beliefs and practices have been too inextricably bound together in history; for centuries they have been too interlaced for their connections possibly to be so external and superficial and for the separation to be so easily consummated. We must not forget that only yesterday they were supported on the same keystone: God, the center of religious life, was also the supreme guarantor of moral order. There is nothing surprising in this partial coalescence; the duties of religion and those of morality are both duties, in other words, morally obligatory practices. It is altogether natural that men were induced to see in one and the same being the source of all obligation. One can easily foresee, by reason of this relationship and partial fusion, that some elements of both systems approached each other to the point of merging and forming only one system. Certain moral ideas became united with certain religious ideas to such an extent as to become indistinct from them. The first ended by no longer having or seeming to have any existence or any reality independent of the second. Consequently, if, in rationalizing morality in moral education, one confines himself to withdraw from moral discipline everything that is religious without replacing it, one almost inevitably runs the danger of withdrawing at the same time all elements that are properly moral. Under the name of rational morality, we would be left only with an impoverished and colorless morality. To ward off this danger, therefore, it is imperative not to be satisfied with a superficial separation. We must seek, in the very heart of religious conceptions, those moral realities that are, as it were, lost and dissimulated in it. We must disengage them, find out what they consist of, determine their proper nature, and express them in rational language. In a word, we must discover the rational substitutes for those religious notions that for a long time have served as the vehicle for the most essential moral ideas.

An example will illustrate precisely what I mean: Even without pushing the analysis, everybody readily perceives that in one sense, a very relative sense as a matter of fact, the moral order constitues a sort of autonomous order in the world. There is something about prescriptions of morality that imposes particular respect for them. While all opinions relating to the material world—to the physical or mental organization of either animals or men—are today entitled to free discussion, people do not admit that moral beliefs should be as freely subjected to criticism. Anybody who questions in our presence that the child has duties toward his parents or that human life should be respected provokes us to immediate protest. The response is quite different from that which a scientific heresy might arouse. It resembles at every point the reprobation that the blasphemer arouses in the soul of the believer. There is even stronger reason for the feelings incited by infractions of moral rules being altogether different from those provoked by ordinary infractions of the precepts of practical wisdom or of professional technique. The domain of morality is as if surrounded by a mysterious barrier which keeps violators at arm's length, just as the religious domain is protected from the reach of the profane. It is a sacred domain. All the things it comprises are as if invested with a particular dignity that raises them above our empirical individuality, and that confers upon them a sort of transcendant reality. Don't we say, casually, that the human person is sacred, that we must hold it in reverence? As long as religion and morals are intimately united, this sacred character can be explained without difficulty since, in that case, morality as well as religion is conceived as an attribute and emanation of divinity, the source of all that is sacred. Everything coming from it participates in its transcendance and finds itself by that very fact implicated in other things. But if we methodically reject the notion of the sacred without systematically replacing it by another, the quasi-religious character of morality is without foundation, (since we are rejecting the traditional conception that provided that foundation without providing another). One is, then, almost inevitably inclined to deny morality. It is even impossible to feel the reality of it, when, as a matter of fact, it could very well be that it is founded in the nature of things.

It may very well be that there is in moral rules something that deserves to be called by this name and that nevertheless could be justified and explained logically without implying the existence of a transcendant being or specifically religious notions. If the eminent dignity attributed to moral rules has, up to the present time, only been expressed in the form of religious conceptions, it does not follow that it cannot be otherwise expressed; consequently, one must be careful that this dignity does not sink with the ideas conventionally associated with it. From the fact that nations, to explain it to themselves, have made of it a radiation and a reflection of divinity, it does not follow that it cannot be attached to another reality, to a purely empirical reality through which it is explained, and of which the idea of God is indeed perhaps only the symbolic expression. If, then, in rationalizing education, we do not retain this character and make it clear to the child in a rational manner, we will only transmit to him a morality fallen from its natural dignity. At the same time, we will risk drying up the source from which the schoolmaster himself drew a part of his authority and also a part of the warmth necessary to stir the heart and stimulate the mind. The schoolmaster, feeling that he was speaking in the name of a superior reality elevated himself, invested himself with an extra energy. If we do not succeed in preserving this sense of self and mission for him—while providing, meanwhile, a different foundation for it—we risk having nothing more than a moral education without prestige and without life.

Here is a first body of eminently complex and positive problems that compel our attention when we undertake to secularize moral education. It is not enough to cut out; we must replace. We must discover those moral forces that men, down to the present time, have conceived of only under the form of religious allegories. We must disengage them from their symbols, present them in their rational nakedness, so to speak, and find a way to make the child feel their reality without recourse to any mythological intermediary. This is the first order of business: we want moral education to become rational and at the same time to produce all the results that should be expected from it.

These questions are not the only ones we face here. Not only must we see to it that morality, as it becomes rationalized, loses none of its basic elements; but it must, through the very fact of secularization, become enriched with new elements. The first transformation of which I have just spoken bore only on the form of our moral ideas. The foundation itself cannot stand without profound modifications. The causes requiring the institution of a secular morality in education are too closely related to the foundation of our social organization for the content of morality itself—indeed, for the content of our duties—to remain unaffected. Indeed, if we have felt with greater force than our fathers the need for an entirely rational moral education, it is evidently because we are becoming more rationalistic.

Rationalism is only one of the aspects of individualism: it is the intellectual aspect of it. We are not dealing here with two different states of mind; each is the converse of the other. When one feels the need of liberating individual thought, it is because in a general way one feels the need of liberating the individual. Intellectual servitude is only one of the servitudes that individualism combats. All development of individualism has the effect of opening moral consciousness to new ideas and rendering it more demanding. Since every advance that it makes results in a higher conception, a more delicate sense of the dignity of man, individualism cannot be developed without making apparent to us as contrary to human dignity, as unjust, social relations that at one time did not seem unjust at all. Conversely, as a matter of fact, rationalistic faith reacts on individualistic sentiment and stimulates it. For injustice is unreasonable and absurd, and, consequently, we are the more sensitive to it as we are more sensitive to the rights of reason. Consequently, a given advance in moral education in the direction of greater rationality cannot occur without also bringing to light new moral tendencies, without inducing a greater thirst for justice, without stirring the public conscience by latent aspirations.

The educator who would undertake to rationalize education without foreseeing the development of new sentiments, without preparing that development, and directing it, would fail in one aspect of his task. That is why he cannot confine himself to commenting upon the old morality of our fathers. He must, in addition, help the younger generations to become conscious of the new ideal toward which they tend confusedly. To orient them in that direction it is not enough for him to conserve the past; he must prepare the future.

Furthermore, it is on that condition alone that moral education fulfills its entire function. If we are satisfied with inculcating in children the body of mediocre moral ideas upon which humanity has been living for centuries, we could, to a certain extent, assure the private morality of individuals. But this is only the minimum condition of morality, and a nation cannot remain satisfied with it. For a great nation like ours to be truly in a state of moral health it is not enough for most of its members to be sufficiently removed from the grossest transgressions—murder, theft, fraud of all kinds.

A society in which there is pacific commerce between its members, in which there is no conflict of any sort, but which has nothing more than that would have a rather mediocre quality. Society must, in addition, have before it an ideal toward which it reaches. It must have some good to achieve, an original contribution to bring to the moral patrimony of mankind. Idleness is a bad counselor for collectivities as well as individuals. When individual activity does not know where to take hold, it turns against itself. When the moral forces of a society remain unemployed, when they are not engaged in some work to accomplish, they deviate from their moral sense and are used up in a morbid and harmful manner. Just as work is the more necessary to man as he is more civilized, similarly, the more the intellectual and moral organization of societies becomes elevated and complex, the more it is necessary that they furnish new nourishment for their increased activity.

A society like ours cannot, therefore, content itself with a complacent possession of moral results that have been handed down to it. It must go on to new conquests; it is necessary that the teacher prepare the children who are in his trust for those necessary advances. He must be on his guard against transmitting the moral gospel of our elders as a sort of closed book. On the contrary, he must excite in them a desire to add a few lines of their own, and give them the tools to satisfy this legitimate ambition.

You can understand better now why I have said that the educational problem poses itself for us in a particularly pressing fashion. In thus expressing myself, I was thinking especially of our system of moral education which is, as you see, to be rebuilt very largely from top to bottom. We can no longer use the traditional system which, as a matter of fact, endured only because of a miracle of equilibrium and the force of habit. For a long time it had been resting on an insecure foundation. It was no longer resting on beliefs strong enough to enable it to take care of its functions effectively. But to replace it usefully, it is not enough to cancel out the old. It is not enough to trifle with certain external features of the system at the risk of jeopardizing what lies beneath. A complete recasting of our educational technique must now engage our efforts. For the inspiration of yesteryear—which, as a matter of fact would awaken in the hearts of men only feebler and feebler echoes—we must substitute a new inspiration. We must discover, in the old system, moral forces hidden in it, hidden under forms that concealed their intrinsic nature. We must make their true reality appear; and we must find what comes of them under present conditions, where even they themselves could not remain immutable. We must, furthermore, take into account the changes that the existence of rational moral education both presupposes and time generates. The task is much more complex than it could possibly appear at first glance. But this should neither surprise nor discourage us. On the contrary, the relative imperfection of certain results is thus explained by reasons that authorize better hopes. The idea of the progress remaining to be made, far from depressing us, can only urge us to more strenuous endeavor. We must resolve to face these difficulties. They become dangerous only when we try to hide them from ourselves and to sidestep them arbitrarily.

# PART I

## The Elements of Morality

# CHAPTER TWO

# ↝ THE FIRST ELEMENT

# OF MORALITY: THE

# SPIRIT OF DISCIPLINE

WE CANNOT USEFULLY TREAT ANY TEACHING PROBLEM, WHATever it may be, except by starting where we are in time and space, i.e., with the conditions confronting the children with whom we are concerned.

In fulfilling this methodological requirement, I tried to emphasize in the last chapter the terms in which the problem of moral education is posed for us.

One can distinguish two stages in childhood: the first, taking place almost entirely within the family or the nursery school—a substitute for the family, as its name suggests; the second, in elementary school, when the child, beginning to leave the family circle, is initiated into a larger environment. This we call the second period of childhood; we shall focus on it in discussing moral education. This is indeed the critical moment in the formation of moral character. Before that, the child is still very young; his intellectual development is quite rudimentary and his emotional life is too simple and underdeveloped. He lacks the intellectual foundation necessary for the relatively complex ideas and sentiments that under-gird our morality. The limited boundaries of his intellectual horizon at the same time limit his moral conceptions. The only possible training at this stage is a very general one, an elementary introduction to a few simple ideas and sentiments.

On the other hand, if, beyond this second period of child-hood—i.e., beyond school age—the foundations of morality have not been laid, they never will be. From this point on, all one can do is to complete the job already begun, refining sensibilities and giving them some intellectual content, i.e., informing them increasingly with intelligence. But the ground-work must have been laid. So we can appropriately fix our attention above all on this stage of development. Moreover, precisely because it is an intermediate stage, what we shall say may be readily applied, *mutatis mutandis*, to the preceding and following stages. On the one hand, in order to show clearly the nature of moral education at this period, we shall be led to indicate how it completes, and carries on from, familial education; on the other hand, to understand what it must later become, it will suffice to project our thinking into the future, taking account of differences in age and situa-tion.

However, this first specification of the problem is not enough. Not only shall I discuss here, at least in principle, only moral education during the second stage of childhood; but I shall limit my subject even more narrowly. I shall deal above all with moral education in this second stage in our public schools because, normally, the public schools are and should be the flywheel of national education. Furthermore, contrary to the all too popular notion that moral education falls chiefly within the jurisdiction of the family, I judge that the task of the school in the moral development of the child can and should be of the greatest importance. There is a whole aspect of the culture, and a most important one, which would otherwise be lost. For if it is the family that can distinctively and effectively evoke and organize those homely sentiments basic to morality and—even more generally—those germane to the simplest personal relationships, it is not the agency so constituted as to train the child in terms of the demands of society. Almost by definition, as it were, it is an inappropriate agency for such a task.

Therefore, focusing our study on the school, we find ourselves precisely at the point that should be regarded as the locus, par excellence, of moral development for children of this age. We have committed ourselves to provide in our schools a completely rational moral education, that is to say, excluding all principles derived from revealed religion. Thus, the problem of moral education is clearly posed for us at this point in history.

I have shown not only that the task to be undertaken is possible but that it is necessary—that it is dictated by all historical development. But at the same time, I have emphasized the complexity of the task. These complications should not discourage us in the least. It is altogether natural that an undertaking of such importance should be difficult; only the mediocre and insignificant tasks are easy. There is, then, nothing to be gained in minimizing the magnitude of the task on which we are working, under pretext of reassuring ourselves.

It is worthier and more profitable to face up to the difficulties, which inevitably accompany such a great change. I have pointed out what these difficulties seem to me to be. In the first place, due to the close bond established historically between morality and religion, we can anticipate—since these are essential elements of morality never expressed save in religious guise—that if we begin to eliminate everything religious from the traditional system without providing any substitute, we run the risk of also eliminating essential moral ideas and sentiments. In the second place, a rational morality cannot have the same content as one that depends upon some authority other than reason. For the development of rationalism does not come about without a parallel development of individualism and, consequently, without a refinement in moral sensitivity that makes certain social relations —the allocation of rights and obligations, which up to the present has not bothered our consciences—appear unjust. Furthermore, there is not only a parallel development between individualism and rationalism, but the latter reacts upon the former and stimulates it. The characteristic of injustice is that it is not founded in the nature of things; it is not based upon reason. Thus, it is inevitable that we shall become more sensitive to injustice in the measure that we respond to the authority of reason. It is not a trifling matter to stimulate free inquiry, to accord a new authority to reason; for the power thus granted cannot but turn against those traditions that persist only insofar as they are divorced from its influence. In undertaking to organize a rational education, we find ourselves confronted with two kinds, two series of problems, the one as compelling as the other. We must take care lest we impoverish morality in the process of rationalizing it; and we must anticipate the complications that it entails and prepare for them.

To attack the first problem, we must rediscover the moral forces basic to all moral life, that of yesterday as well as that of today, without a priori derogation of the former, even if up to the present that morality has only existed in religious guise. We have to seek out the rational expression of such a morality, that is to say, apprehend such morality in itself, in its genuine nature, stripped of all symbols. Secondly, once these moral forces are known, we have to investigate how they should develop and be oriented under present social conditions. Of these two problems, it is the former that, from all evidence, should first concern us. We must first determine, in their essentials, the basic elements of morality before investigating the changes that may be indicated.

To ask what the elements of morality are is not to undertake a complete listing of all the virtues, or even of the most important. It involves an inquiry into fundamental dispositions, into those mental states at the root of the moral life. To influence the child morally is not to nurture in him a particular virtue, followed by another and still another; it is to develop and even to constitute completely, by appropriate methods, those general dispositions that, once created, adapt themselves readily to the particular circumstances of human life. If we are able to push through to their discovery, we shall at once have overcome one of the major obstacles confronting us in the work of our schools. What sometimes creates doubt about the effectiveness of the school in matters pertaining to the moral elements of culture is that these latter apparently involve such a host of ideas, sentiments, and customs that the teacher seems to lack the necessary time, in the few and fleeting moments when the child is under his influence, to awaken and develop them. There is such a diversity of virtues, even if one seeks to fasten on the most important, that if each of them must be at least partially developed, the dissipation of effort over such a large area must necessarily vitiate the enterprise.

To operate effectively, especially since influence can only be exerted during a brief period of time, one must have a definite and clearly specified goal. One must have an *idée fixe*, or a small number of definite ideas that serve as lodestar. Thus, our efforts, pushing always in the same direction, following the same paths, can achieve some results. One must desire strongly whatever he wishes; and few rather than many things. To provide the necessary drive for our educational efforts, we must therefore try to ferret out those basic sentiments that are the foundation of our moral dispositions.

How do we go about it? You are familiar with the way the moralists ordinarily handle this question. They commence with the principle that each of us carries within himself all the elements of morality. Hence, we have only to look inside ourselves with a little care to discover the meaning of morality. So the moralist engages in introspective inquiry and, from amongst the ideas that he has more or less clearly in mind, seizes upon this one or that as seeming to represent the central notions of morality. For some, it is the idea of utility; for others, the notion of perfection; and for still others, it is the conception of human dignity, etc.

I do not wish to discuss at this point whether morality in its entirety resides in each person—whether each individual mind contains in itself all those elements that, simply in their development, constitute morality. Everything that follows leads us to a different conclusion, but we must not anticipate it here. To dispose of this currently fashionable approach I need only point out how subjective and arbitrary it is. After his self-interrogation, all that the moralist can state is his own conception of morality, the conception he has personally contrived. Why is this more objective than the quite unobjective vulgar notions of heat, or light, or electricity? Let us acknowledge that morality may be completely implicit in each mind. Nonetheless, one must know how to get at it. One must still know how to distinguish, amongst all our ideas, those within the province of morality and those that are not. Now, according to what criteria can we make such a distinction? What enables us to say: this is a matter of morality and this is not? Shall we say that that is moral which accords with man's nature? Suppose, then, that we knew quite certainly what man's nature was. What proves that the end of morality is to realize human nature —why might it not have as its function the satisfaction of social needs? Shall we substitute this idea for the other? But first, what justifies us in doing so? And what are the social interests that morality must protect? For such interests are of all sorts—economic, military, scientific, etc. We cannot base practice on such subjective hypotheses as these. We cannot regulate the education that we owe our children on the basis of such purely academic conceptions.

Moreover, this method, to whatever conclusions it may lead, rests throughout on a single premise: that to develop morality empirical analysis is unnecessary. To determine what morality should be, it is apparently thought unnecessary first to inquire what it is or what it has been. People expect to legislate immediately. But whence this privilege? One hears it said today that we can know something of economic, legal, religious, and linguistic matters *only* if we begin by observing facts, analyzing them, comparing them. There is no reason why it should be otherwise with moral facts On the other hand, one can inquire what morality ought to be only if one has first determined the complex of things that goes under this rubric, what its nature is, what ends it serves. Let us begin, then, by looking at morality as a fact, and let us see what we are actually able to understand by it.

In the first place, there is an aspect common to all behavior that we ordinarily call moral. All such behavior conforms to pre-established rules. To conduct one's self morally is a matter of abiding by a norm, determining what conduct should obtain in a given instance even before one is required to act. This domain of morality is the domain of duty; duty is pre-scribed behavior. It is not that the moral conscience is free of uncertainties. We know, indeed, that it is often perplexed, hesitating between alternatives. But then the problem is what is the particular rule that applies to the given situation, and how should it be applied? Since each rule is a general prescription, it cannot be applied exactly and mechanically in identical ways in each particular circumstance. It is up to the person to see how it applies in a given situation. There is always considerable, if limited, leeway left for his initiative. The essentials of conduct are determined by the rule. Furthermore, to the extent that the rule leaves us free, to the extent that it does not prescribe in detail what we ought to do, the action being left to our own judgment, to that extent there is no moral valuation. We are not accountable precisely because of the freedom left us. Just as an action is not a crime in the usual and actual sense of the word when it is not forbidden by an established law, so when it is not contrary to a pre-established norm, it is not immoral. Thus, we can say that morality consists of a system of rules of action that predetermine conduct. They state how one must act in given situations; and to behave properly is to obey conscientiously.

This first statement, which verges on a common-sense observation, suffices nonetheless to highlight an important fact too often misunderstood. Most moralists, indeed, consider morality as entirely contained in a very general, unique formula. It is precisely on this account that they so readily accept the view that morality resides entirely in the individual conscience, and that a simple glance inside ourselves will be enough to reveal it. This formula is expressed in different ways: that of the Kantians is not that of the utilitarians, and each utilitarian moralist has his own. However, in whatever manner it is conceived, everyone assigns it the central position. All the rest of morality consists merely in applying this fundamental principle. This conception expresses the classical distinction between so-called theoretical and applied morality. The aim of the former is to specify the general law of morality; the latter, to investigate how the law thus enunciated should be applied in the major situations and combinations encountered in life. Thus, specific rules deduced by this method would not in themselves have an independent reality. They would only be extensions or corollaries of the general formula as it was reflected throughout the range of life experiences. Apply the general law of morality to various domestic relations and you will have family morality. Apply it to different political relationships and you will have civic morality, etc. These would not be divers duties but a single, unique duty running like a guiding thread throughout life. Given the great diversity of situations and relationships, one can see how, from this point of view, the realm of morality seems quite indeterminate.

However, such a conception of morality reverses the real situation. If we see morality as it is, we see that it consists in an infinity of special rules, fixed and specific, which order man's conduct in those different situations in which he finds himself most frequently. Some define the desirable relationships between man and wife; others, the way parents should behave with their children; and still others, the relationships between person and property. Certain of these maxims are stated in law and sanctioned in clear-cut fashion; others are etched in the public conscience, expressing themselves in the aphorisms of popular morality, and sanctioned simply by the stigma attaching to their violation rather than by some definite punishment. But whether the one or the other, they have their own existence, their own life. The proof lies in the fact that certain of these rules may be found in a weakened state, while others, on the contrary, are altogether viable. In one country, the rules of familial morality may provide all the necessary stability, while the rules of civic virtue are weak and ineffective.

Here, then, are phenomena not only real, but also comparatively autonomous, since they can be realized in different ways depending upon the conditions of social life. This is a far cry from seeing here simple aspects of one and the same general principle that would embrace all their meaning and reality. Quite to the contrary, the general rule, however it has been or is conceived, does not constitute the reality but is a simple abstraction. There is no rule, no social prescription that is recognized or gains its sanction from Kant's moral imperative or from the law of utility as formulated by Bentham, Mill, or Spencer. These are the generalizations of philosophers, the hypotheses of theoreticians. What people refer to as the general law of morality is quite simply a more or less exact way of representing approximately and schematically the moral reality; but it is not that reality itself. It is a more or less satisfactory shorthand statement of characteristics common to all moral rules; it is not a real, established, effective rule. It is to moral reality what philosophers' hypotheses, aimed at expressing the unity of nature, are to that nature itself. It is of the order of science, not of the order of life.

Thus, in fact and in practice, it is not according to theoretical insights or general formulae that we guide our conduct, but according to specific rules applying uniquely to the special situation that they govern. In all significant life situations, we do not refer back to the so-called general principle of morality to discover how it applies in a particular case and thus learn what we should do. Instead there are clear-cut and specific ways of acting required of us. When we conform to the rule prescribing chastity and forbidding incest, is it only because we deduce it from some fundamental axiom of morality? Suppose, as fathers, we find ourselves widowers charged with the entire responsibility of our family. We do not have to hark back to the ultimate source of morality, nor even to some abstract notion of paternity to deduce what conduct is implied in these circumstances. Law and the mores prescribe our conduct.

Thus, it is not necessary to represent morality as something very general, made concrete only to the extent it becomes necessary. On the contrary, morality is a totality of definite rules; it is like so many molds with limiting boundaries, into which we must pour our behavior. We do not have to construct these rules at the moment of action by deducing them from some general principles; they already exist, they are already made, they live and operate around us.

Now, this first statement is of primary importance for us.

It demonstrates that the function of morality is, in the first place, to determine conduct, to fix it, to eliminate the element of individual arbitrariness. Doubtless the content of moral precepts—that is to say, the nature of the prescribed behavior —also has moral value, and we shall discuss this. However, since all such precepts promote regularity of conduct among men, there is a moral aspect in that these actions—not only in their specific content, but in a general way—are held to a certain regularity. This is why transients and people who cannot hold themselves to specific jobs are always suspect. It is because their moral temperament is fundamentally defective—because it is most uncertain and undependable. Indeed, in refusing to yield to the requirements of regularized conduct, they disdain all customary behavior, they resist limitations or restrictions, they feel some compulsion to remain "free." This indeterminate situation also implies a state of endless instability. Such people are subject to momentary impulses, to the disposition of the moment, to whatever notion is in mind at the moment when they must act, since they lack habits sufficiently strong to prevent present inclinations from prevailing over the past. Doubtless it may happen that a fortunate impulse prompts them to a happy decision; but it is a situation by no means guaranteed to repeat itself. Morality is basically a constant thing, and so long as we are not considering an excessively long time span, it remains ever the same. A moral act ought to be the same tomorrow as today, whatever the personal predispositions of the actor. Morality thus presupposes a certain capacity for behaving similarly under like circumstances, and consequently it implies a certain ability to develop habits, a certain need for regularity. So close is the connection between custom and moral behavior that all social customs almost inevitably have a moral character. When a mode of behavior has become customary in a group, whatever deviates from it elicits a wave of disapproval very like that evoked by moral transgressions. Customs share in some way the special respect accorded moral behavior. If all social customs are not moral, all moral behavior is customary behavior. Consequently, whoever resists the customary runs the risk of defying morality.

Regularity, however, is only one element of morality. This same conception of the rule when carefully analyzed will disclose another and no less important feature of morality.

To assure regularity, it is only necessary that customs be strongly founded. But customs, by definition, are forces internalized in the person. It is a kind of accumulated experience within us that unfolds itself, activated, as it were, spontaneously. Internalized, it expresses itself externally as an inclination or a preference. Quite to the contrary, a rule is essentially something that is outside the person. We cannot conceive of it save as an order—or at least as binding advice—which orginates outside ourselves. Is it a matter of rules of hygiene? They come to us from the science that decrees them, or, more specifically, from the experts representing that science. Does it concern rules of professional practice? They come to us from the tradition of the profession and, more directly, from those among our elders who have passed them on to us and who best exemplify them in our eyes. It is for this reason that, through the centuries, people have seen in the rules of morality directives deriving from God.

A rule is not then a simple matter of habitual behavior; it is a way of acting that we do not feel free to alter according to taste. It is in some measure—and to the same extent that it is a rule—beyond personal preference. There is in it something that resists us, is beyond us. We do not determine its existence or its nature. It is independent of what we are. Rather than expressing us, it dominates us. If it were entirely an internal thing, like a sentiment or a habit, there would be no reason why it should not conform to all the variations and fluctuations of our internal states. Of course, we do set for ourselves a line of conduct, and we say, then, that we have set up rules of conduct of such and such a sort. But the word so used generally lacks its full meaning. A plan of action that we ourselves outline, which depends only upon ourselves and that we can always modify is a project, not a rule. Or, if in fact it is to some extent truly independent of our will, it must rest in the same degree on something other than our will—on something external to us. For example, we adopt a given mode of life because it carries the authority of science; the authority of science legitimates it. It is to the science that we defer, in our behavior, and not to ourselves. It is to science that we bend our will.

Thus, we see in these examples what there is in the conception of rules beyond the notion of regularity: *the idea of authority*. By authority, we must understand that influence which imposes upon us all the moral power that we acknowledge as superior to us. Because of this influence, we act in prescribed ways, not because the required conduct is attractive to us, not because we are so inclined by some predisposition either innate or acquired, but because there is some compelling influence in the authority dictating it. Obedience consists in such acquiescence. What are the mental processes at the bottom of this notion of authority, which create this compelling force to which we submit? This we shall have to investigate presently. For the moment, the question is not germane; it is enough if we have the feeling of the thing and of its reality. There is in every moral force that we feel as above or beyond ourselves something that bends our wills. In one sense, one can say that there is no rule, properly speaking, which does not have this imperative character in some degree, because, once again, every rule commands. It is this that makes us feel that we are not free to do as we wish.

Morality, however, constitutes a category of rules where the idea of authority plays an absolutely preponderant role. Part of the esteem we accord to principles of hygiene or of professional practice or various precepts drawn from folk wisdom doubtless stems from the authority accorded science and experimental research. Such a wealth of knowledge and human experience, by itself, imposes on us a respect that communicates itself to the bearers, just as the deference accorded by the devout to things religious is communicated to priests. But, in all these cases, if we abide by the rule it is not only out of deference to the authority that is its source; it is also because the prescribed behavior may very well have useful consequences, whereas contrary behavior would entail harmful results. If, when we are sick, we take care of ourselves, following the doctor's orders, it is not only out of deference to his authority, but also because we hope thus to recover. There is involved here, therefore, a feeling other than respect for authority. There enter quite utilitarian considerations, which are intrinsic to the nature of the act and to its outcomes, possible or probable.

It is quite otherwise with morality. Without doubt, if we violate rules of morality we risk unhappy consequences: we may be blamed, blacklisted, or materially hurt—either in person or our property. But it is a certain and incontestable fact that an act is not moral, even when it is in substantial agreement wtih moral rules, if the consideration of adverse consequences has determined it. Here, for the act to be everything it should be, for the rule to be obeyed as it ought to be, it is necessary for us to yield, not in order to avoid disagreeable results or some moral or material punishment, but very simply because we ought to, regardless of the consequences our conduct may have for us. One must obey a moral precept out of respect for it and for this reason alone. All the leverage that it exerts upon our wills derives exclusively from the authority with which it is invested. Thus, in the case of moral rules, authority operates alone; to the extent that any other element enters into conduct, to that extent it loses its moral character. We are saying, then, that while all rules command. the moral rule consists entirely in a commandment and in nothing else. That is why the moral rule speaks to us with such authority—why, when it speaks, all other considerations must be subordinated. It permits no equivocation. When it is a matter of evaluating the ultimate consequences of an act, uncertainty is inevitable—there is always something indeterminate in the outcome. So many diverse combinations of circumstance can produce outcomes we are unable to foresee. But when it is a matter of duty, since all such calculation is forbidden, it is easier to be sure: all problems are simpler. It is not a matter of anticipating a future inevitably obscure and uncertain. It is a matter of knowing what is prescribed. If duty speaks there is nothing to do but obey. As to the source of this extraordinary authority, I shall not inquire for the time being. I shall content myself with pointing out its incontestable existence.

Morality is not, then, simply a system of customary conduct. It is a system of commandments. We were saying, first of all, that irregular behavior is morally incomplete. So it is with the anarchist. (I use the word in its etymological sense, referring to the man so constituted as not to feel the reality of moral imperatives, the man who is affected by a kind of color-blindness, by virtue of which all moral and intellectual forces seem to him of the same order.) Here we confront another aspect of morality: at the root of the moral life there is, besides the preference for regularity, the notion of moral authority. Furthermore, these two aspects of morality are closely linked, their unity deriving from a more complex idea that embraces both of them. This is the concept of discipline. Discipline in effect regularizes conduct. It implies repetitive behavior under determinate conditions. But discipline does not emerge without authority—a regulating authority. Therefore, to summarize this chapter, we can say that the fundamental element of morality is the spirit of discipline.

However, let us be clear about the meaning of this proposition. Ordinarily, discipline appears useful only because it entails behavior that has useful outcomes. Discipline is only a means of specifying and imposing the required behavior, so it derives its *raison d'etre* from the behavior. But if the preceding analysis is correct we must say that discipline derives its *raison d'etre* from itself; it is good that man is disciplined, independent of the acts to which he thus finds himself constrained. Why? It is all the more necessary to consider this problem, since discipline and rules often appear as constraining—necessary, perhaps, but nonetheless deplorable evils that one must know how to bear while reducing them to a minimum. What, then, makes discipline good? We shall consider this in the next chapter.

# CHAPTER THREE

# ✥ THE SPIRIT OF DISCIPLINE

## (*Continued*)

IN THE LAST CHAPTER WE BEGAN TO INQUIRE INTO THE BASIC properties of the moral temperament, since they must provide the points of leverage for the teacher. We called these the essential elements of morality. In order to understand these essentials, we set ourselves to observe morality from the outside, the way it exists and functions, as we constantly see it about us in the behavior of men. This we have done in order to sort out the genuinely essential elements within the manifold forms in which morality presents itself. That is to say, we sought out those characteristics of moral behavior that, throughout the diversity of man's particular duties, are everywhere the same. Obviously, what is truly basic to morality are those dispositions that prompt us to act morally, not in such and such a particular instance, but generally in men's relationships with one another.

Considered from this point of view, morality may seem at first, in its formal and external aspects, to be of no great significance for us. But morality, not only the sort we practice daily but also what we see in history, consists in the sum of definite and special rules that imperatively determine conduct. Now, from this first proposition there immediately flows as corollary a double consequence. First, since morality determines, fixes, regularizes man's conduct, it presupposes a certain disposition in the individual for a regular existence —a preference for regularity. Obligations are regular, they recur—always the same, uniformly, monotonously the same. Duties are not fulfilled intermittently in a blaze of glory. Genuine obligations are daily ones and the ordinary course of one's life entails their regular performance. Those, then, whose preference for change and diversity prompts a revulsion at all uniformity are certainly in danger of being morally incomplete. Regularity is the moral analogue of periodicity in the organism.

Secondly, since moral requirements are not merely another name for personal habits, since they determine conduct imperatively from sources outside ourselves, in order to fulfill one's obligations and to act morally one must have some appreciation of the authority *sui generis* that informs morality. In other words, it is necessary that the person be so constituted as to feel above him a force unqualified by his personal preferences and to which he yields. We have seen, furthermore, that if this sense of authority constitutes a part of that force with which all rules of conduct, whatever they may be, impose themselves upon us, then authority has an extremely significant function; for here it acts independently. No other feeling or consideration is involved in the moral act. It is in the nature of rules that they are to be obeyed, not because of the behavior they require or the probable consequences of such behavior, but simply because they command. Thus, it is only their authority that accounts for such efficacy as rules may have; consequently, any inability to feel and to recognize such authority wherever it exists— or to demur when it is recognized—is precisely a negation of genuine morality. Doubtless when, as we do, we cut off recourse to theological conceptions justifying the requirements of moral life, we may at first find it surprising that a strictly human conception may exert such an extraordinary influence. But the fact, in itself, is indisputable. We have only to open our eyes to it, as we shall see later when we present an example that will clarify matters. Thus, we assert this second element of morality.

But you have seen that these two elements are basically only one. The meanings of regularity and of authority constitute but two aspects of a single complex state of being that may be described as the spirit of discipline. Here, then, is the first basic element of all moral temperament—the spirit of discipline.

Such a conclusion, however, affronts a widespread human sentiment. Moral discipline has just been presented as a sort of good-in-itself; it certainly seems as though it ought to be of some worth, in and of itself, since we must obey its dictates, not because of the deeds we are required to perform, or their importance, but simply because it commands us. But one tends, rather, to see here a constraint, perhaps necessary, but always troublesome; an evil to which one must resign one's self—since it is inevitable—but which one should also try to reduce to a minimum. Indeed, is not discipline —all discipline—essentially a restraint, a limitation imposed on man's behavior? But to limit, to restrain—this is to deny, to impede the process of living and thus partially to destroy; and all destruction is evil. If life is good, how can it be good to bridle it, to constrain it, to impose limits that it cannot overcome? If life is not good, what is there of worth in the world? To be is to act, to live, and any reduction of life is a diminution of being. He who says discipline says constraint, whether physical or spiritual makes no difference.

Does not all constraint, by definition, do violence to the nature of things? It was just such reasoning that led Bentham to see in law an evil scarcely tolerable, which could only be reasonably justified when it was clearly indispensable. However, because a person's continuing activities involve those

of others, and because in the encounter there is the danger
of conflict, it becomes necessary to specify fair limits of
conduct that must not be transgressed. But such limitation
is in itself an abnormal thing. For Bentham, morality, like
law, involved a kind of pathology. Most of the classical econo-
mists were of the same view. And doubtless the influence of
the same viewpoint has led the major socialist theoreticians
to deem a society without systematic regulation both possible and desirable. The notion of an authority dominating
life and administering law seemed to them to be an archaic
idea, a prejudice that could not persist. It is life itself that
makes its own laws. There could be nothing above or beyond it.

Thus, one is led to enjoin man to develop, not a preference
for balance and moderation, some feeling for moral limits—
which is only another aspect of the sense of moral authority
—but to an altogether contradictory view, that is, an impatience with all restraint and limitation, the desire to encourage
unrestrained and infinite appetite. Man, it seems, is cribbed
and confined when he has not a limitless horizon before him.
Doubtless we know very well that we will never be in a
position to achieve such a goal: but apparently such a perspective, at least, is essential, since it alone can provide us
with a sense of the fullness of life. From such reasoning
derives the veneration that so many nineteenth-century writers
accorded the notion of the infinite. Here we have the lofty
sentiment par excellence, since by means of it man elevates
himself beyond all the limits imposed by nature and liberates
himself, at least ideally, from all restrictions that might
diminish him.

A given teaching method may become totally transformed
depending on the way in which it is carried out; it is carried
out quite differently depending on the way in which it is
conceived. Thus, discipline will produce quite different outcomes according to one's conception of its nature and func-

tion for life in general and for education in particular. We must, therefore, try to specify its function and not leave unanswered the important question it poses. Must one view discipline simply as an external, palpable police force, whose single *raison d'être* is to prevent certain behaviors and which, beyond such preventive action, has no other function? Or, on the contrary, may it not be, as our analysis leads us to suppose, a means *sui generis* of moral education, having an intrinsic value which places its own special imprint upon moral character?

In the first place, it is easy to show that discipline has a social usefulness in and of itself, quite apart from the behaviors it prescribes. In effect, social life is only one of the forms of organized life; all living organization presupposes determinate rules, and to neglect them is to invite serious disturbance. To endure, social life must be so constituted at each moment in time as to be able to respond to the exigencies of the environment; for life cannot suspend itself without death or illness intervening. If it were necessary for a living being to grope *de novo* for an appropriate response to every stimulus from the environing situation, threats to its integrity from many sources would promptly effect its disorganization. This is why, with respect to that which is most vital, the reaction of an organ is predetermined; certain modes of behaving necessarily recur under similar circumstances. This is what one refers to as the function of the organ. Social life is subject to the same imperatives, and regularity is no less indispensable for it. At each point in time, it is necessary that the functioning of familial, vocational, and civic life be assured; to this end, it is altogether necessary that the person be free from an incessant search for appropriate conduct. Norms must be established which determine what proper relationships are, and to which people conform. Deference to established norms is the stuff of our daily duties.

However, such an analysis and justification of discipline is scarcely sufficient. For we cannot account for an institution simply by demonstrating its social utility. Beyond this, it must not encounter insuperable resistance in people. If it does violence to human nature, however socially useful it may be, it will never be born, much less persist since it cannot take root in the conscience. True, social institutions are directed toward society's interests and not those of individuals as such. But, on the other hand, if such institutions threaten or disorganize the individual life at its source, they also disorganize the foundation of their own existence.

We have observed that discipline has often been viewed as a violation of man's natural constitution, since it impedes his unrestricted development. Is this contention sound? Quite to the contrary, an inability to restrict one's self within determinate limits is a sign of disease—with respect to all forms of human conduct and, even more generally, for all kinds of biological behavior. With a certain amount of nourishment a normal man is no longer hungry: it is the bulimiac who cannot be satisfied. Healthy and normally active people enjoy walking; but a mentally deranged walker exhibits a need to go on indefinitely without surcease, without rest or the prospect of repose. Even more general sentiments, such as love of animals—even love of others—when they go beyond a certain point provide indubitable evidence of alienation. It is normal that man should love others and be fond of animals, but only on the condition that neither affection exceed certain limits. If such sentiments develop to the detriment of other feelings it is a sign of derangement, the pathological character of which is well known to clinicians. But one might object that if one satisfies his hunger with a limited quantity of food, it does not follow that one can satiate his intellect with a determinate quantity of knowledge. This is a mistake. At any moment in time the knowledge normally required is narrowly circumscribed by a complex of conditions. First of all, we cannot lead a more vigorous intellectual life than that which is compatible with the condition and over-all development of our central nervous system at that point in time. If we try to go beyond this limit, the foundations of our mental life will be disrupted, and, as a result, the mental life itself. Furthermore, understanding is only one of our psychic functions. Along with purely symbolic faculties there are active ones. If the first are excessively developed, the others will inevitably be atrophied, resulting in an altogether unhealthy inability to take action. In order to get through life we have to accept many things without contriving a scientific rationale for them. If we insist on a reason for everything all our capacities for reasoning and responding are scarcely enough for the perpetual "why." This is what characterizes those abnormal subjects whom the doctors call *douteurs*. What we are saying about intellectual activity holds equally for aesthetic behavior. A nation insensitive to the joys of art is a nation of barbarians. On the other hand, when art comes to play an excessive part in the life of a people, subordinating in the same measure the serious things of life, then its days are numbered.

Thus, in order to live, we have to confront the multiple requirements of life with a limited reserve of vital energy. The amount of energy that we can and should devote to achieving each particular goal is necessarily limited. It is limited by the sum total of the strength at our disposal and the relative significance of the ends we pursue. All life is thus a complex equilibrium whose various elements limit one another; this balance cannot be disrupted without producing unhappiness or illness. Moreover, those activities in whose favor the equilibrium is disrupted become a source of pain for the person—and for the same reason: the disproportionate development accorded them. A need, a desire freed of all restraints, and all rules, no longer geared to some determinate objective and, through this same connection, limited and contained, can be nothing but a source of constant anguish for the person experiencing it. What gratification, indeed, can such a desire yield, since by definition it is incapable of being satisfied? An insatiable thirst cannot be slaked. If certain actions are to give us pleasure, we must feel that they serve some purpose, that is to say, bring us progressively closer to the goal we seek. One cannot bring some objective nearer that, by definition, is infinitely far away. The remaining distance is always the same, whatever route we take. What could be more disillusioning than to proceed toward a terminal point that is nonexistent, since it recedes in the same measure that one advances? Such futile effort is simply marching in place; it cannot fail to leave behind frustration and discouragement. This is why historical periods like ours, which have known the malady of infinite aspiration, are necessarily touched with pessimism. Pessimism always accompanies unlimited aspirations. Goethe's Faust may be regarded as representing par excellence this view of the infinite. And it is not without reason that the poet has portrayed him as laboring in continual anguish.

In order to have a full sense of self-realization, man, far from needing to see limitless horizons unrolling before him, in reality finds nothing as unhappy as the indeterminate reach of such a prospect. Far from needing to feel that he confronts a career without any definite terminus, he can only be happy when involved in definite and specific tasks. This limitation by no means implies, however, that man must arrive at some fixed position where ultimately he finds tranquillity. In intermittent steps one can pass from one special task to others equally specific, without drowning in the dissolving sense of limitlessness. The important thing is that behavior have a clear-cut objective, which may be grasped and which limits and determines it.

Now, any force unopposed by some contrary one necessarily tends to lose itself in the infinite. Just as a body of gas, provided no other matter resists its expansion, fills the immensity of space, so all energy—whether physical or moral—tends to extend itself without limit so long as nothing intervenes to stop it. Hence the need for regulatory organs, which constrain the total complex of our vital forces within appropriate limits. The nervous system has this function for our physical being. This system actuates the organs and allocates whatever energy is required by each of them. But the moral life escapes the physical system. Neither our brain nor any ganglion can assign limits to our intellectual aspirations or to our wills. For mental life, especially in its more developed forms, transcends the organism. Of course, mental life presupposes man's organic make-up, but the link between the two is a rather tenuous one. Moreover, the connection between them becomes looser and more indirect the more developed the intellectual life. Sensations and physical appetites express only the condition of the body, not ideas and complex sentiments. Only a power that is equally spiritual is able to exert influence upon spiritual forces. This spiritual power resides in the authority inherent in moral rules.

Thanks to the authority vested in them, moral rules are genuine forces, which confront our desires and needs, our appetites of all sorts, when they promise to become immoderate. Clearly, such forces are not material things but if they do not influence the body directly, they do activate the spirit. They contain in themselves everything necessary to bend the will, to contain and constrain it, to incline it in such and such a direction. One can say literally that they are forces. We certainly feel them as such every time we undertake to act contrary to their dictates for they present resistance that we cannot always overcome. When a normally constituted man tries to behave in a way repugnant to morality, he feels something that stops him just as clearly as when he tries to lift a weight too heavy for him. What is the source of this remarkable quality? Once again, this is a problem that we defer for the present, but will return to in due time. For the present, we restrict ourselves to the mere statement of the fact, which is indisputable.

On the other hand, since morality is a discipline, since it commands us, it is evident that the behavior required of us is not according to the bent of our individual natures. If morality merely bid us follow our individual natures, it need not speak to us in an imperative tone. Authority is necessary only to halt, to contain rebellious forces, not to encourage existing forces to develop in their own way. It has been said that the function of morality is to prevent the individual from encroaching on forbidden territory; in a sense, nothing is more accurate. Morality is a comprehensive system of prohibitions. That is to say, its objective is to limit the range within which individual behavior should and must normally occur.

We now see what end is served by this necessary limitation. The totality of moral regulations really forms about each person an imaginary wall, at the foot of which a multitude of human passions simply die without being able to go further. For the same reason—that they are contained—it becomes possible to satisfy them. But if at any point this barrier weakens, human forces—until now restrained—pour tumultuously through the open breach; once loosed, they find no limits where they can or must stop. Unfortunately, they can only devote themselves to the pursuit of an end that always eludes them. For example, should the rules of conjugal morality lose their authority, should husband-wife obligations be less respected, should passions and appetites ruled by this sector of morality unleash themselves, being even exacerbated by this same release, then, powerless to fulfill themselves because they have been emancipated from all limitations, such passions would entail a disillusionment which translates itself graphically into statistics of suicide. Again, should that morality governing economic life be shaken, and were the ambitions for gain to become excited and inflamed, knowing no bounds, then one would observe a rise in the annual quota of suicides. One could multiply such examples. Furthermore, it is because morality has the function of limiting and containing that too much wealth so easily becomes a source of immorality. Through the power wealth confers on us, it actually diminishes the power of things to oppose us. Consequently, it lends an increment of strength to our desires, which makes it harder to hold them in check. Under such conditions, moral equilibrium is unstable: it requires but a slight blow to disrupt it.

Thus, we glimpse the nature and source of this malady of infiniteness which we suffer in our day. For man to imagine that he has before him boundless, free, and open space, he must no longer see this moral barrier, which under normal conditions would cut off his view. He must no longer feel those moral forces that restrain him and limit his horizon. But if he no longer feels them, it is because they no longer carry their normal measure of authority, because they are weakened, because they are no longer what they ought to be. The notion of the infinite, then, appears only at those times when moral discipline has lost its ascendancy over man's will. It is the sign of the attrition that emerges during periods when the moral system, prevailing for several centuries, is shaken, failing to respond to new conditions of human life, and without any new system yet contrived to replace that which has disappeared.

Thus, we should not see in the discipline to which we subject children a means of constraint necessary only when it seems indispensable for preventing culpable conduct. Discipline is in itself a factor, *sui generis*, of education. There are certain essential elements of moral character that can be attributed only to discipline. Through it and by means of it alone are we able to teach the child to rein in his desires, to set limits to his appetites of all kinds, to limit and, through limitation, to define the goals of his activity. This limitation is the condition of happiness and of moral health. Certainly the necessary limitation varies according to country and time; it is not the same at different stages in the life career. To the extent that man's mental life develops, in the degree that it becomes more strenuous and complex, in that same measure it becomes necessary that the realm of moral activity be extended. In matters of science, art, or welfare, we can no longer rest content as easily as our fathers did. The educator then will run counter to the aims of discipline if he attempts artificially to restrict its limits. But if discipline must vary, and if one must take account of such variations, it is nonetheless necessary that it exist; and this, for the moment, is all that I wish to establish.

One may perhaps inquire if such happiness is not dearly purchased. Is it not true that to impose any limits upon our faculties is, by the nature of things, a reduction of power? Does not all limitation imply subordination? It seems, then, that any circumscribed activity can only be less valuable, as well as less free and self-determining. Such a conclusion seems to impose itself as a truism. In fact, it is only an illusion of common sense, and on a little reflection it can easily be shown that, quite to the contrary, total and absolute power is only another name for extreme impotence.

Imagine a being liberated from all external restraint, a despot still more absolute than those of which history tells us, a despot that no external power can restrain or influence. By definition, the desires of such a being are irresistible. Shall we say, then, that he is all-powerful? Certainly not, since he himself cannot resist his desires. They are masters of him, as of everything else. He submits to them; he does not dominate them. In a word, when the inclinations are totally liberated, when nothing sets bounds to them, they themselves become tyrannical, and their first slave is precisely the person who experiences them. What a sad picture this presents. Following one upon the other, the most contradictory inclinations, the most antithetical whims, involve the so-called absolute sovereign in the most incompatible feelings, until finally this apparent omnipotence dissolves into genuine impotence. A despot is like a child; he has a child's weaknesses because he is not master of himself. Self-mastery is the first condition of all true power, of all liberty worthy of the name. One cannot be master of himself when he has within him forces that, by definition, cannot be mastered. For the same reason, political parties that are too strong—those that do not have to take account of fairly strong minorities—cannot last long. It is not long to their downfall, simply because of their excess power. Since there is nothing to restrain them, they inevitably go to violent extremes, which are self destroying. A party that is too strong escapes itself and is no longer able to control itself because it is too powerful. The "Chambres Introuvables" kill the very doctrines whose triumph they seem at first to proclaim.*

But, you will say, is it not possible for us to control ourselves through our own individual efforts, without the constant leverage of some external pressure upon us? Certainly, and this capacity for self-control is itself one of the chief powers that education should develop. But in order to set limits ourselves, we must feel the reality of these limits. Someone who was, or believed himself to be, without limits, either in fact or by right, could not dream of limiting himself without being inconsistent; it would do violence to his nature. Internal restraint can only be a reflection, an internal expression of external restraint. The physical milieu that constrains us reminds us that we are only part of a totality surrounding and limiting us; similarly, concerning the moral life, there are only moral forces that can exert on us like influence and

---

* Translator's footnote: This is an ironical designation for the parliament elected after the return of the Bourbons in 1815. The parliament was so rigged that it offered no resistance to a reactionary administration; and the opposition kept asking: where is the Chamber? where is the parliament?

provide this same feeling. What these moral forces are we have indicated.

So we come to this important conclusion. Moral discipline not only buttresses the moral life, properly speaking; its influence extends further. In effect, it follows—as we have just seen—that it performs an important function in forming character and personality in general. In fact, the most essential element of character is this capacity for restraint or—as they say—of inhibition, which allows us to contain our passions, our desires, our habits, and subject them to law.

The individual human being is someone who can leave his imprint upon everything he does, a mark appropriate to himself, constant through time and by means of which he recognizes himself as distinct from all others. But insofar as our inclinations, instincts, and desires lack any counterbalance, insofar as our conduct hangs on the relative intensity of uncontrolled dispositions, these dispositions are gusts of wind, erratic stop-start affairs characteristic of children and primitives, which as they endlessly split the will against itself, dissipate it on the winds of caprice and preclude its gaining the unity and continuity that are the essential preconditions of personality. It is precisely in this development of self mastery that we build up moral discipline. It teaches us not to act in response to those transient whims, bringing our behavior willy-nilly to the level of its natural inclinations. It teaches us that conduct involves effort; that it is moral action only when we restrict some inclination, suppress some appetite, moderate some tendency. At the same time, just as any rule about anything that is relatively fixed or invariable stands above all individual caprice, and as moral rules are still more invariable than all the others, to learn to act morally is also to learn conduct that is orderly, conduct that follows enduring principles and transcends the fortuitous impulse and suggestion. Thus, will is generally formed in the school of duty.

# CHAPTER FOUR

~§   THE SPIRIT OF DISCIPLINE

(Concluded); AND THE SECOND

ELEMENT OF MORALITY:

ATTACHMENT TO SOCIAL GROUPS

HAVING ASCERTAINED THE FIRST ELEMENT OF MORALITY, WE inquired into its function in order to specify its bearing on the training of the child. Morality, we have said, is basically a discipline. All discipline has a double objective: to promote a certain regularity in people's conduct, and to provide them with determinate goals that at the same time limit their horizons. Discipline promotes a preference for the customary, and it imposes restrictions. It regularizes and it constrains. It answers to whatever is recurrent and enduring in men's relationships with one another. Since social life has certain commonalities, since the same combination of circumstances recurs periodically, it is natural that certain modes of action—those found to be most in accord with the nature of things—also repeat themselves with the same regularity. It is the relative regularity of the various situations in which we find ourselves that implies the relative regularity of our behavior.

The practical reason for the limitations imposed by discipline are not so immediately apparent. It seems to imply a violence against human nature. To limit man, to place obstacles in the path of his free development, is this not to prevent him from fulfilling himself? But we have seen that this limitation is a condition of our happiness and moral health. Man, in fact, is made for life in a determinate, limited environment, however extended it may be; the sum total of his life activities is aimed at adapting to this milieu or adapting it to his needs. Thus, the behavior required of us shares in this same determination. To live is to put ourselves in harmony with the physical world surrounding us and with the social world of which we are members; however extended their realms, they are nevertheless limited. The goals we normally seek are equally delimited, and we are not free to transcend the limits without placing ourselves at odds with nature. At each moment of time, our hopes, our feelings of all sorts must be within bounds. The function of discipline is to guarantee such restraint. If such necessary limits are lacking, if the moral forces surrounding us can no longer contain or moderate our passions, human conduct—being no longer constrained—loses itself in the void, the emptiness of which is disguised and adorned with the specious label of the infinite.

Discipline is thus useful, not only in the interests of society and as the indispensable means without which regular cooperation would be impossible, but for the welfare of the individual himself. By means of discipline we learn the control of desire without which man could not achieve happiness. Hence, it even contributes in large measure to the development of that which is of fundamental importance for each of us: our personality. The capacity for containing our inclinations, for restraining ourselves—the ability that we acquire in the school of moral discipline—is the indispensable condition for the emergence of reflective, individual will. The rule, because it teaches us to restrain and master ourselves, is a means of emancipation and of freedom. Above all, in democratic societies like ours is it essential to teach the child this wholesome self-control. For, since in some measure the conventional restraints are no longer effective —barriers which in societies differently organized rigorously restrict people's desires and ambitions—there remains only moral discipline to provide the necessary regulatory influence. Because, in principle, all vocations are available to everybody, the drive to get ahead is more readily stimulated and inflamed beyond all measure to the point of knowing almost no limits.

Education must help the child understand at an early point that, beyond certain contrived boundaries that constitute the historical framework of justice, there are limits based on the nature of things, that is to say, in the nature of each of us. This has nothing to do with insidiously inculcating a spirit of resignation in the child; or curbing his legitimate ambitions; or preventing him from seeing the conditions existing around him. Such proposals would contradict the very principles of our social system. But he must be made to understand that the way to be happy is to set proximate and realizable goals, corresponding to the nature of each person and not to attempt to reach objectives by straining neurotically and unhappily toward infinitely distant and consequently inaccessible goals. Without trying to hide the injustices of the world—injustices that always exist—we must make the child appreciate that he cannot rely for happiness upon unlimited power, knowledge, or wealth; but that it can be found in very diverse situations, that each of us has his sorrows as well as his joys, that the important thing is to discover a goal compatible with one's abilities, one which allows him to realize his nature without seeking to surpass it in some manner, thrusting it violently and artificially beyond its natural limits. There is a whole cluster of mental attitudes that the school should help the child acquire, not because they are in the interests of this or that regime, but because they are sound and will have the most fortunate influence on the general welfare. Let us suggest, further, that moral forces guard against forces of brutality and ignorance. Finally, we must not see in the preference for control certain indescribable tendencies toward stagnation. To move toward clear-cut objectives, one after another, is to move ahead in uninterrupted fashion and not to be immobilized. It is not a matter of knowing whether one must move or not, but at what speed and in what fashion.

Thus, we come to the point of justifying discipline rationally, in terms of its utility, as well as the more obvious aspects of morality. However, we must note that our conception of its function is altogether different from that of certain recognized apologists. In fact, it often happens that, to demonstrate the beneficent results of morality, such apologists rely on a principle that I have criticized: they invoke the support of those who see in discipline only a regrettable, if necessary, evil. Like Bentham and the utilitarians, they take it as self-evident that discipline does violence to human nature; but, rather than concluding that such opposition to man's nature is evil, they consider that it is good because they judge man's nature to be evil. From this point of view, nature is the cause, the flesh is the source of sin and evil. It is not given to man, then, to develop his nature but, on the contrary, he must triumph over it, he must vanquish it, silence its demands. It only provides him the occasion for a beautiful struggle, an heroic effort against himself. Discipline is precisely the means of this victory. Such is the ascetic conception of discipline as it is preached by certain religions.

The idea I have proposed to you is quite otherwise. If we believe that discipline is useful, indeed necessary for the individual, it is because it seems to us demanded by nature itself. It is the way in which nature realizes itself normally, not a way of minimizing or destroying nature. Like everything else, man is a limited being: he is part of a whole. Physically, he is part of the universe; morally, he is part of society. Hence, he cannot, without violating his nature, try to supersede the limits imposed on every hand. Indeed, everything that is most basic in him partakes of this quality of partialness or particularity. To say that one is a person is to say that he is distinct from all others; this distinction implies limitation. If, then, from our point of view, discipline is good, it is not that we regard the work of nature with a rebellious eye, or that we see here a diabolical scheme that must be foiled; but that man's nature cannot be itself except as it is disciplined. If we deem it essential that natural inclinations be held within certain bounds, it is not because that nature seems to us bad, or because we would deny the right to gratification; on the contrary, it is because otherwise such natural inclinations could have no hope of the satisfaction they merit. Thus, there follows this first practical consequence: asceticism is not good in and of itself.

From this first difference between the two conceptions, others may be derived that are no less significant. If discipline is a means through which man realizes his nature, it must change as that nature changes through time. To the extent of historical progress and as a result of civilization, human nature becomes stronger and more vigorous with greater need of expression; this is why it is normal for the range of human activity to expand for the boundaries of our intellectual, moral, and emotional horizons always to roll farther away. Hence, the arrogance of systems of thought— whether artistic, scientific, or in the realm of human welfare —which would prohibit us from going beyond the points reached by our fathers, or would wish us to return there. The normal boundary line is in a state of continual becoming, and any doctrine which, under the authority of absolute principles, would undertake to fix it immutably, once and for all, must sooner or later run up against the force of the changing nature of things.

Not only does the content of discipline change, but also the way it is and should be inculcated. Not only does man's range of behavior change, but the forces that set limits are not absolutely the same at different historical periods. In the lower societies, since social organization is very simple, morality takes on the same character; consequently, it is neither necessary nor even possible that the nature of discipline be clearly elucidated. This same simplicity of moral behavior makes it easy to transform such behavior into habits, mechanically carried out; under these conditions, such automatism poses no difficulties. Since social life is quite self-consistent, differing but little from one place to another, or from one moment in time to another, custom and unreflective tradition are quite adequate. Indeed, custom and tradition have such power and prestige as to leave no place for reasoning and questioning.

On the other hand, the more societies become complex, the more difficult for morality to operate as a purely automatic mechanism. Circumstances are never the same, and as a result the rules of morality require intelligence in their application. Society is continually evolving; morality itself must be sufficiently flexible to change gradually as proves necessary. But this requires that morality not be internalized in such a way as to be beyond criticism or reflection, the agents par excellence of all change. Individuals, while conforming, must take account of what they are doing; and their conformity must not be pushed to the point where it completely captures intelligence. Thus, it does not follow from a belief in the need for discipline that discipline must involve blind and slavish submission. Moral rules must be invested with that authority without which they would be ineffective. However, since a certain point in history it has not been necessary to remove authority from the realm of discussion, converting it into icons to which man dare not, so to speak, lift his eyes. We shall have to inquire later how it is possible to meet these two, apparently contradictory, requirements. For the moment it must suffice to point them out.

This matter leads us to examine an objection that may already have occured to you. We have contended that the erratic, the undisciplined, are morally incomplete. Do they not, nevertheless, play a morally useful part in society? Was not Christ such a deviant, as well as Socrates? And is it not thus with all the historical figures whose names we associate with the great moral revolutions through which humanity has passed? Had their feeling of respect for the moral rules characteristic of their day been too lively, they would not have undertaken to alter them. To dare to shake off the yoke of traditional discipline, one should not feel authority too strongly. Nothing could be clearer.

However, if in critical and abnormal circumstances the feeling for the rule and for discipline must be weakened, it does not follow that such impairment is normal. Furthermore, we must take care not to confuse two very different feelings: the need to substitute a new regulation for an old one; and the impatience with all rules, the abhorrence of all discipline. Under orderly conditions, the former is natural, healthy, and fruitful; the latter is always abnormal since it prompts us to alienate ourselves from the basic conditions of life. Doubtless, with some of the great moral innovators, a legitimate need for change has degenerated into something like anarchy. Because the rules prevailing in their time offended them deeply, their sense of the evil led them to blame, not this or that particular and trainsient form of moral discipline, but the principle itself of all discipline. But it is precisely this that always vitiated their efforts; it is this that rendered so many revolutions fruitless, not yielding results corresponding to the effort expended. At the point when one is rising against the rules, their necessity must be felt more keenly than ever. It is just at the moment when one challenges them that he should always bear in mind that he cannot dispense with rules. Thus the exception that seemed to contradict the principle serves only to confirm it.

In sum, the theories that celebrate the beneficence of unrestricted liberties are apologies for a diseased state. One may even say that, contrary to appearances, the words "liberty" and "lawlessness" clash in their coupling, since liberty is the fruit of regulation. Through the practice of moral rules we develop the capacity to govern and regulate ourselves, which is the whole reality of liberty. Again, it is these same rules that, thanks to the authority and force vested in them, protect us from those immoral and amoral forces besetting us on every hand. "Rules" and "liberty" are far from being exclusive or antithetical terms. The latter is only possible by virtue of the former. The idea of regulation should no longer be accepted with docile resignation; it deserves to be cherished. This is a truth important to remember these days, and one to which public attention can't be too often drawn. For we are living precisely in one of those critical, revolutionary periods when authority is usually weakened through the loss of traditional discipline—a time that may easily give rise to a spirit of anarchy. This is the source of the anarchic aspirations that, whether consciously or not, are emerging today, not only in the particular sects bearing the name, but in the very different doctrines that, although opposed on other points, join in a common aversion to anything smacking of regulation.

We have ascertained the first element of morality and have shown what its function is. But this first element only conveys an idea of the most formal aspect of moral life. We have said that morality consists in a body of rules that govern us; we have analyzed the concept of rule without concerning ourselves with the content of the behavior required of us. We have studied it in a purely formal sense, as a justifiable abstraction. But as a matter of fact, morality has a content that, as one can foresee, itself has moral import. Moral precepts demand of us certain specific behavior; and because all such behavior is moral, since it belongs to the same category—since in other words it shares the same character—it should manifest certain common characteristics. This, or these, common qualities constitute other essential elements of morality, since they are found in all moral behavior, and, consequently, we must try to identify them. Once we understand them, we will have determined, at the same time, another basic element of moral character—that is to say, what it is that prompts man to behave in a way corresponding to this definition. And a new goal will be indicated for the educator.

In order to resolve this problem, we shall proceed as we have in determining the first element of morality. We shall not commence by asking what the content of morality ought to be any more than we asked what the a priori form of morality should be. We shall not inquire what a moral act should be to justify the adjective "moral," commencing with some notion of morality fixed in advance of observation or anything else. On the contrary, we shall observe what kinds of acts they are to which we affix this label. What ways of behaving are approved as moral and what are the characteristics of these modes of behavior? Our task is not to shape the child in terms of a nonexistent morality but in the light of moral concepts as they exist or as they tend to be. In any case, this is our point of departure.

Human behavior can be distinguished in terms of the ends toward which it is directed. Now, all the objectives sought by men may be classified into the following two categories. First, there are those concerning only the individual himself who pursues them; we shall therefore call them *personal*.

Second, there are those acts concerning something other than the individual who is acting; in this case, we shall call them *impersonal*. One can readily see that this last category comprises a considerable number of different kinds of acts, according to whether the ends pursued by the actor relate to other individuals, to groups, or to things. But for the moment it is not necessary to go into these details.

Having made the major distinction, let us see if those acts in the service of personal ends can be called moral.

Personal objectives themselves are of two kinds. We may, first of all, seek simply and purely to sustain life, to preserve ourselves, to seek refuge from those destructive elements that threaten us. Or we may seek personal aggrandizement or personal development. We certainly cannot pass adverse judgment on those acts aimed solely and uniquely at sustaining life. But so far as the public conscience is concerned, such behavior is and always has been quite bereft of moral value. Such acts are morally neutral. Consider someone who takes good care of himself, follows meticulously the rules of hygiene with the single aim of survival. We do not say that his conduct is moral. We deem his conduct prudent, wise; but we do not consider that there is anything in such behavior to which the notion of morality applies. It is outside the realm of morality. Doubtless it is otherwise when we take care of our life, not simply to be able to preserve and enjoy it, but, for example, to be able to preserve our family because we feel that we are necessary to it. In this case our behavior would be considered moral, since it is not a personal end that one has in view, but the interest of the family. Such action is not directed toward personal survival but to enable others than ourselves to live. The objective sought is, thus, impersonal. True, I may seem to run counter to the current conception according to which man has an obligation to perserve his life. This is beside the point. I do not deny that man has an obligation to live, but I say that he does not fulfill a duty, through the sole act of survival, except when life is for him a means of achieving an end that transcends his own life. There is nothing moral in living just for the sake of keeping alive.

The same may be said of all those things we do with a view not only to preserve but to develop and strengthen ourselves—at least if such development is only in our own interest. For example, the man who devotes himself to the cultivation of his intellect or to the refinement of his aesthetic faculties with the single aim of success or, even more simply, for the satisfaction of feeling more complete, richer in knowledge and feelings, for the solitary enjoyment of the picture he presents to himself—such a man does not evoke in us any feeling of morality. One may admire him as one admires a beautiful work of art. But to the extent that he seeks only personal objectives, whatever they may be, we cannot say that he fulfills any obligation. Neither science nor art has any intrinsic moral virtue that can be communicated, *ipso facto* to him who possesses them. Everything hinges on the uses one puts them to, or wishes to make of them. When, for example, one undertakes scientific research in order to reduce human suffering, then by common consent the act is morally praiseworthy. But it is not the same when the research is carried out purely for personal satisfaction.

Here then is our first conclusion: behavior, whatever it may be, directed exclusively toward the personal ends of the actor does not have moral value. It is true that, according to the utilitarian moralists, the moral conscience deceives itself when it judges human conduct in this fashion. According to them, strictly self-centered goals are par excellence the laudable ones. But we do not need to preoccupy ourselves here with the way in which these thinkers evaluate morality; it is this morality itself that we wish to know as it is understood and practiced by all civilized peoples. Put in these terms, the question may be easily resolved. Not only is there not today, but there never has existed any people among whom an egoistic act—that is to say, behavior directed solely to the interest of the person performing it—has been considered moral. Hence, we may conclude that behavior prescribed by the rules of morality is always behavior in pursuit of impersonal ends.

What must we understand by this word? Shall we say that, to act morally, it is enough to look, not to our personal interest, but to that of some other person? Thus, to guard my health would not, according to my contention, be a moral act; but the nature of the act changes when it is the health of someone like myself that I safeguard, when it is his happiness or his enlightenment that I have in view. Such an understanding of this behavior is inconsistent and contradicts itself. Why should that which for me has no moral value have it in the case of others? Why should the health or intelligence of someone who, let us suppose, is like myself —for I leave aside the case in which there are marked discrepancies between the actors—be more sacred than my health and intelligence are to me? On the average, men are of about the same stature, their personalities are more or less alike and may, so to speak, be substituted for one another. If an act calculated to preserve or develop my personality is amoral, why should it be otherwise with an identical act except that it is directed at some other personality? Why is the one more to be valued than the other? Besides, as Spencer has observed, such a morality is applicable only on the condition that it is not universally applied. Indeed, imagine a society in which everyone was prepared to deny himself in favor of his neighbor; then, for the same reason, none could accept the self-denial of others, and renunciation would become impossible because of its universality. For the practice of philanthropy, some must be willing not to—or be in such a position that they cannot—practice it. It is a virtue reserved for some. Morality, on the contrary, must by definition be common and accessible to all. Thus, one can scarcely see in sacrifice or in the devotion of person to person the kind of act we call moral. The essential qualities we are seeking must lie elsewhere.

Shall we find such qualities in action aiming to fulfill, not the interest of someone other than the actor, but the interest of many others; and shall we say that the impersonal goals that alone can confer a moral character upon an act are the particular objectives of a plurality of individuals? Thus, I would be acting morally not when I act on my own behalf, not when I act in the interests of another man, but when I act on behalf of a certain number of my fellows. But how could this be? If each individual taken separately has no moral worth, the sum total of individuals can scarcely have more. The sum of zeros is, and can only be, equal to zero. If a particular interest, whether mine or someone else's, is amoral, several such particular interests must also be amoral.

Moral action pursues impersonal objectives. But the impersonal goals of moral action cannot be either those of a person other than the actor, or those of many others. Hence, it follows that they must necessarily involve something other than individuals. They are supra-individual.

Outside or beyond individuals there is nothing other than groups formed by the union of individuals, that is to say, societies. Moral goals, then, are those the object of which is *society*. To act morally is to act in terms of the collective interest. This conclusion imposes itself in the wake of the foregoing arguments, which were successively eliminated. Now, it is evident that a moral act must serve some living and sentient being and even more specifically a being endowed with consciousnesses. Moral relations are relations between consciousnesses. Above and beyond me as a conscious being, above and beyond those sentient beings who are other individual human beings, there is nothing else save that sentient being that is society. By this I mean anything that is a human group, the family as well as the nation, and humanity, at least to the extent that they constitute societies. We shall have to inquire later if a rank order does not exist among these different groups, if there are not some more significant than others. For the moment, I shall limit myself to proposing this principle, namely, that the domain of the moral begins where the domain of the social begins.

To understand the significance of this major proposition, one must take account of the meaning of society. If we accept what has for a long time been the classical and widely held view, that society is only a collection of individuals, we are thrown back into the foregoing difficulties without any way of surmounting them. If self-interest has no moral value for me, it has no more among my fellows whatever their number, and, consequently, the collective interest, if it is only the sum of self-interests, is itself amoral. If society is to be considered as the normal goal of moral conduct, then it must be possible to see in it something other than a sum of individuals; it must constitute a being *sui generis*, which has its own special character distinct from that of its members and its own individuality different from that of its constituent individuals. In a word, there must exist, in the full meaning of the word, a social being. On this condition only is society able to perform the moral function that the individual cannot.

Thus, the conception of society as a being distinct from the individuals who compose it, a conception demonstrated by sociology at a theoretical level, is here confirmed at the practical level. For the fundamental proposition of the moral conscience is not otherwise explicable. This proposition, in effect, prescribes that man acts morally only when he works toward goals superior to, or beyond, individual goals, only when he makes himself the servant of a being superior to himself and to all other individuals. Now, once we rule out recourse to theological notions, there remains beyond the individual only a single, empirically observable moral being, that which individuals form by their association—that is, society. Unless the system of moral ideas is the product of a general hallucination, that being with which morality links our wills and which is the principal object of our behavior can only be a divine being or a social being. We set aside the first of these hypotheses as beyond the province of science. There remains the second, which, as we shall see, is adequate for our needs and aspirations and which, furthermore, embraces all the reality of the first, minus its symbolism.

One may object that, since society consists only of individuals, it cannot have a character different from that of the individuals who compose it. This is a common-sense argument, which for a long time has impeded and still impedes the development of sociology and the progress of a secular morality for the one depends upon the other. It is an argument that has received more attention than it merits. Indeed, experience demonstrates in a thousand ways that a combination of elements presents new properties that do not characterize any of the elements in isolation. The combination is then something new through the linking of the parts that compose it. In combining tin and copper, basic elements that are soft and malleable, one gets a new substance with an altogether different property. It is bronze, which is hard. A living cell consists entirely of inanimate, mineral molecules. But by the sheer fact of their combination the qualities characteristic of life emerge—the capacity for self-nourishment and reproduction—which are not perceptible in minerals even at the germinal stage.

Thus, it is an invariable fact that a whole may be something other than the sum of its parts. There is nothing here that should surprise us. Simply because the elements, rather than remaining isolated, are associated and connected, they act and react upon one another; it is natural that these actions and reactions, which are the direct result of the association and which did not occur before that association, should give rise to entirely new phenomena, hitherto nonexistent. Applying this general statement to man and to societies, we shall say, then, that because men live together rather than separately, individual minds act upon one another; and as a result of the relationships thus established, there appear ideas and feelings that never characterized these minds in isolation. Everyone knows how emotions and passions may break out in a crowd or a meeting, often altogether different from those that the individuals thus brought together would have expressed had each of them been exposed to the same experiences individually rather than collectively. Things appear to have an altogether different character, are felt in a very different fashion. Thus it is that human groups have a way of thinking, of feeling, and of living differing from that of their members when they think, feel, and live as isolates. Now, what we have said of crowds, of ephemeral gatherings, applies *a fortiori* to societies, which are only permanent and organized crowds.

One fact among many that makes clear this distinction between society and the individual is the way in which the character of the collectivity outlasts the personalities of its members. Early generations are replaced by later ones, and meanwhile society remains with its own structure and its own particular character. There are certainly differences between present-day France and France of the past, but these are, so to speak, differences in age. We have aged, certainly, and the characteristics of the collectivity are consequently modified, just as the individual changes physiologically as he goes through life. However, there is an identity between the France of the Middle Ages and contemporary France that one cannot fail to recognize. While generations of individuals succeed one another, throughout this perpetual flux of particular personalities, society persists, with its own mode of thought, its particular temperament. What is true of political society in its totality and by virtue of the relationship between citizens can apply to each secondary group

through the interaction of its members. The population of
Paris is endlessly renewed; new elements flow in here inces-
santly. Among present-day Parisians, there are very few who
are descendants of Parisians at the beginning of the century.
But the social life of Paris actually presents the same essential
characteristics that it had a hundred years ago. Only now
they are more generally acknowledged. Take the relative
propensity for crime, for suicides, marriage, even the comparatively low fertility—we find the proportionate distribution
among the different age categories analogous. It is, then, the
characteristic influence of the group that imposes these sim-
ilarities on the individuals who continually enter it. This is
the best proof that the group is something other than a
number of individuals.

# CHAPTER FIVE

⋘§   ATTACHMENT TO SOCIAL GROUPS

(*Continued*)

WE HAVE BEGUN TO GET AT THE SECOND ELEMENT OF MO-
rality. It consists in the individual's attachment to a group of
which he is a member. We shall raise the problem presently
whether, among the various groups to which we belong,
there is an heirarchy—whether they are useful to us to the
same extent so far as moral conduct is concerned. But before
embarking on this particular question, it is important to
establish the general principle that the domain of the genuinely moral life only begins where the collective life begins—
or, in other words, that we are moral beings only to the
extent that we are social beings.

To demonstrate this basic proposition I drew upon empirical facts that everyone can verify—in himself, in others, or
better still through the historical study of morality. The fact
is that never, either in the present or in the past, have people
attributed moral value to behavior except as such behavior
was focused on ends other than the personal interest of the
actor. Doutbless, moral conduct has always been thought of as
necessarily producing useful results for some living and conscious being for whom it increases happiness and reduces
misery. But it is not of society they spoke in acknowledging

that the being whose interests were served by morality was the same as the person who was acting. Egoism has been universally classified among the amoral traits.

Now this very elementary proposition is rich in implications. For if self-interest has no moral value for me, evidently it can be of no more worth in others. If my particular interests are not worth anything so far as moral conduct is concerned, how can it be otherwise with my fellows' idiosyncratic interests, which are in no way superior to mine? It follows that, if there is such a thing as morality, it must necessarily link man to goals that go beyond the circle of individual interests. This having been determined, there only remains the task of discovering what these supra-individual goals are, and of what they consist.

We have seen—and it is altogether evident—that beyond the individual there is only a single psychic entity, one empirically observable moral being to which our wills can be linked: this is society. There is, then, nothing but society that can provide the objective for moral behavior. But to be so, the concept of society must satisfy several conditions. First, it is altogether necessary that society not be reduced to a simple collection of individuals; because if the individual interest of each person taken separately is altogether devoid of moral character, the sum of all such interests, however numerous they may be, must also be devoid of morality. If society is to carry out the moral function which, from the standpoint of his particular interests the person cannot do, it must have its own character, have a character distinct from that of its members. We have seen that society does satisfy this condition. Just as the living cell is something other than the simple sum of inanimate molecules constituting it, just as the organism itself is something other than a sum of its cells, so is society a psychic being that has its own particular way of thought, feeling, and action, differing from that peculiar to the individuals who compose it. There is one observation in particular that makes intelligible the unique character of society: this is the way in which a kind of collective personality sustains itself and persists through time, retaining its identity despite the endless changes produced in the mass of individual personalities. Just as the physical and moral traits of the individual remain the same in their essentials, although in the course of a very short period of time all of the material of the organism—i.e., the cells—have been completely renewed; similarly the collective characteristics of society remain essentially the same—barring secondary differences associated with age—despite the incessant replacement of generations. Thus, on the condition that we conceive of society as a being quite distinct from the individual, we finally arrive at something that goes beyond the individual, without any need of straying beyond the realm of experience.

This first condition, however, does not suffice for an understanding of the way in which society can function as we have suggested. Man must still have an interst in linking himself with society. If it were simply something other than the individual, if it were so distinct from us as to be quite alien, such an attachment would be incomprehensible; it would scarcely be possible except to the extent that man in some way surrendered his own nature to become something other than himself. For, in reality, to link one's self with another being is always to merge with him in some measure, to become one with him—even to be ready to substitute the other for one's self if the attachment goes to the point of sacrifice.

Now, is not such renunciation of self quite unintelligible? Why should we subordinate ourselves to such an extent in favor of a being so radically different from ourselves? If society soars above us with no organic connection joining it with us, how can we take it as the goal of our conduct in preference to our self-interest? Because it has greater value, is richer in variegated elements, because it is more highly organized, because, in a word, it has more vitality and reality than a given individuality that must always be of a middling quality in contrast to a "personality" so vast and complex as that of society's? But why should this lofty organization affect us if it does not touch us, at some point? If it does not touch us, why make it the object of our efforts?

One may perhaps say, as has been said, that society is necessarily useful to the individual because of the services it provides him; he ought to desire it since it is in his interest. But then we fall back on the notion of personal interest, which is contradicted by the moral beliefs of all peoples. It was individual interest that was at first considered as the moral goal par excellence, while society was merely a means of attaining that end. However, if we want to be consistent with ourselves and with the facts, and if we intend to take account of this formal principle of the common conscience—rejecting as moral any act exclusively self-centered—then we must regard society as desirable in and of itself and not only to the extent that it is useful to the individual. But how is this possible? We find ourselves confronted with a difficulty quite comparable to that which we encountered before when dealing with the first element of morality. Since morality is a discipline, it has seemed to imply a limitation imposed on human nature. On the other hand, it could appear at first glance that such a limitation was contrary to nature. Similarly, here, the goals that morality assigns us seem to require a renunciation, which apparently has the effect of submerging human personality in some different personality. This impression is re-enforced by some hoary habits of thinking, which oppose society and the individual as two contrary and antagonistic categories, neither of which can expand or develop except at the expense of the other.

Again, this is only a deceptive appearance. Individual and society are certainly beings with different natures. But far from there being some inexpressible kind of antagoism between the two, far from its being the case that the individual can identify himself with society only at the risk of renouncing his own nature either wholly or in part, the fact is that he is not truly himself, he does not fully realize his own nature, except on the condition that he is involved in society. We have shown that the need for containing one's self within determinate limits is demanded by the person's nature. Whenever such limits are breached, whenever moral rules lack the necessary authority to exert, to a desirable degree, a regulatory influence on our behavior, we see society gripped by a dejection and pessimism reflected in the curve of suicides. Similarly, whenever society loses what it should normally have, the power of promoting identification of individual wills with itself, whenever the individual disassociates himself from collective goals in order to seek only his own interests, we see the same result and phenomenon, and suicide rates go up. Man is the more vulnerable to self-destruction the more he is detached from any collectivity, that is to say, the more self-centered his life. Suicide is about three times more frequent among bachelors than among married people, twice as frequent in childless homes as in those with children. It seems, as a matter of fact, inversely related to the number of children. Thus, according as a person is or is not a member of some family group, depending on whether the group is merely the married pair or has the stability conferred by children—to the extent that familial society is more or less cohesive, tightly knit and strong—he clings more or less to life. He also destroys himself less frequently when he has things to concern him other than himself. Crises that activate people's feelings of identity with the group produce the same results. For example, wars, in quickening the sense of patriotism, subordinate preoccupation with the self. The image of the threatened fatherland occupies a place in one's consciousness that it does not have in peace time; consequently, the bond between individual and society is strengthened, and, at the same time, the linkage to life is also re-enforced. The number of suicides declines. Similarly, the greater the cohesiveness of a religious group, and as a result the stronger the bonds between members, the more they are shielded against the thought of suicide. Members of the confessional minorities are always more tightly knit groups because of the opposition to them which they must combat. Also, a given denomination will have fewer suicides in a country where it is in a minority than where it embraces a majority of the people.

The egoist must indeed be a very clever person who understands better than anyone else the art of happiness. Quite to the contrary, he is in a state of unstable equilibrium, which nothing serves to modify. Man possesses all the less of himself when he possesses only himself. How does this come about? It is because man is, in large part, a product of society. It is from society that there comes whatever is best in us, all the higher forms of our behavior.

Language is social in the highest degree: it has been elaborated by society, and society transmits it from one generation to the next. Furthermore, language is not merely a system of words; each language implies a particular mentality, that of the society which speaks it, which thus expresses its own temperament, and it is this mentality which provides the foundation for individual mentality.

Among all the ideas that come to us by virtue of language, we must emphasize those deriving from religion. For religion is a social institution; it has served for many peoples as the foundation of collective life. All religious ideas are social in their origin; and, on the other hand, they still remain the pre-eminent form of public and private thought for the vast majority of men. Today, it is true, among the more advanced thinkers science has replaced religion. Of course, science—in part the heir of religion and having religious origins—is also a work of society. If people have lived isolated from one another, science would have been of no use to them. For under these conditions the human being would have dealt only with the physical milieu immediately surrounding him. Since this environment is simple, restricted, apparently invariable, any new developments aimed at adaptation would themselves have been similarly simple, few in number, and, continually repeating themselves because of the stability of the milieu, they would readily have taken the form of automatic, habitual behavior. Instinct, as among the animals, would have been adequate for everything; and science, which flourishes only when instinct withdraws, would never have been born. That it was born indicates that society needed it. For such a complex and differentiated organization could scarcely function under a rigid system of blind instinct. For the harmonious development of a complicated social order the co-operation of reflective intelligence soon became indispensable. Thus, one sees a kind of crude and nascent science appear in religious myth, but still wrapped in, and mixed up with, all kinds of incompatible elements. Little by little, it separated from these alien elements to establish itself independently under its own name and with its own special methods. This occurred because society, as it became more complex made such a development imperative.

It was, then, as a result of certain collective ends that science was formed and developed. Society called it into being, while compelling its members to instruct themselves. If one were to withdraw from the human mind everything that is a product of scientific culture, a huge void would be created. What I say of intelligence could be repeated with respect to all our other faculties. If we have an ever more compelling need for various activities, if we are less and less satisfied with the rather slow and dull life that man leads in less developed societies, it is because our society requires more and more intensive labors and more and more industry so that it has become habitual, and, through time, habit has become a need. But there is nothing elemental in us that incites us to this continual and painful effort.

Must we then acknowledge the antagonism between the individual and society, which so many theoreticians have cavalierly asserted? Quite to the contrary, there is in us a host of states which something other than ourselves—that is to say, society—expresses in, or through, us. Such states constitute society itself, living and acting in us. Certainly society is greater than, and goes beyond, us, for it is infinitely more vast than our individual being; but at the same time it enters into every part of us. It is outside us and envelops us, but it is also in us and is everywhere an aspect of our nature. We are fused with it. Just as our physical organism gets its nourishment outside itself, so our mental organism feeds itself on ideas, sentiments, and practices that come to us from society.

It is society that we consider the most important part of ourselves. From this point of view, one can readily see how it can become the thing to which we are bound. In fact, we could not disengage ourselves from society without cutting ourselves off from ourselves. Between it and us there is the strongest and most intimate connection, since it is a part of our own being, since in a sense it constitutes what is best in us. Under these conditions, one can understand how uncertain the life of the self-centered person, the egoist, is. For he goes contrary to nature. The egoist lives as though he were a whole, one who has in himself his *raison d'être* and who is sufficient unto himself. But this is an impossibility, a contradiction in terms. In vain do we sever—or attempt to sever—the bonds that connect us to others. We find ourselves unable to do so. We cling necessarily to the milieu surrounding us. It pervades us, it blends with us. Consequently, there is in us something other than ourselves if for no other reason than this: when we hold to ourselves, we

hold to something other than ourselves. Furthermore, one
can even say that the absolute egoist is an unrealizable abstraction. In order to live a purely egoistic life we would
have to strip away our social nature, which is quite as impossible as escaping our shadows. All we can do is to approximate more or less this abstractly conceived limit. But the
more we approach such a limit, the more we depart from
nature—the more abnormal does our life become, which
suggests that life soon becomes unbearable. Except under
some exceptionally favorable combination of circumstances,
such a distorted mode of life, so deflected from its normal
objectives, could result in nothing but frustration and pain.
Such exceptional circumstances are altogether lacking. Furthermore, during periods when society is disorganized and,
as a result of its decadence has less power to exact the commitment of individual wills, and when, consequently, egoism
has freer reign—these are calamitous times. The cult of the
self and the notion of the infinite often go together. Bud-
dhism is the best illustration of this relationship.

Thus, just as morality limits and constrains us, in response
to the requirements of our nature, so in requiring our commitment and subordination to the group does it compel us
to realize ourselves. It only commands us to do what is indicated by the nature of things. In order to be men worthy
of the name, we must, as soon as possible, put ourselves in
communication with that central source of the mental and
moral life that characterizes human kind. This source is not
within us; it is in society. Society is the producer and repository of all the riches of civilization, without which man
would fall to the level of animals. We must, then, be receptive to its influence, rather than turning back jealously
upon ourselves to protect our autonomy. It is precisely such
sterile cutting-off that morality condemns when it makes
commitment to the group the duty par excellence. Furthermore, this basic obligation, first among all others, far from

implying some incomprehensible renunciation, has only the effect of requiring conduct that develops our personalities.

We said before that the notion of personality presupposes, as its central element, a self-mastery that we can achieve only in the school of moral discipline. This primary and necessary condition is not sufficient. A person is not only a being who disciplines himself; he is also a system of ideas, of feelings, of habits and tendencies, a consciousness that has a content; and one is all the more a person as this content is enriched. For this reason, is not the civilized man a person in greater measure than the primitive; the adult, than the child? Morality, in drawing us outside ourselves, and thrusting us into the nourishing milieu of society, puts us precisely in the position of developing our personalities. Someone who does not live exclusively of, and for, himself, who offers and gives himself, who merges with the environing world and allows it to permeate his life—such a person certainly lives a richer and more vigorous life than the solitary egoist who bottles himself up and alienates himself from men and things. This is why a man who is genuinely moral—not the middling and mediocre morality that goes no further than certain elementary restrictions—a man with an active and positive morality, cannot fail to have a strong personality.

Society, therefore, goes beyond the individual; it has its own nature distinct from that of the individual; consequently, it fulfills the first necessary condition for serving as the object of moral behavior. But, on the other hand, it rejoins the individual. There is no gulf between it and him. It thrusts into us strong and deep roots. The best part of us is only an emanation of the collectivity. This explains how we can commit ourselves to it and even prefer it to ourselves.

Up to this point we have talked of society only in a general way, as if it there were only one. As a matter of fact, man always lives in the midst of many groups. To mention only the more important, there is the family in which one is born, the nation or the political group, and humanity. Ought one to commit himself to one of these groups to the exclusion of others? This is out of the question. Despite certain simplistic statements that have been made, there is no necessary antagonism between these three loyalties, as if one were only able to be a citizen of his country to the extent that he was alienated from the family, or could not fulfill his obligations as one of mankind except as he forgot his duties as citizen. Family, nation, and humanity represent different phases of our social and moral evolution, stages that prepare for, and build upon, one another. Consequently, these groups may be superimposed without excluding one another. Just as each has its part to play in historical development, they mutually complement each other in the present: each has its function. The family involves the person in an altogether different way, and answers to different moral needs, than does the nation. It is not a matter then of making an exclusive choice among them. Man is morally complete only when governed by the threefold force they exercise on him.

If these three groups can and should coexist concurrently, if each of them constitutes a moral objective worthy of our effort, it does not follow that these different goals have the same value. They constitute a hierarchy. The evidence suggests that familial goals are and should be subordinated to national objectives, if for no other reason than that the nation is a social group at a higher level. Because the family is closer to the individual, it provides less impersonal—and hence, less lofty—goals. The circle of familial interests is so restricted that it is in large measure the same as individual interests. Furthermore, to the extent that societies advance and become centralized, the general life of society—that which is shared by all its members and which finds its beginning and end in the political group—continually pre-empts more of the individual's thought and energies, while the relative and even the absolute part played by the family tends to decline. Public affairs of all sorts—political, judicial, international—as well as economic, scientific, and artistic events that affect the whole nation, draw the person out of the familial milieu and fix his attention on other things. Even the distinctively domestic activities have declined, since the child often leaves home at a very young age to get a public education, and since as an adult he will move away and start his own family, which, in turn, he will have with him but a short time. The center of gravity of moral life, formerly in the family, tends increasingly to shift away from it. The family is now becoming an agency secondary to the state.

If there can be no question on this point, the problem of whether humanity ought to be subordinate to the state, cosmopolitanism to nationalism, is on the contrary one of those that arouses the greatest controversy today. There could not be a graver issue, since the orientation of moral activity will be altogether different and moral education understood in almost contrary fashion, depending on the group to which priority is accorded.

What lends weight to the discussion is the strength of the arguments on both sides. On the one hand, this argument is persuasive: increasingly, those moral objectives that are most abstract and impersonal, those that are farthest removed from all conditions of time and place and race are also those which emerge as pre-eminent. Nations grow upon the foundations of the small tribal groups of former times; then the nations themselves are joined in even greater social organizations. Consequently, the moral objectives of society have been more and more generalized. Morality continuously disengages itself from particular ethnic groups or geographical areas precisely because each society, as it becomes larger, embraces a greater diversity of climatic and geographic conditions, and all these differing influences mutually cancel themselves. The national ideal of the early Greeks and

Romans was more narrowly focused on those tiny societies that were the cities of Greece and Italy: the ideal was, in a sense, a municipal ideal. By the time of the feudal collectivities of the Middle Ages, the ideal already involved a greater and more general group, which grew and was re-enforced to the extent that European societies became more extended and centralized. There seems no reason to assign certain arbitrary limits to such a continuous progressive development. Now mankind's goals are still higher than the loftiest national goals. Then should not supremacy be accorded the objectives of mankind in general?

On the other hand, in contrast with the nation, mankind as source and object of morality suffers this deficiency: there is no constituted society. It is not a social organism having its own consciousness, its own individuality, and its own organization. It is only an abstract term by which we designate the sum of states, nations, and tribes, which in their totality constitute mankind. The state is actually the most highly organized form of human organization in existence, and if one may believe that in the future states even greater than those of today may be formed, there is nothing to justify the supposition that there will never emerge a state embracing the whole of humanity. However, in any case, such an ideal is so far distant that there is no reason for considering it at this time. Now, it would seem impossible to subordinate and sacrifice a group that does in fact exist, that is at the present a living reality, to one not yet born and that very probably never will be anything but an intellectual construct. According to what we have said, conduct is moral only when it has for its object a society having its own structure and character. How can humanity have such a character and fill such a role since it is not a constituted group?

So it seems that we are confronted here with a contradiction. On the one hand, we can scarcely help conceiving of moral ends that are loftier than national goals; on the other hand, it seems quite impossible that these loftier ends can be embodied in a human group perfectly adequate to them. The only way of resolving this difficulty, which troubles public thinking, is to seek the realization of the human ideal through the most highly developed groups that we know, through those closest to mankind as a whole, but without confusing the two—that is to say through the efforts of specific nations. To eliminate all such contradictions, thus satisfying the requirements of our moral consciousness, it suffices that the state commit itself as its main goal not to expanding, in a material sense, to the detriment of its neighbors, not to gaining greater strength than they, or to becoming richer than they; but to the goal of realizing among its own people the general interests of humanity—that is to say, committing itself to an access of justice, to a higher morality, to organizing itself in such a way that there is always a closer correspondence between the merit of its citizens and their conditions of life with the end of reducing or preventing individual suffering. From this point of view, all rivalry between different countries disappears and, consequently, all contradiction between cosmopolitanism and patriotism.

Everything depends, after all, on the way in which patriotism is conceived; it can take two very different forms. Insofar as it is centrifugal, so to speak, it points national activity outside its boundaries and prompts nations to encroach upon one another, to stress their incompatibilities. Then they are put in a situation of conflict and, at the same time, put national sentiment in conflict with commitments to mankind. Or, conversely, the sentiment of patriotism may be altogether internally oriented, fixing upon the tasks of the internal improvement of society. In this case, it prompts all nations that have achieved comparable moral development to collaborate toward the same end. The first way is aggressive, military; the second is scientific, artistic, and, in a word, basically pacific.

Under these conditions, one no longer must ask whether

the national ideal should be sacrificed for the ideals of mankind, since the two merge. Moreover, this fusion does not by any means imply that the particular national character is doomed to disappear. For each can have its own particular way of conceiving this ideal in accord with its own character, temperament, and history. Scientists in a given society and even throughout the world all share a common objective, which is to extend the domain of human intelligence; but each scientist has, nonetheless, his own intellectual and moral individuality. Each sees the world—or better, a given part of the world—from his own perspective; but all of these various points of view, far from being exclusive, mutually correct and complement one another. Similarly, each particular country represents, or at least may represent a special point of view toward mankind; these various ways of conceiving the same object, far from being antagonistic, call forth one another because of their differences. For they are only different perspectives on the same reality—a reality whose infinite complexity can be expressed only through an infinity of successive or simultaneous approximations. Thus, as a result of whatever it is beyond or outside of particular societies that inclines them to the same ideal, that provides a common orientation for their moral behavior, it by no means follows that their differing individualities must vanish, losing themselves in one another. For this suprasocietal ideal is too rich in its variegated elements to be expressed and realized in its totality through the character of any one such state. There must be a kind of division of labor between the two, which is and will continue to be their reason for existence. Doubtless, the specific national characters that currently obtain will die away. They will be replaced by others, probably greater ones. But however vast they may be, so far as we now can see, there will always be a plurality of states, whose collaboration will be required to realize the goals of mankind.

Thus, we have ascertained more precisely the second element of morality. Basically, it consists in the attachment to a social group. If man is to be a moral being, he must be devoted to something other than himself; he must feel at one with a society, however lowly it may be. This is why the first task of moral education is to reunite the child with the society immediately surrounding him, that is to say, with the family. In a general sense, morality begins where and when social life begins, but there are nonetheless different degrees of morality, if for no other reason than that all human societies are not of equal moral value. Now there is one that enjoys a real primacy over all the others—the political society, the nation. However, it can enjoy moral primacy only on the condition that it is not conceived of as an unscrupulously self-centered being, solely preoccupied with expansion and self-aggrandizement to the detriment of similar entities; but as one of many agencies that must collaborate for the progressive realization of the conception of mankind. The school has, above all, the function of linking the child to this society. As for the family, it itself suffices to arouse and sustain in the hearts of its members those sentiments necessary for its existence. On the contrary, as for the nation— as here understood—the school is the only moral agent through which the child is able systematically to learn to know and love his country. It is precisely this fact that lends pre-eminent significance to the part played by the school today in the shaping of national morality.

# CHAPTER SIX

# ATTACHMENT TO SOCIAL GROUPS (*Concluded*); AND THE LINKAGE OF THE FIRST TWO ELEMENTS

We have specified the second element of morality. It consists in the individual's attachment to those social groups of which he is a member. Morality begins, accordingly, only in so far as we belong to a human group, whatever it may be. Since, in fact, man is complete only as he belongs to several societies, morality itself is complete only to the extent that we feel identified with those different groups in which we are involved—family, union, business, club, political party, country, humanity. Invariably, however, these groups do not have an equal moral significance, and they perform functions by no means equally important in the collective life. We cannot, therefore accord them an equal place in our considerations. There is one association that among all the others enjoys a genuine pre-eminence and that represents the end, par excellence, of moral conduct. This is the political society, i.e., the nation—but the nation conceived of as a partial embodiment of the idea of humanity.

The nation, as it lays claim to the contemporary conscience, is not the inflated and jealous state that knows no rules other than those directed toward its own interest and that deems itself emancipated from all the discipline of morality. What gives the nation its moral value is that it most closely approximates the society of mankind, at present unrealized in fact and perhaps unrealizable, yet representing the limiting case, or the ideal limit toward which we always strive.

We must be careful lest we see in this conception of the nation some kind of utopian fantasy. It is easy to see that it becomes more and more of a reality in history. If for no other reason than that society becomes increasingly big, the social ideal becomes more and more remote from all provincial and ethnic conditions and can be shared by a greater number of men recruited from the most diverse races and places. As a result of this alone, it becomes more abstract, more general, and consequently closer to the human ideal.

The statement of this principle allows us to resolve a difficulty encountered in the preceding chapters, the solution of which we postponed.

Since the actor's self-interest does not constitute a moral end, we concluded that others' individual interests could not be so regarded either, since there is no reason that another like one's self should be in a preferred position. But there is no doubt, as a matter of fact, that conscience confers a certain moral character on actions undertaken on behalf of one's fellow man. In a general sense, altrustic conduct in all its forms is universally considered as morally praiseworthy. Now is the public conscience wrong in thus evaluating man's conduct?

Such an assumption is clearly inadmissible. Given the generality of such a view, one can scarcely see it as the result of some kind of fortuitous aberration. An error is an accidental thing that can be neither so universal nor so lasting. But it is not at all necessary to attribute this kind of aberration to people's moral judgments to make the facts fit what we have said. For all that we have established is that charity, in the ordinary and popular sense of the word, the charity of person to person, has no moral value in itself and cannot by itself constitute the normal end of moral conduct.

It is still possible, nonetheless, that charity promotes morality indirectly. Although the interest in others' welfare is not moral in itself and cannot be accorded any moral priority, it may nonetheless be that the tendency to seek it in preference to our own promotes the development of morality, because such tendencies prepare and incline one to seek ends geuninely and correctly moral. As a matter of fact, this is what happens. There are no genuinely moral ends except collective ones. There is no truly moral force save that involved in attachment to a group. However, when one is committed to that society of which he is a member, it is psychologically impossible not to be bound to the people who compose it and through whom it comes into being. For although society is something other than the individual, although it is not completely in any one of us, there is nonetheless no one in whom it is not reflected. As a result, it is altogether natural that the sentiments we have for it are borne back upon those in whom society is partially embodied. To hold to society is to cling to the social ideal; and there is a little of this ideal in each of us. Each one of us has a hand in this collective ideal, which makes for the integrity of the group, which in turn is the sacred thing, par excellence. Consequently, each of us shares the religious deference inspired by this ideal. The bond to the group thus implies, in an indirect but almost necessary way, the bond to other individuals; when the group ideal is only a particular manifestation of the human ideal—when the citizen-ideal merges in large measure with the generic ideal of mankind— then it is to man *qua* man that we are bound, at the same time feeling more strongly linked with those in whom we find most clearly our society's particular conception of humanity.

This is what explains the moral character ascribed to sentiments of interpersonal sympathy and the acts prompted by such feelings. In themselves, they do not constitute intrinsic elements of the moral temperament; but they are closely linked to the most basic moral dispositions, while their absence may be taken to indicate—and not unreasonably—an inferior morality. If one loves his country, or humanity in general, he cannot see the suffering of his compatriots—or, more generally, of any human being—without suffering himself and without demonstrating, consequently, the impulse to relieve it. Conversely, if one is too immune to all pity, he is relatively unable to identify himself with anything other than himself and unable, *a fortiori*, to attach himself to the group of which he is part.

Charity, then, has moral value only as a symptom of a moral state with which it is associated; because it points to a moral propensity to sacrifice, to go beyond one's self, to go beyond the circle of self-interest, it clears the way for a true morality. Moreover, various other sentiments have the same significance—those which attach us to things other than men, to which we are related, such as animals, or the things surrounding us, such as birthplaces, etc. There evidently is nothing apparently moral in attachment to inanimate things. Yet whoever cuts himself off too easily from the familiar things of life gives evidence—evidence that is alarming from a moral point of view—of a break in the bond linking him with something other than himself, that is to say, in sum, an inferior capacity for committing himself.

It is true that the charity of person for person thus occupies a secondary and subordinate place in the system of moral behavior. This is not surprising. It should not be accorded a loftier status. In reality, it would be easy to show that this kind of unselfishness is usually poor in its outcomes. In fact, the lone individual, reduced to his own resources, is unable to alter the social situation. One can act effectively upon society only by grouping individual efforts in such a way as to counter social forces with social forces. The ills that specific acts of charity seek to cure or mitigate derive basically from social causes. Taken apart from particular cases, the nature of the distress in a given society is a function of the conditions of economic life and of the way in which it operates—that is to say, a function of its particular organization.

If today we have a large number of social vagrants, people from all ranks of society, it is because there is something in our European societies promoting such a condition. If alcoholism increases apace, it is because the intense stresses of civilization arouse needs which, if no other means are provided, are satisfied by means of alcohol. Such obviously social evils require social treatment. The lone individual can do nothing against them. The only effective remedy lies in the collective organization of welfare. Individual energies must be grouped, concentrated, organized to produce any effect. At the same time, such action takes on a higher moral character precisely because it serves more impersonal, more general ends. It is doubtless true that in this case one no longer has the pleasure of seeing with his own eyes the outcomes of willing sacrifice; but precisely because selflessness is more difficult, because it is less facilitated by obvious impressions, it is of more value. To follow any other course, to deal with each specific ill without seeking to act on its causes, is to behave like a doctor who treats the external symptoms of a disease without trying to get at the deeper cause of which the symptom is only an external manifestation. Now doubtless one is sometimes obliged to limit himself to symptomatic medicine when he is powerless to do anything better. It is not a question of condemning or discouraging all individual charity, but merely of determining the extent to which morality is involved.

These, then, are the first two elements of morality. To discriminate and define them we have had to study them separately. The result is that they must have seemed, up to now, to be distinct and independent. Discipline seems to be one thing, and the collective ideal to which we are committed another, quite different thing. As a matter of fact, however, there is a close connection between the two. They are only two aspects of the same, single reality. To understand what makes them one and thus to achieve a more coherent and concrete view of moral life, it will suffice to inquire into the authority that we have recognized in moral rules, deference to which constitutes discipline: what does it consist of and whence does it spring? So far, we have deferred this question, but we are now ready to attack it.

We have seen that moral rules have a particular authority, by virtue of which human wills abide by their prescriptions simply because they so ordain, and independent of the possible outcomes that the acts thus prescribed may have. To do one's duty because it is a duty—this is to abide by the rule because it is a rule. How does it happen that a rule, humanly contrived, can have such ascendance, that it can so bend the wills of those human beings who themselves make it? Certainly, since the fact itself is incontestable, we could assert the proposition even though we were in no position to offer an explanation, and even, it could be maintained, although we shall not be able to explain it. But we must be careful not to deny the moral reality simply because the present state of knowledge does not allow us to account for it. As a matter of fact, however, what has been established in the preceding chapters will permit us to resolve this mystery without any recourse to hypotheses of a non-empirical order.

We have just shown that the function of morality is to link the individual to one or several social groups and that morality presupposes this very attachment. So it is that morality is made *for* society. Is it not, then, a priori evident that it is made *by* society? What or who could be the author of morality? The individual? But of all that which transpires in the vast moral milieu constituted by a great society like ours, amidst the infinite number of actions and reactions recipro-cally involving millions of social units at each instant of time, we sense only the few repercussions that reach our limited personal spheres. We can certainly perceive the great events that unfold in the full light of public awareness; but the internal operations of the machine, the silent functioning of the internal organs, in a word, all that makes up the very substance and continuity of collective life—all this is beyond our purview, all this escapes us. Undoubtedly, we hear the muffled sounds of the life surrounding us; and we understand very well that there is, all around us, an enormous and com-plex reality. But we have no direct awareness of it, any more than of the physical forces informing our physical environ-ment. Only the effects get through to us.

Therefore, it is impossible for the individual to have been the author of the system of ideas and practices that do not directly relate to him, but that aim at a reality other than himself and of which he has only an ever so vague feeling. Society in its totality has independently a consciousness ade-quate to the job of establishing this discipline, the object of which is to represent itself, at least to the extent that it is self-aware. Consequently, this conclusion asserts itself logi-cally. If a society is the end of morality, it is also its producer. The individual does not carry within himself the precepts of morality designed in some schematic form, so that he has nothing more to do than sharpen and develop them. On the contrary, such precepts do not emerge except through the relationships of associated individuals, as they translate and reflect the life of the relevant group or groups.

The logic of this view is confirmed, moreover, by historical proofs that may be regarded as decisive. For the fact that morality varies from society to society certainly shows that it is a social product. That of Greek and Roman cities is not ours, just as that of primitive tribes is not the morality of the city. It is true that people have sometimes tried to explain this variation in moral ideals as the result of errors based upon our imperfect understanding. It has been contended that, if Roman morality was different from ours, it is because human intelligence was then veiled and obscured by all kinds of prejudices and superstitions since erased. But if there is one fact that history has irrefutably demonstrated it is that the morality of each people is directly related to the social structure of the people practicing it. The connection is so intimate that, given the general character of the morality observed in a given society and barring abnormal and pathological cases, one can infer the nature of that society, the elements of its structure and the way it is organized. Tell me the marriage patterns, the morals dominating family life, and I will tell you the principal characteristics of its organization.

The notion that the Romans could have practiced a different morality is, really, an historical absurdity. Not only would they have been unable to do so, but they should not have had any other. Let us suppose, in fact, that through some miracle they opened themselves to ideas such as those that are the basis for our present-day morality. Roman society could not have survived. For morality is a work of life, not of death. In a word, each social type has the morality necessary to it, just as each biological type has a nervous system that enables it to sustain itself. A moral system is built up by the same society whose structure is thus faithfully reflected in it. It is quite the same with what we call the moral individual. It is society that prescribes our obligations toward ourselves. It requires us to develop in ourselves an ideal type, and it requires this because it has a vital interest in doing so. Society, in fact, cannot exist except on the condition that all of its members are sufficiently alike—that is to say, only on the condition that they all reflect, in differing degree, the characteristics essential for a given ideal, which is the collective ideal. That is why this aspect of morality, like all the others, has differed according to the type and country.

So much acknowledged, the question we have posed finds a ready answer. If society itself has instituted the rules of morality, it must also be society that has invested them with their authority, which we seek to explain.

What is it, in fact, that we label authority? Without pretending to settle a problem as complex as this in a few words, we can nonetheless suggest the following definition: authority is a quality with which a being, either actual or imaginary, is invested through his relationship with given individuals, and it is because of this alone that he is thought by the latter to be endowed with powers superior to those they find in themselves. It is of no importance, as a matter of fact, whether these powers are real or imaginary. It is enough that they exist as real in peoples' minds. The sorcerer is an authority for those who believe in him. This is why authority is called moral: it is because it exists in minds, not in things.

Having stated the definition, it is easy to demonstrate that the being that best fulfills the necessary conditions as constituting an authority is the collective being. For it follows from all that we have said that society infinitely surpasses the individual, not only in material scope, but beyond that, in moral power. Not only does it command incomparably greater power, since it derives from the mutual re-enforcement of all the individual forces, but in it is found the source of that intellectual and moral life to which we turn to nourish our thought and our morality. For the fashioning of a newly born generation implies the assimilation, little by little, of the cultural milieu; it is only gradually as the animal—as we are born—incorporates the elements of his culture that the human being emerges. For it is society that is the repository of all the wealth of civilization; it is society that accumulates and preserves these treasures transmitting them from age to age; it is through society that these riches reach us. Thus it is that we are obligated to society, since it is from society that we receive these things.

One can understand, therefore, how a powerful morality, of which our conscience is merely a partial embodiment, must be invested with such authority. Even that element of mystery that seems inherent in all conceptions of authority is not lacking in the feeling we have for society. As a matter of fact, it is natural that any being having superhuman powers should baffle man's intelligence. This is why authority achieves its maximum impact above all in some religious form.

Now, we have just been observing that society is full of mystery for the individual. We constantly have the impression of being surrounded with a host of things in the course of happening whose nature escapes us. All sorts of forces move themselves about, encounter one another, collide near us almost brushing us in their passage; yet we go without seeing them until that time when some impressive culmination provides a glimpse of a hidden and mysterious event which has occurred under our noses, but of which we had no suspicion and which we begin to see only in terms of its results. There is above all one fact that constantly re-enforces this feeling: it is the pressure which society continually exerts upon us and of which we cannot be unaware. Whenever we deliberate as to how we should act, there is a voice that speaks to us, saying: that is your duty. When we fail in the duty with which we have been confronted the same voice is heard reproaching our action. Because it speaks to us in an imperative tone we certainly feel that it must come from some being superior to us; but we cannot see clearly who or what it is. This is why, in order to explain this mysterious voice that does not speak with a human accent, people imagine it to be connected with transcendant personalities above and beyond man, which then become the object of a cult—the cult being, in the final analysis, only the external evidence of the authority attributed to the superhuman beings. It is our task to divest this conception of the mythical forms in which it has been shrouded in the course of history, and to grasp the reality beneath the symbolism. This reality is society. In molding us morally, society has inculcated in us those feelings that prescribe our conduct so imperatively; and that kick back with such force when we fail to abide by their injunctions. Our moral conscience is its product and reflects it. When our conscience speaks, it is society speaking within us. The tone with which it speaks is the best demonstration of its remarkable authority.

Not only is society a moral authority, but there is every reason to consider it the type and the source of all moral authority. We would, of course, be pleased to believe that there are at least some individuals who owe their eminence only to themselves and their natural superiority. But to what, exactly, do they owe it? To their greater physical strength? Precisely because contemporary society is unwilling to accord anything of a moral nature to sheer physical superiority, this does not confer upon people a whit of moral authority. Not only do we not respect sheer physical strength; we scarcely fear it. For our social organization is inclined to prevent the abuse of power and consequently to make it less formidable. Would great intelligence or remarkable scientific ability suffice to confer on such people an authority in proportion to their intellectual superiority? Once again, public opinion must first see in science something of moral value. Galileo was stripped of all authority by the tribunal that condemned him. The greatest scientific genius would be given no preferred position by a people who do not believe in science. How about a person of great moral character: would this endow him with more authority? Again, such a morality would have to be precisely that demanded by society. For behavior not deemed moral, whatever it might be, could not increase people's esteem of the actor. For most of their fellow citizens, Christ and Socrates were immoral and were not accorded any authority by them. In a word, authority does not reside in some external, objective fact, which logically implies and necessarily produces morality. It consists entirely in the conception that men have of such a fact; it is a matter of opinion, and opinion is a collective thing. It is the judgment of the group. Furthermore, it is easy to understand why all moral authority must be social in its origin. Authority is that quality in a man who is lifted above other men; he is a superman. But the more intelligent man, or the stronger, or the one who is more righteous is still a man; it is only a matter of degree that differentiates him from his fellows. Only society is beyond the individual. It is therefore from society that all authority emanates. It is society that invests such and such human qualities with this property *sui generis*, this prestige that elevates the persons possessing it beyond themselves. They become supermen because they share in the superiority, in this sort of transcendance, of society vis-à-vis its members.

Let us apply what we have just said to the rules of morality, and we shall readily understand the authority with which they are invested. It is because morality is a social thing that it seems to us—and has always appeared to man—as endowed with a kind of ideal transcendance; we feel that it belongs to a world beyond us, and it is this that has prompted people to see here the dicta and the laws of a superhuman power. If, again, the authority of the group focuses particularly on certain beliefs and sentiments, these are certainly moral ideas and moral feelings. There is nothing so closely bound to the very core of the collective conscience: these beliefs and sentiments are the vital part of it.

Thus, what we said earlier about the way in which moral rules act upon our wills becomes clear and specific. When we spoke of them as forces that contain and restrain us, it may have seemed that we were hypostatizing or reifying abstractions. What, as a matter of fact, is a rule other than a simple combination of abstract ideas? And how can a purely verbal formula exert such influence? But now we see that underneath the formula, which is only the symbolic exterior, there are some genuine forces that are the essence of it. Thou shalt not kill, thou shalt not steal—these maxims, which for centuries have been transmitted from generation to generation, evidently do not have in themselves any magic virtue requiring us to respect them. But beyond the maxim, there are collective sentiments, the condition of public opinion that renders effective the rules merely expressing that maxim. For this collective sentiment is a force quite as real and active as the forces that fill the physical world. In a word, when we are constrained by moral discipline it is really society setting the limits and restraining us. Here is the concrete and living being that assigns us certain limits; and when one understands what it is and how it surpasses the individual's moral energies he is no longer surprised at the power of its influence.

At the same time, we see how the two elements of morality re-enforce one another and what makes for their unity. Far from being two distinct and independent things, which by some mysterious circumstance meet at the foundation of our moral life, they are on the contrary only two aspects of one and the same thing—that is, society. What is discipline, in fact, if not society conceived of as that which commands us, which dictates to us, which hands down its laws to us? As for the second element, the attachment to the group, it is again society that we discover, but conceived this time as a thing desirable and good, such as a goal which attracts us, an ideal to be realized. On the one hand, it seems to us an authority that constrains us, fixes limits for us, blocks us when we would trespass, and to which we defer with a feeling of religious respect. On the other hand, society is the benevolent and protecting power, the nourishing mother from which we gain the whole of our moral and intellectual substance and toward whom our wills turn in a spirit of love and gratitude. In the one case, it is like a jealous and formidable God, the stern lawmaker allowing no transgression of His orders. In the other case, it is the succoring deity to whom the faithful sacrifice themselves with gladness. Society owes its dual aspect and dual role to the single and unique property by virtue of which it is a thing superior to individuals. For it is because it is beyond us that it commands us as an imperative authority. If it were at our own level, it could only proffer advice that would put us under no obligation and would not impose itself upon our wills.

Similarly, because society is beyond us it constitutes the only possible goal of moral conduct. For precisely because this goal is beyond our own individual goals, we cannot seek to achieve it without elevating ourselves in the same measure beyond ourselves—without surpassing our individual nature, which is the highest ambition that man can pursue or ever has pursued. That is why the major historical figures, those who seem to us infinitely greater than all others, are not the great artists, or the men of profound wisdom, or statesmen, but those who have achieved—or are thought to have achieved—the greatest moral triumphs: Moses, Socrates, Buddha, Confucius, Christ, Mohammed, and Luther, to mention only a few of the greatest names. We consider them so not only because they are great men—that is to say persons like ourselves although endowed with more talent; but because in our minds they identify themselves with the impersonal ideal that they embodied and the great human groupings that they personified, we see them as raised beyond the condition of human beings and transfigured. This is why popular imagination, if it has not deified them, has nevertheless felt a need to set them apart and to identify them as closely as possible with divinity.

Far from doing violence to the ordinary conceptions, the conclusion at which we have just arrived finds in them a confirmation and at the same time brings to them a new exactness. Everyone, really, more or less clearly distinguishes two elements in morality, which correspond precisely to those we ourselves have just distinguished. The moralists refer to them as the good and the necessary. The necessary is morality insofar as it prescribes and proscribes. It is the morality of coercive prescriptions, strict and harsh, the instructions one must obey. The good is morality insofar as it seems to us a desirable thing, a cherished ideal to which we aspire through a spontaneous impulse of the will.

However, the concepts of duty and of the good are by themselves a pair of abstractions which, insofar as they aren't linked with any living reality, remain, so to speak, in the air; consequently, they altogether lack that which is needed to touch the heart and mind—above all, the minds and hearts of children. Doubtless whoever is keenly sensitive to things of a moral nature can discuss them with some passion—and this is contagious. But should a rational education involve emotional exhortation that makes its appeal only to the passions, however noble the passions that are evoked? Such an education is no different from that which we hope to supersede, since passion is not only a manifestation of prejudice, but prejudice in its most conspicuous form.

Of course, it is essential to stimulate the emotions, since they are the moving forces of conduct. But it is all the more necessary to arouse them through the justiciable procedures of reason; it is all the more necessary that they not be blind passions; it is all the more necessary that they be countered with ideas that clarify and guide them. If one limits himself to repeating and elaborating in emotional language such abstract words as *duty* and *good*, there can only result a parrot-like morality. The child must be put in contact with the concrete and living realities, which such abstract terms can only express in the most general way. We have demonstrated what this reality is, and thus moral education has a sound and certain foundation. It is not simply confronted with some fuzzy concepts. It has a point of support in reality. It knows what forces it must use and what should be brought to bear on the child to make of him a moral being.

# CHAPTER SEVEN

~§ CONCLUSIONS ON THE FIRST TWO

ELEMENTS OF MORALITY; AND

THE THIRD ELEMENT:

AUTONOMY, OR

SELF-DETERMINATION

THE POINT OF THE METHOD WE HAVE BEEN PURSUING IN THE study of moral facts is to transform the confused, popular notions of morality into precise and clear-cut notions. Our aim is to see morality clearly as it is, to reveal it in the midst of the diverse and confused preferences and ideas that beset it. This cannot be done simply by substituting our own conceptions for it. It is the moral reality with which we must begin and to which we must always return. Morality itself is our only possible point of departure: where else can we observe morality as it exists in fact? Moral theory that does not begin by observing morality as it is in order to understand its nature—its essential elements, its functions—necessarily lacks all foundation. Thus, we turn to the judgments of the common conscience as they can be observed. These constitute the only possible object of our inquiry. But, on the other hand, it is to this common conscience that we must return at the end of the quest, in order to try to clarify it by substituting more precise and methodically elaborated ideas for confused conceptions of it. Therefore, at each successive point of our discussion, and with respect to every major idea that we established, I have made it a practice to inquire what there was in customary moral notions corresponding to these ideas—what the ill-articulated impressions are, of which these ideas are the scientific expression.

Therefore, after having distinguished the two essential elements of morality, I undertook to show that such a distinction— not identical but analogous, and taking different forms—is universally made. There is in fact scarcely a moralist who has not sensed that there were two quite different things involved in morality, currently designated by the words *good* and *duty*. Duty is morality insofar as it commands. It is morality conceived of as an authority that we must obey because, and only because, it is authority. The good is morality conceived as a desirable thing that attracts our wills to it spontaneously, quickening our desire for it. Now, it is readily seen that duty is in fact society insofar as it imposes rules on us, specifies limits to our natural inclinations; while the good is society insofar as it constitutes a richer reality than our own individual selves and in which we cannot be involved without enriching ourselves. The same sentiment expresses itself in both ways. Morality appears to us under a double aspect: on the one hand, as imperative law, which demands complete obedience of us; on the other hand, as a splendid ideal, to which we spontaneously aspire.

This distinction is not merely of theoretical interest. The good and the required are indeed abstract terms, but substantive ones that resume the characteristics of a reality that is good and that has the quality of bending our wills. What is this reality? Morality? But morality is itself a totality of general judgments, of general maxims. What is the reality expressed and represented by these judgements? This question, which is by no means articulated in the common conscience, we have tried to resolve; at the same time, we have provided education with a method—and the only one—of rationally shaping the child's moral temperament. For there is only one method for eliciting such ideas and sentiments in the child's mind without recourse to irrational devices, without relying exclusively on the appeal to blind emotion. This is to link the child as directly as possible with that to which these ideas and feelings refer. It is only this that, through its influence on the consciousness, can stimulate those mental states expressing it. Education through direct experience affects the moral as well as the intellectual elements of culture. Now that we understand what these things are, what the concrete reality is that is expressed by moral sentiments, the way of proceeding with moral education is sketched out. In order to introduce it in the school, it will suffice to make it a part of the school context, to present it to children in its various aspects in such a way as to imprint it in their consciousness. At least the principle of pedagogical practice has been ascertained.

At the same time that these two elements of morality are found to be thus connected in reality, we can see better what promotes this unity. The question of how the good re-enforces the necessary and vice versa has often embarrased the moralists, and they have seen no way of resolving the problem than by deducing one of these conceptions from the other. For the one group, the good is the basic notion from which duty is derived. We are obliged, they argue, to conform to the rule because the prescribed act is good. But then the idea of duty is thrust into the background and disappears almost completely. On the contrary, however, duty almost necessarily implies the idea of resisting one's inclinations. At the bottom of the notion of obligation there is the idea of a moral constraint.

On the other hand, another school of thought has tried to

deduce the good from duty, contending that the only good derives from doing one's duty. But then, conversely, morality is stripped of everything attractive, of all that smacks of sentiment, of all that can stimulate spontaneous behavior. It becomes, instead, a strict and altogether coercive command, which must be obeyed regardless of whether the required behavior corresponds in any way to our natures or to our interests. In this case, the notion of the good vanishes. Yet it is no less indispensable than the other; for it is impossible for us to act if our behavior does not seem good in some respect, or if we are not in some measure interested in performing it.

Thus, all such attempts to reduce these two concepts to a single unity, by deducing the one from the other, result in discarding one of them, absorbing the concept of duty in the concept of the good or vice versa. Put in these terms the problem is insoluble.

However, the problem is readily resolved as soon as we understand that the two elements of morality are only two different aspects of the same reality. Their unity stems not from the fact that one is the corollary of the other or vice versa; it is the unity, expressed in different forms of behavior, of a real entity. Because society is beyond us, it commands us; on the other hand, being superior to everything in us, it permeates us. Because it constitutes part of us, it draws us with the special attraction that inspires us toward moral ends. It is not a matter, then, of trying to deduce the good from duty or the other way around. But according as we represent society to ourselves in one or the other of these aspects, it is viewed as a power that lays down the law for us or as a cherished being to which we give ourselves. According as our behavior is influenced by the one or the other view of society, we act out of respect for duty or through a desire of the good. Since we can probably never regard society from one of these viewpoints to the complete exclusion of the other; since we can never basically separate two aspects of one and the same reality; since, through natural association, the idea of the one can scarcely fail to be present, however inconspicuously, when the idea of the other is uppermost in our consciousness; it follows that, speaking rigorously, we never act completely out of duty, nor ever completely through love of the ideal. In practice, one of these sentiments must always accompany the other, at least as an auxiliary or complementary sentiment. There are certainly few if any men who are able to do their duty for the sole reason that it is their duty and without having at least some vague sense that the prescribed act is in some respect good—in a word, without being disposed to it by some natural inclination of their feelings. Conversely, although society may be within us and although we merge partially with it, when we act morally the collective ends we pursue are so far beyond us that in order to succeed to their heights—to go beyond ourseves to this extent—an effort is generally required of which we would be incapable were it not for the idea of duty, the feeling that we ought so to act, that we are obliged to do so, which re-enforces and sustains our commitment to the group.

However close the connection linking these two sentiments to one another, however they may be mutually implicated, it is important to note that they are still different things. The proof lies in the fact that among individuals, as among peoples, they develop inversely. With the individual, it is always the one or the other of these sentiments that dominates and colors in a special way the person's moral temperament. In this regard, one can distinguish two extreme and opposed types in men's moral character, which of course span a host of intermediate conditions.

With some people, it is the sensitivity to the rule, a disposition for discipline that predominates. They do their duty as they see it, completely and without hesitation, simply because it is their duty and without any particular appeal to their hearts. These are the men of substantial intellect and strong will—Kant is an ideal example—but among whom the emotional faculties are much less developed than those of the intellect. As soon as reason speaks, they obey; but they hold their feelings at a distance. Thus, their bearing suggests firmness and resolution and at the same time conveys a sense of coldness, severity, rigidity. The power of self-control is characteristic of them. This is why they do not go beyond their rights, do not trample on those of others. But they also have little capacity for those spontaneous impulses in which the individual gives or joyfully sacrifices himself.

Other people are characterized not by self-control and a tendency to withdraw but by a love of spending themselves, by an outward expansiveness. They love to attach, and devote themselves to others. These are the loving hearts, the ardent and generous souls. But their behavior, by contrast, is regulated only with difficulty. If they are capable of great deeds, they find it hard to tie themselves down to the performance of mundane obligations. Their moral conduct lacks, then, that consistent logic, that beautiful moral bearing of the former. One is less sure of these passionate men. For passions, even the most noble, blow successively hot and cold under the influence of chance circumstances and in the most erratic ways.

In sum, these two types contrast with one another like the two kinds of morality. Those of one type have the self-mastery, the power of inhibition, the authority over themselves that is developed by the performance of duty. The others are characterized by active and creative energy that is developed through the most continuous and intimate communication with the very source of moral energy—that is to say, society.

As with individuals, so with societies. Sometimes the one, sometimes the other element predominates; and the character of the moral life changes accordingly. When a people has achieved a stage of equilibrium and maturity, when the various social functions, at least temporarily, are articulated in an ordered fashion, when the collective sentiments in their essentials are incontestable for the great majority of people, then the preference for rule and order is naturally preponderant. Even generous impulses, if they suggest in any way a disturbance of traditional ideas and established rules inspire nothing but distaste. It may even happen that this state of mind is such as to make its influence felt, not only in the customs, but also in the arts and letters, which express, after their fashion, the moral situation of the country. This is what characterizes certain periods such as that of Louis XIV or that of Augustus, when society had come to be quite fully integrated. On the contrary, in times of flux and change, the spirit of discipline cannot preserve its moral vigor since the prevailing system of rules is shaken, at least in some of its parts. At such times, it is inevitable that we feel less keenly the authority of a discipline that is, in fact, attenuated. As a result, it is the other element, the need for some objective to which one can commit himself, an ideal to which he can dedicate himself—in a word, the spirit of sacrifice and devotion—that becomes the province, par excellence, of morality.

Now—and this is the conclusion toward which we have been driving—we are going through precisely one of these critical phases. Indeed, history records no crisis as serious as that in which European societies have been involved for more than a century. Collective discipline in its traditional form has lost its authority, as the divergent tendencies troubling the public conscience and the resulting general anxiety demonstrate. Consequently, the spirit of discipline itself has lost its ascendancy. Under these conditions, the only recourse is to the other element of morality. Doubtless, at any given moment, the sense of discipline is not to be neglected. We ourselves noted that it was especially essential to feel the necessity of moral rules at the time when one was working to change them. We must sustain this feeling for discipline in the child. This is a task that the educator should never give up. We shall see, shortly, how he should go about it. But moral discipline can have its full and useful effect only when morality is established, since its aim is to fix and sustain those essential traits that this morality presupposes. When, on the contrary, morality has yet to be established, when it is still nebulous and unformulated, then to achieve this end we must have recourse to the active and imaginative forces of the conscience, rather than to purely conservative forces—since it is not a matter of conserving anything. While we must certainly not lose sight of the need for the disciplinary element of morality, the educator should apply himself first and above all to evoking and developing this morality. This means, above all else, that the capacity for giving, for devoting one's self, should be stimulated and nourished. It is necessary to involve individuals in the pursuit of great collective ends to which they can devote themselves; to train them to cherish a social ideal, for the realization of which they may some day work. Otherwise, if this second source of morality does not make up for what is temporarily but necessarily lacking in the first, the nation cannot fail to fall into a state of moral debility, entailing danger even for its physical existence.

For if society lacks the unity that derives from the fact that the relationships between its parts are exactly regulated, that unity resulting from the harmonious articulation of its various functions assured by effective discipline, and if, in addition, society lacks the unity based upon the commitment of men's wills to a common objective, then it is no more than a pile of sand that the least jolt or the slightest puff will suffice to scatter. As a result, under present conditions, it is above all the faith in a common ideal that we must seek to elicit. We have seen how the spirit of devotion to patriotic objectives can furnish this necessary end. New ideas of justice and solidarity are now developing and, sooner or later, will prompt the establishment of appropriate institutions. Today the most pressing goal of moral education is to work to unravel such notions, still confused and sometimes unconscious; to bring children to cherish them without eliciting a sense of resentment against ideas and practices bequeathed to us by the past, which are the source of our current predicament. Above all, we have to develop a *spirit*; and this we have to prepare in the child. Undoubtedly there is the risk that the moral life developing in this way may very well be a discordant and confused business, since it will not materialize immediately in an organized fashion; but it will come, and once aroused, everything allows us to hope that in time it will order and discipline itself.

We are now at the point of checking whether the results of the analysis that we have just offered conform reasonably well to the program that we outlined. We proposed at the beginning to discover the rational forms of those moral beliefs that, up to the present, are scarcely expressed except in a religious form. Have we succeeded? To answer this question, let us look into the moral ideas that have found relatively adequate expression in religious symbolism.

First of all, in associating morality with a transcendental power, religion has made the authority inherent in moral precepts easily represented. Rather than appearing as an abstraction without any roots in reality, the imperative quality of the rule was readily explained as soon as the rule itself was conceived of as an emanation from the sovereign will. Moral obligation had an objective foundation from the moment when there was outside and beyond us a being to whom we had obligations; to convey such feelings to the child, it was only required to make him feel the reality of this transcendant being through appropriate methods.

God is not only conceived of as a lawmaker and the guardian of the moral order: he also represents an ideal which

the individual strives to realize. Ὁμοίως τω Θεω,* to seek to
live in God's image, to merge with Him; such is the basic
principle of all religious morality. If in one sense God exists,
and in another He is an endless becoming, then He must
realize himself progressively in the world insofar as we em-
ulate and reproduce Him in ourselves. If He can serve thus
as man's ideal and model there must be something which we
have in common with him; because no matter how superior
He is to each of us, there is some part of Him in us. The most
significant part of our being, which we call the soul, comes
from Him and expresses Him through us. This is the divine
element of our nature, and it is the element that we have to
develop. Through such reasoning, the human will found
itself oriented toward supra-individual ends, and at the same
time the duty of person to person was not eliminated but
linked to a higher source from which it flowed. Since we all
carry the imprint of divinity, the feelings that divinity inspire
in us must naturally be carried over to those who go with us,
in seeking God. It is God whom we revere in them, and it is
on this condition that our commitment will have a moral
value.

Now, it is apparent that we succeeded in expressing all
these moral realities in rational terms. All that we needed
was to substitute for the conception of a supernatural being
the empirical idea of a directly observable being, which is
society—provided that we do not view society as an arithmetic
sum of individuals, but as a new personality distinct from individual personalities. We have shown how society so conceived constrains us since it dominates us; and how it draws
our wills to it because, at the same time that it dominates us
it enters into us. Just as the faithful see in the loftier part of
conscience a bit, a reflection, of divinity, we have seen here
an element and a reflection of the collectivity. The parallel is

---

* Translator's note: The Greek may be translated as "becoming like God";
or "approximating the Godhead."

indeed so complete that in itself it already constitutes a first demonstration of the hypothesis often suggested here, namely, that divinity is the symbolic expression of the collectivity.

Some will perhaps object that the prospect of other-worldly sanctions must be a better guarantee of the authority of moral rules than simple social sanctions, whose applications, subject as they are to error, are always uncertain. However, the fact that some great religions have not relied on these sanctions, shows clearly that this is not the real reason for the effectiveness of religious morality: this was the case with Judaism until a very recent point in its history. Furthermore, everyone today recognizes that, to the extent that the weighing of sanctions —whatever their nature—conditions action, to that same extent the behavior lacks moral value. One cannot then attribute any moral relevance to a conception—the idea of sanctions— that cannot enter into conduct without changing its moral character.

We can be sure, then, that we have not impoverished moral reality by thus expressing it in rational terms. Moreover it is easy to see, as we anticipated, that this change in form implies other changes in content. Now, given our objective, it is certainly no trivial outcome to have shown that, without any diminution or distortion, morality can be completely derived from empirical realities and that, consequently, education is in the nature of things as applicable to the moral as to the intellectual elements of culture. Beyond this, such a substitution of one form for another also results in high-lighting certain qualities and elements of morality that otherwise would have remained hidden. Not, certainly, that a simple scientific and logical enterprise such as we have undertaken can create them out of nothing or suffices to bring them into being. Science explains what is; it does not create things. It cannot by itself endow morality with properties that morality lacked altogether. But it can help to make apparent certain qualities henceforth existing, but which, since they are of too recent an origin, religious symbolism cannot properly express. As a result, religious symbolism tends to deny or at least to minimize them.

Already, then, merely by virtue of the fact that it is rationalized, morality is freed of the paralysis to which it is logically condemned when founded on a religious base. When it is viewed as the law of an eternal and immutable being, evidently it must be conceived as unchangeable, like the image of God. On the contrary, if, as I have tried to show, it constitutes a social function, then it shares both the relative permanence and the relative variability seen in societies. A society remains, in some measure, the same throughout all the course of its existence. Throughout the changing conditions to which it is subject, there is a basic character that is always the same. The prevailing moral system presents, then, the same degree of identity and constancy. There are certain common qualities in the morality of the Middle Ages and that of our time. On the other hand, just as society, while retaining its identity nonetheless evolves continually, morality undergoes a parallel transformation. To the extent that societies become more complex and pliable, these transformations become more frequent and more significant. Thus we could say, a while ago, that our main task today is to create a morality. Therefore, if the moral life expresses above all the nature of the social, without being so fluid as to prevent altogether a provisional state of affairs, it is susceptible to continuous development.

However marked the change effected simply by conceiving of morality in a secular fashion, there is something else still more important. There is an aspect of morality that we have not discussed up to now and that can only emerge in a rational morality.

Heretofore we have, in effect, viewed morality as a system of rules, external to the individual, which impose themselves on him from outside; not, certainly, by any physical force, but by virtue of the ascendancy that they enjoy. From this point of view, it is certainly true that the individual will seems to be controlled by a law not of its own making. It is not we, in effect, who create morality. Doubtless, since we constitute part of the society that elaborates it, in a sense each of us collaborates in the development giving rise to morality. But the part played by each generation in the evolution of morality is quite restricted. The morality of our time is fixed in its essentials from the moment of our birth; the changes it undergoes during the course of an individual's life—those in which we can share—are infinitely limited. Great moral transformations always presuppose a long period of time. Furthermore, each of us is only one among innumerable units who collaborate in such a change. Our personal contribution is therefore never more than a minute factor in the complex result in which it disappears anonymously. Thus, one cannot fail to recognize that if the moral rule is a collective product, we receive much more than we contribute. Our posture is much more passive than active. We are influenced to a greater extent than we influence.

Now, this passivity is in opposition to an actual tendency of the moral consciousness—one that becomes continually stronger. Indeed, one of the fundamental axioms of our morality—perhaps even *the* fundamental axiom—is that the human being is the sacred thing par excellence. He merits the respect that the faithful of all religions reserve for their Gods. We ourselves express this when we make the idea of humanity the end and the *raison d'être* of the nation.

As a result of this principle, any kind of restriction placed upon our consciences seems immoral since it does violence to our personal autonomy. Today, everyone acknowledges, at least in theory, that never in any case should a predetermined mode of thought be arbitrarily imposed on us, even in the name of moral authority. It is not only a rule of logic but of morality that our reason should accept as true only that which it itself has spontaneously recognized as such. If so, it could not be otherwise with behavior. For since the end and *raison d'être* of an idea is to guide behavior, what does it matter that thought be free if behavior is controlled?

Some people, it is true, dispute the right of the moral conscience to claim such autonomy They point out that in fact we are perpetually subject to restraints, that the social context molds us, that it imposes all kinds of views, which we have not thought through, to say nothing of those irrevocable tendencies that are genetically determined. They add that, not only in fact but as a matter of right, personality can be nothing but a product of its environment. For where does it come from? One must either say that it is born of nothing, that it exists one and indivisible through all eternity, a veritable psychic atom implanted in some incomprensible manner in the body; or, if it does have some source, it must necessarily be a composite result of various forces derived from biological or social sources. Now, we have shown how it could not have developed out of any other source. But however indisputable these facts, it is altogether quite as certain that the moral conscience protests more and more emphatically against this subservient position and emphatically claims for the person an ever greater autonomy. Given the universality and persistence of this claim and the ever increasing clarity with which it is affirmed, it is impossible to view it as the product of some kind of delusion of the public conscience. It must certainly correspond to something real. It is itself a fact of the same order as those that would contradict it; rather than denying it or disputing its right to exist, we must, since it does in fact exist, try to understand it.

Kant is certainly the moralist who has had the keenest sense of this double necessity. To begin with, no one has felt more strongly than he the imperative quality of the moral law: he makes it a veritable ordinance to which we owe a kind of passive obedience. "The relationship between human will and this law," he says, "is one of dependence [*Abhängichkeit*]; we call it obligation [*Verbindlichkeit*] which indicates a constraint [*Nöthigung*]." At the same time, he refuses to acknowledge that the will can be completely moral when it is not autonomous, when it defers passively to a law of which it is not the maker. "The autonomy of the will," he says, "is the unique principle of all moral laws and of all their corresponding duties: all heteronomy in matters of the will . . . is opposed . . . to the morality of the will." Kant hopes to resolve this contradiction as follows: By itself, he says, the will is autonomous. Were the will not subordinated to the influence of the senses, if it were so constituted as to conform only to the precepts of reason, it would move spontaneously toward duty through the impulse of its nature alone. For a purely rational being, the law then loses its obligatory quality, its coercive aspect. Autonomy would then be complete. But in fact, we are not beings of pure reason; we have sensibilities that have their own nature and that are refractory to the dictates of reason. While reason is geared to the general and the impersonal, our senses, on the contrary, have an affinity for the particular and the individual. The law of reason is, then, a restraint upon our inclinations; we feel it as constraining and obligatory because it exerts a genuine constraint over the senses. But it constitutes an obligation, an imperative discipline only in connection with the senses. Pure reason, on the contrary, depends only on itself: it is autonomous. It itself makes the law that it imposes on the inferior aspects of our beings. Thus, the contradiction is resolved in terms of the dualism of our nature: autonomy is the product of reasoned will, heteronomy the product of the senses.

Obligation, in this case, would be some kind of accidental quality of the moral law. Of itself, the law would not necessarily be obligatory, but would be clothed with authority only when it found itself in conflict with the passions. Such an hypothesis is altogether arbitrary. Everything suggests, on the contrary, that the moral law is invested with an authority that imposes deference even upon reason. We do not only feel that it dominates our senses, but our whole nature, even our rational nature. Kant has shown better than anyone that there is something religious in the sentiment that moral law inspires even in the loftiest reason. But we can only have a religious feeling for some being—actual or ideal—that seems to us to be superior to the faculty that conceived it. That is why obligation is an essential element of the moral precept; and we have suggested the reason for this. Our whole nature has the need to be limited, contained, restricted—our reason as well as our senses. For our reason is not a transcendant faculty; it is implicated in society and consequently conforms to the laws of society. Everything in the world is limited, and all limitation presupposes forces which do the limiting. In order to conceive a pure autonomy of the will, even in the terms that I have just put them, Kant was obliged to admit that the will, at least the will insofar as it is purely rational, does not depend on the laws of nature. He was obliged to create a reality apart from the world, on which the world exerts no influence, and which, reacting on itself, remains independent of the action of external forces. It does not seem profitable just now to discuss this metaphysical conception, which can only mislead us in our thinking.

# CHAPTER EIGHT

# ~~§ AUTONOMY, OR

# SELF-DETERMINATION (*Concluded*)

AT SEVERAL POINTS ALREADY WE HAVE ENCOUNTERED APPARENT contradictions between the various elements of morality: the contradiction between the good and the obligatory, between the individual and group, between the limitation imposed by the role and the self-willed unfolding of human nature. There is nothing in the frequency of these antitheses that should surprise us. Moral reality is at once complex and a single whole. However, its unity derives from that of the concrete being that serves as its foundation, the nature of which is expressed in morality—that is to say, society. When, on the contrary, one represents the elements of morality in the abstract, without relating them to anything concrete, the ideas then formed of morality seem necessarily discontinuous; and it becomes almost impossible, without miracles of logic, to reunite these various elements and assign each its place. Thus, we get these antithetical points of view, these contraries, or those forced reductions in which the thinking of certain theoreticians has so often been trapped.

It was this sort of thing that gave rise to the new antithesis that we encountered at the end of the last chapter. On the one hand, moral rules seem, from all the evidence, external to the will. They are not of our fashioning, consequently, in conforming to them, we defer to a law not of our own making. We undergo a constraint that, however moral, is nonetheless real. On the other hand, it is certain that conscience protests such dependency. We do not regard an act as completely moral except when we perform it freely without coercion of any sort. We are not free if the law by which we regulate our behavior is imposed on us, if we have not freely desired it. The tendency of the moral conscience to link the morality of an act with the autonomy of the actor is a fact one cannot deny and which must be accounted for.

We have seen the solution Kant proposed for this problem—a problem whose difficulties he certainly sensed; indeed, he was the first to have posed it. According to him, autonomy is the principle of morality. In effect, morality consists in realizing impersonal and general ends, independent of the person and his particular interests. Now, reason, by virtue of its natural makeup, is oriented toward the general and the impersonal, for it is the same among all men—even among all reasoning beings. There is only one reason. As a result, insofar as we are only moved by reason, we act morally and with full autonomy because we are simply following the law of our reasoning nature.

Whence, then, the feeling of obligation? It is because in fact we are not purely rational beings; we are also emotional creatures. Temperament is the quality by which persons are distinguished from one another. My joys are mine alone and only reflect my personal temperament. Our sensibilities, then, incline us toward individual, egoistic, irrational, and immoral ends. Between the law of reason and our temperaments, there is a genuine antagonism, and, consequently, the former can impose itself upon the latter only through exercising a very real constraint. It is the sense of this constraint that gives rise to the feelings of obligation. With God, all is reason, and there is no room for feelings of this kind; with Him, morality is realized with an absolutely autonomous spontaneity. But it is not so with man—a complex and heterogeneous being divided against himself.

From this point of view, obligation or discipline becomes only an adventitious attribute of moral laws. By themselves, moral laws are not necessarily imperative; they take on this quality only when in conflict with the temperament and when they must exercise authority to overcome impassioned resistances. But this hypothesis is altogether arbitrary. Obligation is an essential element of every moral precept, and we have given the reason for this. Our whole nature has a need to be constrained, bounded, restricted—our intellectual as well as our emotional nature. In reality, reason is not a transcendent faculty; it is part of nature and consequently is subject to the laws of nature. The universe is limited, and all limitation presupposes some forces which do the limiting. Furthermore, to conceive of a purely autonomous will, Kant is obliged to acknowledge that the will, insofar as it is purely rational, is not subject to the law of nature. He has to make of it a faculty set aside from the world, over which nature has no influence. Turning back on itself, it is withdrawn from the influence of external forces. It seems useless to discuss a conception so obviously contrary to the facts and which can only imperil the moral ideas with which it may be associated. One might as well renounce all kinds of autonomy, if autonomy of will must be purchased at the price of such a violent separation from nature. Moreover, how can reason, which is postulated as outside of things and beyond reality, establish the laws of the moral order, if, as we have established, such laws express the nature of the concrete reality that is society?

Such a solution is quite abstract and dialectic. The autonomy that it confers on us is logically possible; but it has not and never will have anything to do with reality. Since we are and always will be sensate as well as rational human beings, there will always be conflict between these two parts of ourselves, and heteronomy will always be the rule in fact if not by right. What the moral conscience demands is an effective autonomy, it is true; not only for some unspecified ideal being, but for such beings as we ourselves are. Indeed, the fact that our requirements on this score are continually increasing certainly suggests that it is not a matter of a simple logical possibility, always equally true in the sense of an altogether abstract truth, but of something that grows, is progressively becoming, that evolves through history.

To understand the nature of progressive autonomy, let us look first at the way it materializes in our relations with the physical universe. It is not only in the realm of moral ideas that we seek and gain a greater independence. We are increasingly liberated from direct dependence on things, and we are quite aware of this process. But we cannot regard man's reason as the legislator of the physical universe. It has not received its laws from us. If we have in some respects liberated ourselves, it is not the result of our own efforts. It is to science that we owe this relative liberation. To simplify the argument let us suppose that we have complete knowledge of things and that each of us has this knowledge. Thus, the world, properly speaking, is no longer outside us; it has become a part of ourselves, since we have within us a system of symbolic representations that adequately express it. Everything in the physical world is represented in our consciousnesses by an idea; and, since these ideas are scientific—that is to say, distinct and clearly defined—we can manipulate them, combine them readily, as we do, for example, with the propositions of geometry. Consequently, in order to know at a given moment in time what the physical world is like and how we should adapt to it, we no longer need go beyond ourselves to understand physical phenomena. It is enough to look within ourselves and

to analyze our ideas about the objects we deal with, just as
the mathematician can determine the relationships between
magnitudes through a simple mental calculation and without having to observe the actual relationships of such magnitudes as they obtain outside of him.

Thus, to understand the world and to order our conduct
as it should be in relationship to it, we only have to take
careful thought, to be fully aware of that which is in ourselves. This constitutes a first degree of autonomy. Moreover,
because we then understand the laws of everything, we also
understand the reasons for everything. We can then understand the reason for the universal order. In other words,
to resurrect an old expression, if it is not we who made
the plan of nature, we rediscover it through science, we
re-think it, and we understand why it is as it is. Hence, to
the extent that we see that it is everything it ought to be—
that it is as the nature of things implies—we can conform,
not simply because we are physically restrained and unable
to do otherwise without danger, but because we deem it
good and have no better alternative. What prompts the faithful to see that the world is good in principle because it is
the work of a good being, we can establish a posteriori to the
extent that science permits us to establish rationally what
faith postulates a priori. Such conformity does not amount
to passive resignation but to enlightened allegiance. Conforming to the order of things because one is sure that it is
everything it ought to be is not submitting to a constraint.
It is freely desiring this order, assenting through an understanding of the cause. Wishing freely is not desiring the
absurd. On the contrary, it implies wishing what is rational
—that is to say, it implies the desire to act in agreement
with the nature of things. True, it happens that things
sometimes depart from their own nature under the influence
of abnormal or accidental circumstances. But then science
warns us, while at the same time providing means for bal-

ancing and rectifying things, since it gives us knowledge of the normal and natural state of things and the sources of these abnormal deviations.

Of course, what we have just been discussing is altogether hypothetical. Knowledge of nature is not and never will be complete. But what I have just dealt with as a *fait accompli* is an ideal limit that we approach asymptotically. To the extent that science builds itself, we, in our relationship with the physical universe, tend increasingly to rely only on ourselves. We liberate ourselves through understanding; there is no other means of liberation. Science is the wellspring of our autonomy.

In the moral order there is room for the same autonomy; and there is place for no other. Since morality expresses the nature of society and since this nature is no more directly apprehended by us than the nature of the physical world, individual reason can no more be the lawmaker for the moral world than that of the physical world. The layman's confused notions of society express the reality of society no more adequately than our auditory and visual sensations express sound or color, the objective nature of physical phenomena to which they correspond. However, it is possible through science to get hold of this order, which the individual, *qua* individual, has not created and for which he has not deliberately wished. We can investigate the nature of these moral rules, which the child receives from without, through education, and which impose themselves on him by virtue of their authority. We can investigate the reasons for their being, their immediate and more remote conditions. In a word, we can create a scientific study of the moral order.

Let us suppose a science of morality is an accomplished fact. Our ascendancy has gained its goal. We are masters of the moral order. It is no longer external to us, since from this point on it is represented in us through a system of clear and distinct ideas; and we understand all the relationships between these ideas. Now we are able to check on the extent to which the moral order is founded in the nature of things—that is, in the nature of society—which is to say to what extent it is what it ought to be. In the degree that we see it as such, we can freely conform to it. For to wish that it be other than is implied by the natural make-up of the reality that it expresses would be to talk nonsense under the pretext of free will. We can also see to what extent it is not based on the order of things, for it is always possible that society may involve some abnormal elements. In this case, we should have available, thanks to the same sciences we are supposing established, the means of restoring it to a normal state. Thus, on condition of having adequate knowledge of moral precepts, of their causes and of their functions, we are in a position to conform to them, but consciously and knowing why. Such conformity has nothing of constraint about it. Doubtless we are still further from this ideal state for matters concerning our moral life than for those bearing on the physical world; for the science of morality dates from yesterday, and its results are still indescisive. But that does not matter. There remains, nonetheless, the means of liberating ourselves; and this is what lends substance to the general aspiration for greater moral autonomy.

But, one may ask, from the moment that we understand the *raison d'être* of moral rules, from the moment that we conform voluntarily to them, do they not promptly lose their imperative quality? And then are we not ourselves vulnerable to the criticism just levelled at Kant, that is to say, of sacrificing one of the essential elements of morality to the principle of autonomy? Indeed, doesn't the idea of consent freely given exclude the notion of the imperative command, although we have seen in the imperative quality of the rule one of its most distinctive traits? This misses the point, however. In reality, a thing does not stop being itself because we know the why of it. Because we know the nature and the law of life, it does not at all follow that life loses a single one of its specific characteristics. Similarly, because the science of morality teaches us the reason for the imperative quality inherent in moral rules, these latter do not on that account lose their imperative character. Because we know that there is something useful in that which is commanded, it follows not that we fail to obey but that we obey voluntarily. We can understand very well that it is in our nature to be limited by forces outside us; accordingly, we accept this limitation freely, because it is natural and good without being any the less real. Only through the fact of our informed consent it is no longer a humiliation and a bondage.

Such autonomy, then, leaves to moral principles all their distinctive qualities, even those for which it seems to be—and in a sense is—the negation. The two antithetical terms are reconciled and rejoined. We are still limited, for we are finite beings; and, in a sense, we are still passive with respect to the rule that commands us. However, this passivity becomes at the same time activity, through the active part we take in deliberately desiring it. We desire it because we know the reason for its existence. It is not passive conformity that, taken by itself, constitutes a reduction of our personality. It is passive obedience to which we consent without full knowledge of the cause for it. When, on the contrary, we blindly carry out an order of whose meaning and import we are ignorant, but nonetheless *understanding why* we should lend ourselves to the role of a blind instrument, we are as free as when we alone have all the initiative in our behavior.

This is the only kind of autonomy to which we have any claim; and the only kind having value for us. It is not an autonomy that we get prefabricated from nature, that we find at birth among our constituent attributes. Rather, we fashion it ourselves to the extent that we achieve a more complete knowledge of things. It does not imply that the human being, in any of his aspects, escapes the world and its laws. We are an integral part of the world; it acts on us, it penetrates every part of us, and it must be so; without this pervasive influence our consciousness would be empty of all content. Each of us is the point of convergence for a certain number of external forces, and our personalities result from the intersection of these influences. Should the forces no longer converge here, there would remain nothing more than a mathematical point, an empty place where conscience and personality could not be built up. But if in some measure we are the product of things, we can, through science, use our understanding to control both the things that exert an influence upon us and this influence itself. In this way, we again become our masters.

Thought is the liberator of will. This proposition, which everyone will freely acknowledge insofar as it concerns the physical world, is no less true of the moral world. Society is a product of innumerable forces of which we are only an infinitesimal fraction—forces which, far from our having desired or contrived them, combine according to laws and forms of which we are ignorant. Furthermore, we inherit a great part, already made, from the past. It is necessarily thus with morality, an expression of the social nature. So it is a dangerous illusion to imagine that morality is a personal artifact; and that consequently we have it completely and from the beginning under our control, that it is never anything but what we wish it to be. It is an illusion, such as that of the primitive who thinks he can stop the course of the sun, control the storm, or unleash the winds by an act of will, the expression of a desire, or by some forcible injunction. We can only conquer the moral world in the same fashion that we conquer the physical world: by building a science of moral matters.

Thus, we have ascertained a third element of morality. To act morally, it is not enough—above all, it is no longer enough—to respect discipline and to be committed to a group. Beyond this, and whether out of deference to a rule or devotion to a collective ideal, we must have knowledge, as clear and complete an awareness as possible of the reasons for our conduct. This consciousness confers on our behavior the autonomy that the public conscience from now on requires of every genuinely and completely moral being. Hence, we can say that the third element of morality is the understanding of it. Morality no longer consists merely in behaving, even intentionally behaving, in certain required ways. Beyond this, the rule prescribing such behavior must be freely desired, that is to say, freely accepted; and this willing aceptance is nothing less than an enlightened assent.

Here it is, perhaps, that the moral conscience of contemporary peoples is confronted with the greatest change: intelligence has become and is becoming increasingly an element of morality. Morality, which originally was completely a function of the act, the content of the behavior that constituted the act, now depends more and more upon knowledge. For a long time now we have imputed social value only to an act that was intentional, that is to say when the actor pictured ahead of time what the act involved and what bearing it had on the rule. But now, beoynd this first level of awareness, we require another, which goes deeper into the nature of things—the symbolic explanation of the rule itself, its causes and reasons for being. This explains the place we accord the teaching of morality in our schools. For to teach morality is neither to preach nor to indoctrinate; it is to explain. If we refuse the child all explanation of this sort, if we do not to try to help him understand the reasons for the rules he should abide by, we would be condemning him to an incomplete and inferior morality. Such teaching, far from harming the public morality—as has sometimes been alleged—is henceforth its necessary condition. Of course, it is very difficult, for it must rest upon a science that is just in the process of developing. In the present state of sociological studies, it is not always easy to link each particular obligation to a definite characteristic of the social organization that explains it. However, as of our day, there is some general information that can be usefully given, and of such a kind as to help the child understand not only his duties but the reasons for these duties. We shall return to this question when we attack directly the problem of what moral instruction in the school ought to be.

The third and last element of morality is the principal differentiating characteristic of a secular morality since, logically, it can have no place in a religious morality. It implies, in fact, that there is a human science of morality and consequently that moral facts are natural phenomena that emerge through reason alone. Science is impossible except as it is based upon nature, that is to say, upon observable reality. Because God is beyond the world, he is above and beyond science. If, then, morality comes from God and expresses His nature, it must at the same time be beyond the grasp of our reason. Indeed, as a result of the identification of religious systems and morality for some centuries, morality has retained an indescribable kind of magic quality, which still, for some people, puts it outside the legitimate domain of science. They deny the right of the human mind to grapple with morality as with the rest of the world. It seems that with morality one enters a realm of mystery, where the ordinary procedures of scientific inquiry are no longer appropriate; undertaking to treat it as a natural phenomenon stirs up a sort of scandal, as if it were a profanation. Doubtless such dismay is justified if one cannot rationalize morality without stripping it of the authority and dignity which belong to it. But we have seen that it is possible to explain its majestic nature while giving it a purely scientific expression and without destroying or even diminishing its authority.

Such are the principal elements of morality—those at least that we actually perceive. Before inquiring into the methods by which they can be developed in the child, let us try to draw together briefly the conclusions we have just arrived at, *seriatim*, and view morality as it has emerged from our analysis as an integrated concept.

From the beginning, we have been able to see what a multiplicity of aspects morality has. It is a morality of duty, and we have continually insisted on the necessity of the rule and of discipline as an aspect of morality; but at the same time it is a morality of the good, since it assigns to human activity an end that is good and that involves everything needed to arouse desire and attract the will. The taste for regularity in life, the preference for moderation, the need for limits, self-mastery—these are reconciled readily with the need to give, in a spirit of devotion and sacrifice; reconciled, in a word, with the active and expansive forces of moral energy. But above all, it is a rational morality. Indeed, we have not only explicated all the elements of morality in terms that are intelligible, secular, and rational; but we have in addition made advancing knowledge of morality itself an element *sui generis* of morality. We have not only shown that reason could be applied to moral phenomena but we have further asserted that the application of reason to morality is increasingly becoming a condition of virtue, and we have indicated the grounds for this statement.

People have sometimes objected to the method we are following in the study of moral phenomena as being of no practical use, and as restricting man by emphasizing deference to the status quo—not opening to him any vistas on the ideal (this because we have made it a rule to observe moral reality objectively as experience reveals it, rather than attempting to determine it a priori). One can see, now, how little substance there is in such an objection. We have viewed morality as essentially idealistic. What, indeed, is an ideal if not a body of ideas that soar above the individual while vigorously stimulating certain behavior? Now, society, which we have made the objective of moral conduct, infinitely surpasses the level of self-centered interests. What we must above all cherish in society—that to which above all we must devote ourselves—is not society in its physical aspects, but its spirit. And what is this thing that people call society's soul or spirit but a complex of ideas, of which the isolated individual would never have been able to conceive, which go beyond his mentality, and which come into being and sustain themselves only through the interaction of a plurality of associated individuals?

On the other hand, while it is essentially an idealistic conception, this morality has its own realism. For the ideal with which we are dealing is not extraspatial or extratemporal. It clings to reality; it is part of it; it informs society—that concrete, living entity which, so to speak, we see and touch and are involved in. Furthermore, such an idealism does not run the danger of degenerating into passive rumination or pure but sterile reveries. For it links us, not to some simple internal things that the mind contemplates more or less passively, but to things outside ourselves, which enjoy and suffer as we do, which have needs as we do, and which as a result call forth our responses altogether naturally. One can easily foresee the educational results of this theoretical conception. From this point of view, the way of developing the child morally is not to repeat to him, with however much emotion and conviction, a certain number of very general maxims valid eternally and everywhere; but to make him understand his country and his times, to make him feel his responsibilities, to initiate him into life and thus to prepare him to take his part in the collective tasks awaiting him.

Finally, and for the same reason that it is idealistic, this conception of morality obviously imposes on man an unselfish posture. But by a curious reciprocation the indivdual finds his reward in this selflessness. The two antithetical terms that moralists have opposed to one another for centuries are readily reconciled in reality. For it is through doing his duty that man achieves a preference for moderation—that self —limitation which is the necessary condition of happiness and health. Similarly, it is in attaching himself to the group that he comes to share in the superior life residing in the group. Should he try to shut himself off from the outside world, to turn in on himself, to bring everything to bear on the self, then he is no longer able to lead anything but a precarious existence and one contrary to nature. Thus, duty and sacrifice no longer seem to us a sort of miracle through which man somehow does violence to his nature. Quite to the contrary, it is in submitting to rules and devoting himself to the group that he becomes truly a man. Morality is a pre-eminently human thing, for in prompting man to go beyond himself it only stimulates him to realize his own nature as a man.

You see how immensely complicated the moral life is, since it even embraces apparent contradictions. We recall this passage, in which Pascal tries to make man sense all the contradictions in him: "If he boasts, I humble him; if he humbles himself, I praise him; and constantly contradict him until he understands that he is an incomprehensible monster." In a way it is something like this with morality. The ideal that it draws for us is a remarkable mixture of subordination and power, of submission and autonomy. When we try to rebel against it, we are harshly recalled to the necessity of the rule. When we conform to it, it liberates us from this subservience by allowing reason to govern the same rule that constrains us. It prescribes that we must give ourselves, subordinate ourselves, to something other than ourselves. How inadequate, therefore, the formulae of those moralists who would reduce the whole of morality to one of its elements, when in fact morality is one of the richest and most complex of realities.

If, then, I have dwelt long on this preliminary analysis, it is because I wanted to give some feeling for this richness and complexity. For in order to take up wholeheartedly the task that devolves upon the educator, one must be interested in it, devoted to it; and to devote one's self to it, one must feel everything that is vital in it. When one compresses the whole of morality into a few lessons on morality as prescribed in the curriculum—lessons that recur periodically, at more or less short intervals during the week, it is hard to become very enthusiastic for a task that, because of its intermittent character, scarcely appears adequate for leaving on the child any deep or durable mark, without which he cannot acquire anything of the moral culture. But if lessons in morality have their place in moral education it is only one part of it. Moral education cannot be so rigidly confined to the classroom hour: it is not a matter of such and such a moment; it is implicated in every moment. It must be mingled in the whole of school life, as morality itself is involved in the whole web of collective life. This is why, while at bottom it retains its unity, it is as variegated as life itself. There is no formula that can contain and express it adequately. If indeed there is any basic criticism that can be levelled against our analysis it is that it is very probably incomplete. Now, quite surely, a deeper analysis will enable us to see, presently, some elements and aspects we have not detected. We do not pretend that the conclusions at which we have arrived constitute anything like a tightly knit, closed system. On the contrary, it is only a provisional approximation of moral reality. But however imperfect this approximation may be, it has nonetheless enabled us to sort out some essential elements of morality. Some definite goals are thus assigned to the role of teacher. These goals having been thus specified, the time has come to inquire by what means they can be attained.

# PART II

## How to Develop the Elements of

## Morality in the Child

# CHAPTER NINE

# ∽§ DISCIPLINE AND THE

# PSYCHOLOGY OF THE CHILD

HAVING DETERMINED THE SEVERAL ELEMENTS OF MORALITY, we are about to inquire how they can be built into, or developed in, the child. We begin with the first of those elements that we have distinguished, that is to say, the spirit of discipline.

The nature of the question itself determines the way of attacking it. We know the end to be attained, that is to say, the goal where we must lead the child. But the way in which it is appropriate to lead him there, the route we should follow, depends necessarily on the point of departure. The influence of education is not applied to a *tabula rasa*. The child has his own nature, and in order to act intelligently on this nature, we must first of all seek to understand it. Thus, we should first ask in what way and to what extent the child is accessible to that state of mind we wish to stimulate in him. Among his natural aptitudes, which may we build upon in order to get the desired result? The time has come, then, to inquire into the psychology of the child, which alone can provide us with the necessary information on this point.

We were saying in our first chapter that the mental states that education must arouse in the child exist only as very general conditions, quite remote from the specific form that they are required to take. This proposition will be verified particularly as regards the spirit of discipline. One can in fact say that neither of the elements of which discipline is composed exist completely formed in the child's consciousness.

There are two elements of the spirit of discipline. There is first of all the preference for regularity of existence. Because duty is always the same under the same circumstances, and because the principal circumstances of life are determined once and for all by our sex, our civil status, our occupations, our social situation, it is impossible that one should delight to do his duty and yet resist the regular and habitual. The whole of the moral order rests upon this regularity. Collective life could not function harmoniously if each of those charged with a social function—whether familial, civic, or professional—were not to dispose of his job at the time and in the manner prescribed.

Childish behavior on the contrary, is characterized by its complete irregularity. The child shifts from one impression to another, from one activity, one sentiment, to another with extraordinary speed. His disposition is by no means stable. He breaks out in anger and is mollified with the same suddenness. Tears succeed laughter, friendliness displaces hatred or vice versa, without any apparent reason or at most under the influence of the slightest circumstance. The games which occupy him do not hold his interest long; he is quickly bored and passes on to something else. One sees this same mobility in the tireless curiosity with which the child follows his parents and his teachers. Some have occasionally seen in this a first manifestation of a scientific instinct. Such a comparison cannot be accepted without reservation. Doubtless, when the child raises questions he demonstrates a need to classify the things he sees and the impressions that he experiences in that limited system of ideas, in process of formation, which constitutes his mind; and this need of intellectual organization is certainly at the root of scientific knowledge. But how flighty and changeable it is in the child! Whatever the object that has attracted the attention of this small observer, it retains his attention only for a matter of seconds. He does not hold still until whatever it is, is done; or until someone has given him an idea that satisfies him. Scarcely has somebody answered him when his mind is already elsewhere. "The feeling of ignorance," says Sully,

is not yet completely developed in the child; the desire to know is not sustained, it is not fastened on each particular object with a sufficiently definite interest; so that parents will often state that the little questioner's mind is already far from the subject and his imagination roving elsewhere even before the answer has been given him.[1]

It is instability, a fleeting quality, which dominates childish curiosity.

On this point, furthermore, as on many other scores, the child only reproduces one of the distinctive characteristics of early man. People who have not yet advanced from the most elementary forms of civilization are in fact marked by this same inconstancy in ideas and feelings, the same lack of continuity in individual conduct. The most insignificant conduct is enough to activate the most astonishing transformations in the adult consciousness. A pleasing gesture, a grimace, a word, and the most ferocious rage is transformed into benevolent feelings; or contrariwise, threat of death takes the place of the warmest show of friendship. It is a psychological peculiarity that explorers know well and that they have often used in their own interests. Besides, it is easy enough to understand how the desire for regularity, for sequence and continuity of behavior, could only be the product of a sufficiently advanced civilization. In the very simple, primitive societies, there is not much in the way of concerted activities; as a result there is not much regulated behavior. The collective life lacks that sequence and continuity

---

1. James Sully, *The Teacher's Handbook of Psychology; On the Basis of "Outlines of Psychology"* (New York: D. Appleton and Co., 1888), p. 401.

that it has in more advanced societies. It does, of course, evidence itself whenever the tribe assembles to undertake collectively some religious ceremony, or to discuss tribal matters, or to organize for the hunt or a military sortie. But aside from these sporadic occasions, the individual is left to his own devices, to all the promptings of his own whims. He is not charged with specified functions that he has to fulfill at a fixed time and in a definite manner. Society leaves him to do as he will with his time and, consequently, does not require of him the regularity that always presupposes a more or less painful effort.

In large societies like ours, however, labor is very finely divided, and the different jobs to which people are committed reciprocally affect one another. They are like so many functions that are implied by and act upon one another. So it is impossible to leave them to individual whim; it is necessary to regulate them in order to make co-operation possible. Hence, the measured regularity of our existence. There is scarcely a moment in the day when we are not acting as instruments of the social order; for economic activities themselves, although less directly regulated than public functions, are also collective. We have often scoffed at the unskilled worker who goes through the same motions day after day. But this is only a caricature, an exaggerated instance, of a way of life that all of us lead to some extent. The plan of our activities is in large part predetermined and will be always more so. The fact that this regularity is an outcome of civilization explains readily how it is lacking in the child.

From a second point of view, the spirit of discipline involves as we have said, the moderation of desires and self-mastery. Everyday experience is enough to prove that it is completely lacking up to a fairly advanced age. The child has no feeling that there are normal limits to his needs: when he is fond of something, he wants it to satiety. He neither restrains himself nor does he readily comply when someone else imposes limits on him. He is not kept in check by the conception the adult has of the necessity of natural laws; he has no sense of their existence. He cannot distinguish between the possible and the impossible, and, consequently, he has no sense of the way that reality sets insurmountable barriers to his desires. It seems to him that everything should yield to him, and he is irritated at the resistances of things as well as those of people.

There is one emotion that shows with particular force the character of the child's temperament. This is anger. Anger, as we know, is quite frequent with the child, and it often assumes an extreme form. "When young children become infuriated," Darwin says, "they roll on the ground, on their backs, on their stomachs, crying, flailing with their feet, scratching and striking out at anything within range." It is said, and truly so, that the child can't make enough fuss to assuage his feelings. Now, there is no mental state more clearly opposed to the self-mastery implied by discipline; for it consists precisely in a temporary derangement of personality. We say of people who are enraged that they no longer feel, that they no longer know what is going on about them. There are few passions so exclusive. When it breaks upon us, above all if it is intense, it drives out all other feelings. It drives out any other emotion that might contain it and dominates all of consciousness. Nothing neutralizes it; and this explains its limitless quality. It continually drives straight ahead as long as energy remains. The frequency of anger in the child and the violence it often has, prove better than words the natural intemperance of the child. Besides, on this point again, the child only reproduces a well-known trait of primitive mentality. Indeed, we know of the intractability of primitive passions, their inability to restrain themselves, their natural tendency to excess.

We can see what a gulf there is between the child's point of departure and the goal toward which he must be led:

on the one hand, a mind endlessly moving, a veritable ka-
leidoscope that changes from one moment to the next, emotional behavior that drives straight ahead to the point of
exhaustion; and, on the other hand, the preference for regular and moderate behavior. It has taken centuries for man
to travel this distance. Education must enable the child to
cover it in a few years. It is not, then, simply a matter of
activating and stimulating certain latent tendencies, which
ask only to be elicited and developed. Rather, we have to
build completely from original elements not formed in the
native make-up of the child. However, if nature does not
predispose the child in appropriate ways—in such a way
that we have only to superintend and direct his natural
development—if it leaves almost everything for us to do, we
could not on the other hand succeed in our labors if the
child's nature were opposed to us, if it were completely
refractory to the orientation that must be developed in him.
The child's nature is not so malleable that one can make it
take on forms for which it is in no way fitted. So there must
be in the child, if not precisely those conditions we must
develop, at least certain general predispositions that help us
in achieving the goal and that act as levers through which
educational influence is transmitted to the roots of the child's
consciousness. Were this not so, it would be closed to us.
Through physical coercion, we can require the child to perform in certain ways; but the wellsprings of his inner life
escape us. There would be drilling and training, but not
education.

There are in fact at least two basic predispositions, two
built-in characteristics of the child's nature, which expose
him to our influence: first, his character as a creature of
habit; and second, his suggestibility, especially his openness
to imperative suggestion.

Through a contrast that may seem peculiar but is nonetheless certain—and which we will presently explain further—

the child whom we have just described as inconstancy itself
is at the same time a veritable creature of habit. Once he has
developed certain habits, they dominate his behavior to a far
greater extent than with adults. Once he has repeated a given
act several times he shows a need to reproduce it in the same
way. He abhors the slightest variation. We know, for example,
how the order of his meal, once established, becomes sacred
and inviolable for him. He even pushes this adherence to
habit to the point of the most compulsive detail. He wants
his cup, his napkin in the same place. He wants to be served
by the same person. The slightest deviation distresses him.
We have just seen how readily he shifts from one kind of
play to another. But on the other hand, once he has become
accustomed to a certain game he will repeat it indefinitely.
He will reread the same book to the point of satiety. He will
dwell on the same pictures without becoming bored. How
many times have we told our children the same old stories:
one might say that they are forever new for children. Similarly, some innovation, implying even an unimportant change
in daily routines, stimulates a genuine aversion in the child.
"One of the things which most disconcerts the child," says
Sully, "is a sudden change in place. As an infant, the child
does not show any anxiety when he is moved into a new
room; but later, once he has become accustomed to a certain
room, he will have a feeling of strangeness if he is moved
from one room to another."[2] A change in the group of persons ordinarily around him produces the same effect. Preyer
claims that his son, around six or seven months of age, broke
out in tears upon seeing a stranger. A simple change in cloth-
ing can give rise to a similar upset. The same son of Preyer
was distraught when he was seventeen months old upon seeing his mother in a black dress. Color has much to do with
producing such an effect; for according to a report of Sully's,

---

2. James Sully, *Studies of Childhood* (London: Longmans, Green and
Co., 1896). Durkheim's reference is to p. 274 of a French translation published in 1898. (Ed.)

"a child will burst into tears upon seeing its mother in a dress of color or design which is altogether new to him; while another, from age seventeen months to two-and-a-half years showed such a marked aversion to new clothes that they had the greatest conceivable trouble in getting him to put them on." The child, although inconstant, has a veritable hatred for the new.

It is not only that he cherishes his own habitual ways of doing things; it is the same with the behavior of others around him. When he notices that everybody about him always behaves in the same way under the same circumstances, he thinks it quite impossible to behave otherwise. Any derogation of the customary seems scandalous to him. It excites a surprise in which feelings of rebellion and indignation readily enter. Doubtless the adult is also given to such fetishism; but to a much less extent than among children. If even the most insignificant gestures are repeated before the child in the same manner, they become for him integral elements of an immutable order that must not be challenged. Hence, the child's taste for ceremonial formalities. If his parents embrace him in a given way, he treats his dolls—his children—in exactly the same manner. And this traditionalism has further implications since it is more general. The child applies it, not only to his own conduct, but to everything in his small world. He almost comes to see in it a kind of general law valid for everything that in his eyes pertains to humanity.

However peculiar this coexistence of conventionality and inconstancy may seem, it is not peculiar to the child. One also encounters it among primitives. We have seen how the primitive is volatile, changing in his character to the extent that he is quite unpredictable. We likewise know that traditionalism is nowhere stronger. Nowhere has custom such authority; everything to which it applies is regulated to the last detail. Inflections of voice and the least gestures are predetermined, and everyone conforms scrupulously to the customary. Hence, the very considerable development of ceremonials in such societies. Thus, novelties or innovations are hard to come by. Behaviors once established are repeated without variation for centuries. However, it is not necessary to go back to the beginnings of history to establish the juxtaposition of these two states of mind, which seem at first blush irreconcilable. Peoples whose temperaments are most volatile, those whose thinking shifts most readily from one extreme to another—those, consequently, among whom revolutions are most frequent and who swing violently to opposite extremes—these are not peoples who demonstrate the greatest capacity for change. Far from it; these are precisely the ones among whom old traditions and routines are more solidly rooted. They only change superficially; at bottom they remain always the same. On the surface there is an uninterrupted stream of continually new events. But this superficial mobility disguises the most monotonous uniformity. It is among the most revolutionary peoples that bureaucratic routine is often the most powerful.

For extremes of fluctuating and of stable behavior only seem to exclude one another. In reality, vagrant notions and fleeting impressions, precisely because they do not last and are promptly replaced by others, cannot block the path of customary behavior when the latter is established. For there is in custom a force augmented through repetition, which is simply not true of transient and inconstant states that are gone as soon as they appear, that push one another out of consciousness, and that contradict and mutually neutralize one another. When one compares such tenuous behavior, these fragile states of fluid and emphemeral consciousness, with the consistency, with, so to speak, the density of established custom, one can readily understand that the person must follow the direction indicated by the latter. It reigns supreme because it is the only established driving force. It is in a way a mechanical necessity that the center of gravity of

conduct be in the realm of custom. If the adult, especially
the cultivated person, is not subservient to custom, it is because his sequence of ideas and feelings have continuity and
persistence; they are not simply flashes glowing for a moment
and then promptly extinguished. The mind holds them for
some time. They are real forces that can oppose custom and
limit it. Because the inner life has more continuity, because
it is not overthrown every moment, custom is not the sole
master. Thus, excessive change, far from being incompatible
with routines, paves the way for it and re-enforces its dominance.

If this tendency toward traditionalism does not in itself
constitute a moral condition, it is nonetheless a source of
support for the influence that we must exert over the child.
For we can use the power that—as a result of the instability
of his mental life—habit has over the child to correct and
curb instability itself. It suffices to lead the child to acquire
regular habits with respect to everything bearing on the chief
circumstances of his life. Under these conditions, his life will
no longer present the contradictory spectacle of extreme inconstancy endlessly alternating with an almost compulsive
routine; but that which is fugitive and inconstant will find
its place; it will regularize and organize itself in the whole
complex of behavior which is a first step toward the moral life.
The child already has, in his attachment to habitual conduct
and in his discomfort when he fails to find people and other
objects in their customary places, an obscure feeling that
there is a normal order in things, which alone is based in
nature and which, so understood, is opposed to the fortuitous
and should therefore be preferred to happenstance. It is a
distinction of this sort that is at the base of the moral order.
Of course, an idea as confused and unconscious as this needs
to be clarified, sharpened, re-enforced, and developed. It is
nonetheless true that we have here an opening, through which
a really moral influence can be introduced into the child's

spirit. And so, too, we know one of the wellsprings of his inner life, which enables us to orient him in a proper direction.

This taste for regularity in life is not, as we know, the whole of the spirit of discipline. In addition, there is the preference for moderation, the ability to restrain one's desires, and the notion of normal limits. It is not enough that the child be accustomed to repeat the same behaviors under the same conditions. He must have the feeling that beyond him there are moral forces that set bounds for him, forces that he must take into account and to which he must yield. Since these forces are moral the child does not see them with his eyes. He has no sensory apparatus that allows him to detect the distinctive characteristics of moral authority. On every hand, there is a whole world that surrounds him but that, in a sense, is invisible to him. Now doubtless he sees very well the corporeal aspects of people and things that constitute his immediate milieu—I mean his family. He certainly senses that the adults he finds here, his parents, are in a position to make him submit to their wills. But this physical constraint cannot in any way give him the impression of the drawing power *sui generis* exerted by moral forces, prompting a spontaneous deference of the will to their demands—a deference prompted by respectful acquiescence and not by sheer physical coercion. How do we evoke in him this necessary feeling? We do so by building on his great receptivity to suggestions of all sorts.

Guyau was the first to have noted that the child is naturally in a psychological situation strongly analogous to that of the hypnotized subject. What are the conditions for hypnotic suggestion? There are two principal ones: First, the hypnotized subject is as completely passive as possible. His will is paralyzed. His mind is blank. He sees and hears nothing but the hypnotist. Whatever is happening around him leaves him untouched. The idea suggested under these conditions fixes itself in the mind with so much force because it encounters no resistance. There is no other idea competing with it, since the mind is a perfect void. As a result, it tends to be transformed into action. For an idea is not a purely speculative and intellectual thing; it always entails the beginning of behavior in which it is realized, and the action so begun continues if no contrary state intervenes to inhibit it. However, if the suggested act is surely to occur, this first condition is not generally sufficient. The hypnotist must say: I will it. He must make the subject feel that a refusal is inconceivable, that he must obey. If he equivocates, if he debates the matter, his power is gone.

These two conditions are fulfilled by the child in his relationships with parents and teachers. First, he finds himself quite naturally in the condition of passivity in which hypnotic procedures place the subject. If his mind is not completely blank, it is nonetheless poor in its symbolic life and has few fixed tendencies. Consequently, any new idea introduced into this sparsely populated mental milieu encounters very little resistance and tends readily to pass into action. This is what makes the child so vulnerable to the contagion of example, so inclined to imitate. When he sees certain behavior, the image that he has of it tends to materialize in a similar act. As for the second condition, it is quite naturally fulfilled in the imperative tone in which the teacher puts his orders. To impose his will he must be firm, and he must affirm with resolution. Without doubt, it is only at the beginning that the suggestion of the teacher has the whole of its powerful influence, its dominance over external behavior. When the child has come to understand more clearly his moral dependency vis-à-vis his parents and his teachers, his need for them, their intellectual superiority over him, and the worth of that superiority, then the ascendancy with which they are henceforth continually invested communicates itself to their prescriptions and re-enforces them. But it is nonetheless true that the imperative character of the suggestions is the original source of its efficacy; and it remains for a long time a more or less important factor.

Through an interesting experiment, Messrs. Binet and Henry have demonstrated this natural suggestibility of the child. Schoolchildren were asked to look attentively at lines of different length. Once the image of these lines had been well fixed in memory, the students were asked to find them in another figure, which, besides the original line, contained others of all lengths. When the child thought he had found the matching line and had pointed it out, the investigator asked him, without any particular stress, this single question: are you sure that this is the single correct line? This one question was enough to prompt 89 per cent of the elementary school children to change their first response. In the middle group and the advanced group the percentages were respectively 80 per cent and 54 per cent. Even when children responded correctly, they altered their first response to the rather considerable extent of 56 per cent. Here the turn-about is entirely the result of suggestion. You will note, in addition, the unequal suggestability of children depending upon age. To the extent that the child's mind is furnished, he develops more power of resistance to suggestion.

The fact, then, is established and no longer questioned by teachers. The amazing credulity, docility, good will, obedience, inconsistency, and the whims manifested in a host of traits among young children recall the phenomena observed in the hypnotized adult. For example, if to a two-and-a-half-year-old about to take his first bit of biscuit and just beginning to nibble I say categorically—without giving any reasons, with an assurance permitting no contradiction, and in a fairly loud voice but without frightening him: "Now the child has eaten enough, he is full," the child, without having gotten to the point of nibbling the biscuit, will withdraw it from his mouth, put it on the table and end his meal. It is easy to persuade children, even at age three or four, that the pain following a blow, for example, has gone; that they no longer are thirsty; —that they are no longer tired—on the condition that the assertion countering their complaints is altogether preemptory.

We have here, then, an external check that can be opposed to the child's desires and passions; consequently, we can accustom him at an early point to self-control and moderation; we can make him feel that he should not yield without reservation to his inclinations, but that there is always a limit beyond which he ought not to go. And the child will clearly feel in this case that he is yielding to the influence of a force that is not acting on him like physical forces, but that has altogether peculiar qualities. He has, in fact, a clear awareness that this force is in a sense external to him, that he would not have acted in the same way if the initiative for the act had been completely his, since he has yielded to an order received. On the other hand, he takes account of the fact that he has not submitted to a physical constraint. The determinate cause of his act was not some physical pressure, as when someone imposes such and such an attitude upon him by force, but an altogether inner state, that is to say, an idea suggested; and there are intrinsic qualities of this idea that determined its efficacy. It is out of such elements that the first notion probably developed—among men and also with children—of that which we call a moral force or moral authority. For moral authority has precisely this characteristic: it acts on us from outside, through the intermediation of an inner state, and without physical coercion—either actual or threatened. Without doubt, many other elements soon gather little by little around this original nucleus.

Due alone to the fact that the child has obeyed a given person many times, he is quite naturally brought to borrow from this same person certain attributes associated with the influence exerted over him by the latter. He thinks of that person as having a power *sui generis*, which elevates him to the highest position in the child's imagination. For the moment, however, we needn't pursue the development of this idea; it suffices to show the point at which it makes contact with the child's nature.

We must, then, be reassured. Thanks to the fact that habit so easily dominates the mind of the child, we can accustom him to regularity and develop his taste for it; thanks to his suggestibility, we can at the same time give him his first feeling for the moral forces which surround him and upon which he depends. So we have two powerful tools in our hands, so powerful that they must be handled with the greatest discretion. When one imagines how open to influence the mind of the child is, how readily it retains the slightest, most vagrant impression, one is more inclined to fear the abuse of such power than to be skeptical of the teacher's influence. There are many kinds of precautions that must be taken to protect the child against the omnipotence of education. How, under these conditions, could we dream, as was recently proposed, of permitting the child to spend his entire life in the hands of a single instructor? Such an education would, by force of circumstance, easily lead to subservience. The child could not fail to reproduce passively the single model placed before him. The only way of preventing this kind of servitude, of insuring that education does not make of the child a carbon copy of the teacher's shortcomings, is to multiply the teachers in order that they may complement one another, and so that the various influences prevent any one from becoming too exclusively preponderant.

However powerful our means of influencing the child, we are still far from the goal. What a distance between this very general receptivity of the child to habit and suggestion, on the one hand, and the clear conception of moral law, on the other. In order that these indefinite and unspecified germs or tendencies may develop into the definite and complex sentiments of morality, education must cultivate and transform them. In the next chapter we shall see by what means such a transformation should be effected.

# CHAPTER TEN

# ◄§ THE DISCIPLINE OF THE SCHOOL

WE HAVE SOUGHT OUT THOSE NATURAL PREDISPOSITIONS IN the child that might help us in inculcating in him the spirit of discipline. We saw how, thanks to his marked propensity for habitual behavior, we can limit his inconstancies, his constitutional instabilities, and build in him a preference for an ordered life; and how, thanks to his extreme suggestibility, we can give him something like a first feeling for moral authority. Thus, we have in our hands two powerful modes of action—so powerful that they may be used only with restraint and discretion. Indeed, when one considers the undeveloped and vulnerable mind of the child, so susceptible that the least external impression may leave deep and durable marks, one may fear the abuse of power into which the teacher may fall, rather than his lack of power. Rather than there being no danger that the influence of teacher and parents is ever excessive, certain steps are indispensable to protect the freedom of the child against them. One of the most effective precautions that can be undertaken in this respect is to ensure that children are not trained exclusively under the influence of a single milieu or, still worse, by a single and unique person. This is one of a number of reasons that make education within the family inadequate. The child reared exclusively in his family becomes its creature: he reproduces all its pecularities, all its characteristics, even to the point of the tics of the familial physiognomy; but he will not be able to develop his own personality. The school frees the child from this excessive dependency. But even at school, and for the same reason, he should be successively entrusted to different teachers. If, as was recently proposed for our secondary schools, the child remains for several years subject to the influence of one and the same instructor, he must necessarily become a slavish copy of the one model placed constantly before him. Such subjection of man to man is immoral; it is only the abstract and impersonal rule that should command such deference of the human will.

However powerful these modes of influence thus offered us by virtue of the child's nature, they certainly cannot alone produce the desired moral effects. By themselves, these predispositions do not constitute moral states properly speaking —states that are henceforth achieved or realized. But according to how one uses them, they can promote the most contradictory objectives. One can enlist the dominance of habit, so readily established in the child, to give him a preference for an ordered life. Conversely, if one does not intervene in time and in an appropriate manner, the child may well become accustomed to irregularity; once this habit is developed and rooted in him he will find it hard to undo. Similarly, as we have just observed, one can capitalize on the child's extreme suggestibility to bend his will to some other's, to strip him of all initiative, rather than making him more open to the liberating action of an impersonal discipline.

And so we do not mean to suggest that the child receives genetically certain predetermined moral predispositions. The weapons that nature puts at our disposal cut two ways; everything depends on how they are used. Hence, the futility of those recurrent discussions as to whether the child is born moral or immoral, or whether he has in him more or less of the positive elements of morality or immorality. So put, the problem is not amenable to any clean-cut solution. To act morally is to conform to the rules of morality. Now, the moral law is outside the consciousness of the child; it is elaborated independent of him; he begins to have contact with it only after a given point in his life. Therefore, it is altogether impossible that, at the moment of birth, he should have some indescribable kind of anticipatory conception, just as he could not have any inherited picture of the external world before opening his eyes. All that he has at birth are some very general dispositions, which are crystallized in one way or another according to how the educator exerts his influence, that is, according to the manner in which this potential is put to work.

We have already had occasion to remark that this putting to work can and must begin in the family and from the cradle. We indicated, along the way, how there was already something like the beginning of moral education here, if for no other reason than that the family requires the rather sudden development of regular habits; and how the parents have at their disposal the means of developing in the child, at an early point, something like a first feeling for moral authority. Thus, we may suppose that when the child enters school he is not in the state of moral neutrality that characterized him at birth; and that these very general predispositions of which we have been speaking have already revealed themselves and begun to crystallize. More particularly, it is certain that by living a regular family life the child will more readily develop a taste for regularity; or, more generally, if he is reared in a family that is morally wholesome, he will share in that moral health through the contagion of example.

Although this familial education is an excellent first preparation for the moral life, its usefulness is quite restricted—above all, with respect to the spirit of discipline. That which is essential to the spirit of discipline, that is to say, respect for the rule, can scarcely develop in the familial setting. The family, especially today, is a very small group of persons who know each other intimately and who are constantly in contact with one another. As a result, their relationships are not subject to any general, impersonal, immutable regulation; they always have and normally should have an air of freedom and ease, which makes them resistant to strict regulation. Familial duties cannot be fixed once and for all through definite precepts that are always applicable and in the same manner; rather they are likely to accommodate themselves to differences in personality and circumstance. It is a matter of temperament, of mutual accommodation, that promotes affection and adjustment. By virtue of its natural warmth, the family setting is especially likely to give birth to the first altruistic inclinations, the first feelings of solidarity; but the morality practiced in this setting is above all a matter of emotion and sentiment. The abstract idea of duty is less important here than sympathy, than the spontaneous impulses of the heart. All the members of this small society are too near one another; and, as a result of this proximity, they have too much feeling for their reciprocal needs; they have too much consciousness of one another for it to be necessary, or even useful, to guarantee their co-operation through regulation. Doubtless, there were times when the family was a quite considerable society comprising a number of households, slaves, and associated people. Then it was necessary that the father of the family, the chief of the group, be clothed with a higher authority. He was lawmaker and magistrate, and all domestic relationships were subject to a genuine discipline. This is no longer the case, for the family numbers only a few persons. Family relationships have lost their earlier impersonality and have a personal and quite volitional character, which does not fit regulation very well.

But meanwhile the child must learn respect for the rule; he must learn to do his duty because it is his duty, because he feels obliged to do so even though the task may not seem an easy one. Such an apprenticeship, which can only be quite incomplete in the family, must devolve upon the school. In fact, there is a whole system of rules in the school that predetermine the child's conduct. He must come to class regularly, he must arrive at a specified time and with an appropriate bearing and attitude. He must not disrupt things in class. He must have learned his lessons, done his homework, and have done so reasonably well, etc. There are, therefore, a host of obligations that the child is required to shoulder. Together they constitute the discipline of the school. It is through the practice of school discipline that we can inculcate the spirit of discipline in the child.

Too often, it is true, people conceive of school discipline so as to preclude endowing it with such an important moral function. Some see in it a simple way of guaranteeing superficial peace and order in the class. Under such conditions, one can quite reasonably come to view these imperative requirements as barbarous—as a tyranny of complicated rules. We protest against this kind of regulation, which is apparently imposed on the child for the sole purpose of easing the teacher's task in inducing uniformity. Does not such a system evoke feelings of hostility in the student toward the teacher, rather than the affectionate confidence that should characterize their relationship?

In reality, however, the nature and function of school discipline is something altogether different. It is not a simple device for securing superficial peace in the classroom—a device allowing the work to roll on tranquilly. It is the morality of the classroom, just as the discipline of the social body is morality properly speaking. Each social group, each type of society, has and could not fail to have its own morality, which expresses its own make-up.

Now, the class is a small society. It is therefore both natural and necessary that it have its own morality corresponding to its size, the character of its elements, and its function. Discipline is this morality. The obligations we shall presently enumerate are the student's duties, just as the civic or professional obligations imposed by state or corporation are the duties of the adult. On the other hand, the schoolroom society is much closer to the society of adults than it is to that of the family. For aside from the fact that it is larger, the individuals—teachers and students—who make it up are not brought together by personal feelings or preferences but for altogether general and abstract reasons, that is to say, because of the social function to be performed by the teacher, and the immature mental condition of the students. For all these reasons, the rule of the classroom cannot bend or give with the same flexibility as that of the family in all kinds and combinations of circumstances. It cannot accommodate itself to given temperaments. There is already something colder and more impersonal about the obligations imposed by the school: they are now concerned with reason and less with feelings; they require more effort and greater application. And although —as we have previously said—we must guard against overdoing it, it is nevertheless indispensable in order that school discipline be everything that it should be and fulfill its function completely. For only on this condition will it be able to serve as intermediary between the affective morality of the family and the more rigorous morality of civil life. It is by respecting the school rules that the child learns to respect rules in general, that he develops the habit of self-control and restraint simply because he should control and restrain himself. It is a first initiation into the austerity of duty. Serious life has now begun.

This, then, is the true function of discipline. It is not a simple procedure aimed at making the child work, stimulating his desire for instruction, or husbanding the energies of the teacher. It is essentially an instrument—difficult to duplicate —of moral education. The teacher to whom it is entrusted cannot guard it too conscientiously. It is not only a matter of his own interest and peace of mind; one can say without exaggeration that the morality of the classroom rests upon his resolution. Indeed, it is certain that an undisciplined class lacks morality. When children no longer feel restrained, they are in a state of ferment that makes them impatient of all curbs, and their behavior shows it—even outside the classroom. One can see analagous situations in the family when domestic education is overly relaxed. In school, this unwholesome ferment or excitement, the result of a failure of discipline, constitutes a more serious moral danger because the agitation is collective. We must never lose sight of the fact that the class is a small society. Thus, no member of this small group acts as though he were alone; each is subject to the influence of the group, and this we must consider most carefully.

Collective action, according to the way its influence is used, may enhance the good or increase the evil. Should its influence be abnormal, then, precisely because it excites and intensifies individual energies, it drives them on the road to catastrophe with all the greater energy. This accounts for immorality developing so readily in mobs and quite often reaching an exceptional degree of violence. The mob, we know, kills easily. A mob or crowd is a society, but one that is inchoate, unstable, without regularly organized discipline. Because it is a society the strong emotional forces generated in the crowd are especially intense. Therefore, they move quickly to excesses. A forceful and complex system of regulation is required to enclose them within normal limits, to prevent them from bursting all bounds. By definition, however, mob lacks constituted rules, regulatory organs of any sort. The forces thus set loose are left entirely to themselves; consequently, it is inevitable that they allow themselves to go beyond all limits, that they know no moderation and spill out into tumultuous, destructive, and, as a result, almost necessarily immoral disorders.

A class without discipline is like a mob. Because a given number of children are brought together in the same class, there is a kind of general stimulation deriving from the common life and imparted to all the individual activities—a stimulation that, when everything goes along normally and is well directed, emerges as more enthusiasm, more concern about doing things well than if each student were working individually. But if the teacher has not developed the necessary authority then this hyperactivity degenerates into an unwholesome ferment, and a genuine demoralization sets in, the more serious as the class is larger. This demoralization becomes obvious in that those elements of least moral value in the class come to have a preponderant place in the common life; just as in political societies during periods of great flux, one sees hosts of harmful elements come to the surface of public life, while in normal times they would be hidden in the shadows.

It is important, therefore, to react against the discredit into which, for a number of years, discipline has tended to fall. Doubtless when one examines the rules of conduct that the teacher must enforce, in themselves and in detail, one is inclined to judge them as useless vexations; and the benevolent feelings, which childhood quite naturally inspires in us, prompt us to feel that they are excessively demanding. Is it not possible for a child to be good and yet fail to be punctual, to be unprepared at the specified time for his lesson or other responsibilities, etc.? If, however, instead of examing these school rules in detail, we consider them as a whole, as the student's code of duty, the matter takes on a different aspect. Then conscientiousness in fulfilling all these petty obligations appears as a virtue. It is the virtue of childhood, the only one in accord with the kind of life the child leads at that age, and consequently the only one that can be asked of him. This is why one cannot cultivate it too conscientiously. If, in a given class, the challenge to discipline results in a kind of partial demoralization, at least one may hope that it will be only a passing thing; but if the disturbance is general, if the whole system is discredited in public opinion and in the view of teachers themselves, then public morality is touched at one of its vital sources.

Furthermore, what should help prevent us from yielding too readily to an overweening acceptance of childhood weakness is the fact that children themselves are the first to appreciate good discipline. It has often been said that if nations are to be happy they must be well governed; it is the same with children as with men. They also need to sense a law beyond them which constrains and sustains them. A well-disciplined class has an air of health and good humor. Each one is in his place and finds it good to be there. The absence of discipline, on the contrary, produces confusion, from which those suffer most who would seem to flourish on it. One no longer knows whether this is good or bad, whether this should or should not be done, whether this is permitted or is illegitimate. Hence a state of nervous agitation, of contagious feverishness unfortunate for the child. Then his inconstancy of temperament is at its peak; he shifts very rapidly from one extreme to another, from laughter to tears and conversely. For the child, like the man, is no longer operating under normal conditions when he feels nothing beyond him setting limits, moderating his behavior, and obliging him not to go beyond his nature. This is all the more true of the child in whom the need for restraint and moderation has not yet had time to organize itself so as to enable it to function spontaneously.

School discipline can produce the useful results that it should achieve only by confining itself within certain limits. Of course, it is necessary that in its major aspects the life of the class be pretty much fixed; but, on the other hand, it is not necessary that regulation should go to the point of the most detailed minutiae. It is indispensable that there be rules; it is unfortunate if everything is regulated. Not all adult behavior is subject to the regulation of morality. There are some things that one may or may not do, or may do as he sees best. In a word, some behavior is independent of moral considerations. Similarly, it is not necessary that school discipline embrace all of school life. It is not necessary that children's attitudes, their bearing, the way they walk or recite their lessons, the way they word their written work or keep their notebooks, etc. be predetermined with great precision. For a discipline so extended is as contrary to the interests of real discipline as superstition is contrary to the interests of true religion, and for two reasons. First, the child sees in such requirements only detestable or absurd procedures aimed at constraining and annoying him—which compromises the authority of the rule in his eyes. On the other hand, if he submits passively and without resistance, he becomes accustomed to doing nothing except upon somebody's order—which destroys all initiative in him. Now, above all, under actual conditions of moral conduct, when the individual is required to act on his own and to play a personal role in the collective life, a pattern of regulation so encompassing could not fail to have the most unfortunate influence on the child's morality. If it did not make a rebel, it would make a morally impoverished person of him.

However serious the consequences of such abuse of discipline, the teacher is only too easily inclined to commit it; and it is important that he take this into account. Since any uncontained power tends to expand endlessly, without limit, the regulatory power at his disposal needs to be contained. Within the class, the teacher is alone with the children who are in no position to resist him. He must, then, resist himself, his own inclinations. It was probably these excesses in school-room regulation, permitted for many years, which gave rise to the reaction against discipline, which itself runs the risk of going too far.

Now that we understand school discipline and its function,

let us see how it should be handled in order to bring children to practice it. In order to develop in them a taste for discipline, it will not do to impose it by force or to accustom them to it mechanically. The child must come to feel himself what there is in a rule which determines that he should abide by it willingly. In other words, he must sense the moral authority in the rule, which renders it worthy of respect. His obedience is not truly moral except when it is the external manifestation of an inner feeling of respect. How is such a feeling inculcated?

Since it is through the teacher that the rule is revealed to the child, everything depends upon him. A rule can scarcely have any authority other than that with which the teacher invests it—that is to say, the idea of which he suggests to the children. The question comes to this: what conditions must the teacher fulfill in order to radiate authority?

Of course, certain personal qualities are necessary. Notably, the teacher should be decisive, have some will power. Since the imperative character of the rule derives from the fact that it silences all doubts and hesitations, the rule cannot appear obligatory to the child if applied indecisively—if those charged with teaching it to him do not seem always certain of what it should be. However, these are really secondary considerations. What is above all important is that the teacher really feel in himself the authority he must communicate and for which he must convey some feeling. It constitutes a force that he can manifest only if he possesses it effectively.

Now, what is the source of the teacher's authority? Does it derive from a physical power with which he is armed, from his right of punishment and reward? The fear of punishment is something altogether different from respect for authority. It has a moral character and moral value only if the penalty is regarded as just by those subjected to it, which implies that the authority which punishes is itself recognized as legitimate. However, this is what is in question. It is not from the outside, from the fear he inspires, that the teacher should gain his authority; it is from himself. This cannot come to him except from his innermost being. He must believe, not perhaps in himself or in the superior quality of his intelligence or will, but in his task and the greatness of that task. It is the priest's lofty conception of his mission that gives him the authority that so readily colors his language and bearing. For he speaks in the name of a God, who he feels in himself and to whom he feels himself much closer than the laymen in the crowds he addresses. So, the lay teacher can and should have something of this same feeling. He also is an instrument of a great moral reality which surpasses him and with which he communicates more directly than does the child, since it is through his intermediation that the child communicates with it. Just as the priest is the interpreter of God, he is the interpreter of the great moral ideas of his time and country. Whatever is linked with these ideas, whatever the significance and authority attributed to them, necessarily spreads to him and everything coming from him since he expresses these things and embodies them in the eyes of children.

In this authority, which derives from a quite impersonal source, nothing of arrogance, vanity, or pedantry must enter. It is entirely brought about through the teacher's respect for his role or, if one may put it this way, for his ministry. This respect is transmitted through word and gesture from his mind to that of the child, where it is imprinted. Of course, I do not mean to say that one must take some indescribable kind of priestly tone in dictating a duty or explaining a lesson. It is by no means necessary that this feeling be always foremost in order to produce its effect. It is enough that it assert itself at the desired moment, and that, although it is only latent and does not openly manifest itself ostentatiously, it nonetheless colors the attitude of the teacher in a general manner.

However, the dominant part played by the teacher in generating this feeling—the personal role that he plays—entails a danger that we must guard against. Indeed, there is reason to fear lest the child develop the habit of associating the notion of rule itself too narrowly with the person of the teacher—lest he view the regulations of the school too concretely as the expression of the teacher's will. So it is that people throughout time have needed to view laws of conduct as instituted by a divine personality. Such a conception runs contrary to the end we want to achieve. The rule is no longer a rule if it is not impersonal and if it is not represented as such in our minds. The teacher must therefore be committed to presenting it, not as his own personal doing, but as a moral power superior to him, and of which he is the instrument not the author. He must make the students understand that it imposes itself on him as it does on them; that he cannot remove or modify it; that he is constrained to apply it; and that it dominates him and obliges him as it obliges them. On this condition alone will he be able to evoke a sentiment that, in a democratic society like ours, is or ought to be at the very foundation of the public conscience: this is the respect for legality, the respect for impersonal law deriving its ascendancy from impersonality itself. From the moment when the law is no longer embodied in a specific person who represents it in a palpable manner, the mind must necessarily seize upon some general and abstract conception of law and respect it as such. Indeed, is it not true that the only thing that survives or can survive in a society where the prestige of class and dynasties is no longer recognized is the impersonal authority of law? For it cannot weaken without all of collective discipline giving way. Unfortunately, we cannot hide the fact that such an idea runs counter to customs deeply rooted for centuries, and that a whole education is necessary to imbue men's minds with it. The school would fail in one of its principal obligations if it disregarded this task.

Now we have come to see, in succession, both the nature of the discipline of the school and how it is possible to make the child feel its authority. We have been able to handle both of these questions without introducing any ideas about the sanctions attached to the rule. Sanctions, therefore, do not have the preponderant role sometimes assigned to them in the development of the spirit of discipline. However, since there are no rules without sanctions there must certainly be a connection between the idea of the rule and the idea of sanction; and the latter must serve in some manner in the functioning of the former. What is this connection?

To answer this question it is appropriate to examine separately the two kinds of sanctions related to school rules, as well as to moral rules and judicial rules: punishment, on the one hand, and rewards, on the other. We shall begin with the former. What is the function of punishment in the school?

# CHAPTER ELEVEN

# ∼§ THE USE OF PUNISHMENT

# IN THE SCHOOL

HAVING INVESTIGATED THE MORAL FUNCTION OF SCHOOL DISCI-
cipline—how it should serve to inculcate respect for the abstract and impersonal rule, training the child in self-control and
self-restraint—we inquired into the manner and conditions for
achieving the goal which is its *raison d'être*. In order for the
child to subject himself to the prescriptions of the rule, he
must feel what there is in it worthy of respect, that is to say,
the moral authority with which it is invested. Now, since the
child comes to understand the rule through the teacher and
since it is the teacher who reveals it to him, it can have only
such authority as the teacher communicates to it. The behavior
prescribed by the rule—behavior perhaps boring and restrictive
—has nothing intrinsic that imposes itself on one's will. Its
necessary ascendancy can only come from outside itself—from
the teacher. Hence, the only question is how such authority
comes to be vested in the teacher. We have seen that the
only source from which it can spring is within himself, that
is to say, in the conception he has of his work, in the moral
ideal to which he is committed and to which he endeavors
to commit the children.

What enables a man to speak with authority is the warmth

of his convictions, the faith he has not only in the abstract truth of the ideas he expresses but, above all, in their moral value.

For moral authority—this complex of qualities that lift us above empirical selves, beyond the average of our fellow-men —can only come from the closest and most intimate devotion to the only reality truly beyond us: our attachment to the moral reality. External signs may be misleading; if the inner feeling is present and vital it will assert and transmit itself more often than not. That is why, and not without reason, we make authority the *sine qua non* of the teacher. Not only is it the condition of an outward orderliness, but the moral life of the class depends on it. Certainly, this authority vested in the teacher may accrue through the respectiful confidence he inspires in the children, simply because he devotes himself to his work and recognizes its significance. He believes more in what he is doing because he is not alone in this belief; because the children believe in it with him. Their faith re-enforces and fortifies his own. Just as the statesman can govern people only if they have a good opinion of him, so the teacher can govern his classroom only if the class believes in him.

The collective feeling that sustains the teacher is already an outcome of the authority vested in him. The feeling children have for authority is translated in this way. Because it is like an echo from all the little minds with which he deals, it rebounds toward him enlarged by all these repercussions. The effect reacts on the cause and intensifies it. The authority possessed by the teacher nonetheless remains the initial cause, the great motivating force that activitates everything else; and however important these repercussions may be, they nonetheless constitute only secondary phenomena.

Need I add that when we speak of the teacher's authority, of the need for it, we by no means intend to say that he must lead a class as though it were a regiment? Of course, nothing is more contrary to the spirit of discipline than to disguise it with a sugary facade. We distort it by presenting it as Montaigne wished—as something easy and pleasant. Everything in life is not beer and skittles; the child needs to prepare himself for exertions and hardship. Consequently, it would be a calamity to allow him to believe that everything can be done as though it were play. However, to begin with, social life is not military life; and if the child must be introduced to the sober things of life, we must never lose sight of the fact that it is only a matter of an initiation, a first introduction, and that the child is not a man and should be handled in accordance with his nature as a child. The teacher's authority should then be tempered with benevolence so that firmness never degenerates into boorishness or harshness. We have said often enough that duty has two aspects: on the one hand, it appears as strict and demanding; on the other, as desirable and attractive. In the family, the second element is preponderant; in the school, the former should assume more importance. However, the moral make-up of the child is still too delicate and shifting to be able to face profitably the pure austerity of duty.

Be that as it may, we see that respect for discipline does not originate in the fear of sanctions curbing violations of the rule. Indeed, whoever has had any experience with school life knows very well that a well-disciplined class is one wherein there is little punishment. Punishment and unruliness generally go together. Thus, in the uses of discipline—in school as well as in life—sanctions do not play the preponderant role sometimes assigned to them by certain theoreticians, although it is certainly true that there must be some fairly close connection between the idea of rule and the idea of punishment curbing infraction of the rule. Not without reason have sanctions always been linked to the rules specifying the child's conduct, just as they are to the rules determining adult behavior.

What, then, is the bond joining these two terms to one another? In other words, why is it necessary to punish? Some very different—even contradictory—solutions have been proposed for this question, which seems at first blush so simple. From an altogether practical point of view, it is important to examine these solutions; for the way in which one uses punishment obviously depends on one's idea of sanctions in the school and their function.

Two theories confront each other. For some, punishment is a simple way of preventing defections from the rule. We must punish the child, they say, so that he doesn't misbehave again and to prevent others from imitating him. It is purely a matter of a close mental association between two ideas— the idea of given misbehavior and the idea of suffering, fear of which prevents recurrence of the forbidden act. In other words, the function of punishment is essentially preventive, due entirely to the intimidation resulting from the threat of punishment.

Certainly punishment must produce in some measure the effect thus attributed to it. We cannot deny, a priori, that fear of punishment is able to exert a salutary influence on certain wills. But this is neither the unique nor even the chief reason for punishment. For if it had no other object, the functions it performs would be of altogether secondary importance, and one might well ask whether they are worth the quite considerable disadvantages. In reality, since punishment acts from the outside and on externals, it cannot touch the moral life at its source. It can, in a degree that we shall presently specify, mechanically train the child to eschew certain behavior; but as to the predisposition that involves him in misbehavior, it cannot elicit a contrary inclination toward the good. Although intimidation may be effective, it does not, by itself, make for improvement. If, then, chastisement had no function other than to constrain unacceptable impulses through intimidation, one might very well see in it a way of guaranteeing overt and superficial propriety—a police procedure; but it would not be in any sense a moralizing instrument. Furthermore, even from this particular viewpoint, its efficacy is very limited. Examples of Italian criminals have strikingly demonstrated that the prophylactic influence of punishment has been exaggerated beyond all reality; and it is easy to see why its influence must be very limited.

Doubtless the suffering caused by punishment is a hardship, and the prospect of it must enter into the calculations of the actor. But duty is also a hardship that constrains one. One is inconvenienced in doing his duty. Whatever the duty, there is an element of privation, sacrifice and renunciation which is above all painful when one is not naturally inclined toward it. Why, of these two hardships, is it the sanction of punishment that seems the most formidable? On the contrary, it would seem that because the consequences are remote in time, because many and various combinations of circumstances allow one to hope that he may evade the hardship, the thought of punishment would hardly outweigh the certain hardship imposed in resisting a present temptation or renouncing an immediate joy. In sum, the penalty is the professional risk of the delinquent career.

Now, there are many careers in which the professional risk is quite considerable and which nonetheless recruit their members without difficulty. Miners, workers in dangerous industries, Icelandic fishermen, etc.—the example of the death or illness of fellow-workers or their predecessors does not stop them. They prefer to expose themselves to certain and serious danger rather than give up their work, a kind of activity they love. Why should the risk courted by the delinquent be more effective in preventing him from following his inclinations? No doubt punishment can easily prevent those who have no sense of a calling, if one may put it so—the mediocre souls who vacillate, hesitate between two alternatives; and so their action is limited.

What we have said about the adult delinquent applies equally well to the delinquent student. When the natural indolence of the child is countered only by the prospect of extra school jobs, there is every reason to fear that in most cases the former will win out. If, then, schoolroom punishment has no reason for being other than to spare us some misbehavior, the outcomes certainly do not correspond to the position it now and always has occupied in all educational systems—especially when one thinks about all that it costs: wasted energy, the squandering of time, and, still more, the risk of eliciting bad feelings in the child.

Furthermore, there is one fact that clearly shows that punishment must have another function. We all know that punishment should somehow fit the crime. No more in the school than in real life can we conscientiously accept equivalent sanctions for unequal offenses, or vice versa. But if, as the theory we are examining would have it, punishment aims only at preventing the forbidden act—restraining, by means of a threat, the tendency to commit it—then punishment ought to be geared not to the seriousness of the act but to the strength of the inclination. The inclination to petty misdeeds, the venial ones, may be much more intense and resistant to correction than the penchant for major schoolroom offenses. For example, there are very few children who are strongly inclined toward overt rebellion against the teacher, to be openly insolent, to harm their fellows. On the other hand, there are many who are inclined to be indolent, to be distracted, etc. However, we cannot punish slight infractions —even where they are chronic and almost constitutional— more severely than an act of open rebellion. Such an unsuitable punishment would seem unjust to the guilty party and would risk inciting rebellion against the teacher and the order of things that he represents. And if punishment is deemed just, that is to say, proportional to the seriousness of the violation, its sole object cannot be to intimidate. Its connection with the moral value of the act that it suppresses gives witness that it must have some other function.

According to one school of moralists, which opposes the preceding viewpoint, this function consists not in preventing recidivism but in expunging it. Punishment should have in itself a value compensating for the evil involved in the offense. We must punish, they say, not to intimidate but to atone for the infraction and its outcomes. "Punishment," says M. Janet, "must not only be a threat assuring the execution of the law, but an atonement or an expiation which sets the violation to rights." So understood, punishment is a kind of counteroffense, which nullifies the offense and restores things to their proper state. It turns not toward the future but toward the past. Thanks to it, the past would be as though it had never happened. Some misdeed has disturbed the order; punishment re-establishes that disrupted order. How does this come about? By the suffering that it implies. "The order disrupted by a rebellious will," says the same author, "is re-established through that suffering which is the consequence of the offense committed." The misery inflicted on the guilty party atones for the evil he caused; it restores the antecedent order because it expiates. Punishment becomes essentially an expiation. From this point of view, the proportionality between crime and punishment is easily explained. For if punishment is to counterbalance and expunge the offense, it must be the equivalent of that offense. If it is to neutralize the crime, it must increase as the evil increases.

Some have objected, and not unreasonably, that the principle on which this conception rests is absurd and irrational. Misery in itself is always bad, they contend. In what way can the evil inflicted on the guilty person compensate for the evil he has done? The first of these evils is added to the second, not subtracted. We see here only a spurious symmetry. It is, says Guyau, as though a physician, in order to heal a diseased arm, began by amputating the other arm. In a word, punishment conceived as expiation is merely a not very novel brand of the old retaliation; and the law of retaliation, they say, is no longer acceptable to the contemporary moral conscience.

Nonetheless, there is something to hold on to in this theory. What must be saved is this notion that punishment erases, or more or less makes amends, so far as possible, for the offense. However, it is not the suffering that gives rise to this quality of reparation. Pain *is* an evil, and it is clearly absurd to think that one evil can compensate for another or nullify it. But punishment does not consist entirely in the suffering that it causes. Indeed, suffering is much less significant than we think in the repression of illegitimate conduct. The essence of penalties and punishment lies elsewhere.

To understand how punishment can make up for the misdeed, let us see first of all what moral wrong is caused by an offense, and what must be done to reduce or expunge it.

With the child as with the adult, moral authority is a creature of opinion and draws all its force from opinion. Consequently, what lends authority to the rule in school is the feeling that the children have for it, the way in which they view it as a sacred and inviolable thing quite beyond their control; and everything that might attenuate this feeling, everything that might induce children to believe that it is not really inviolable can scarcely fail to strike discipline at its very source. To the extent that the rule is violated it ceases to appear as inviolable; a sacred thing profaned no longer seems sacred if nothing new develops to restore its original nature. One doesn't believe in a divinity against which the vulgar lift their hands with impunity. Any violation of the rule tends, also, to whittle away the child's faith in the intangible quality of the rule. The child submits to it because it is endowed with a prestige—a kind of moral force—whose energy corresponds to the potency of its control over behavior. If children see it unanimously obeyed, it will seem to them as very powerful simply in terms of the importance of its effects. On the other hand, if they see willful deviation they will deem it weak and without influence. This is the real moral harm caused by misbehavior. It shatters the child's faith in the authority of school law, just as it shakes the faith of the adult in the authority of moral law, and consequently actually diminishes that authority. In a word, if nothing happens to neutralize its effects, a moral violation *demoralizes*. What must there be to rectify the evil thus produced? The law that has been violated must somehow bear witness that despite appearances it remains always itself, that it has lost none of its force or authority despite the act that repudiated it. In other words, it must assert itself in the face of the violation and react in such a way as to demonstrate a strength proportionate to that of the attack against it. Punishment is nothing but this meaningful demonstration.

It is true that in speaking of a law that affirms itself, that reacts, I may seem to be reifying abstractions. But everything that has just been said can be easily put in quite concrete terms. Certainly it is not the rule that reacts and asserts itself; it reacts and affirms itself through the intermediation of its instrument, that is to say, through the intermediation of the teacher. We know in reality that if the child believes in the rule it is because he believes in his teacher. He respects it because his teacher affirms it as worthy of respect and respects it himself. But if the teacher allows violation without intervening, such a tolerance will seem to offer proof that he no longer believes in it with the same conviction, that he no longer feels it worthy of respect in the same degree; and in the same measure the student will cease to believe in it. Even the mere appearance of doubt by the teacher entails doubt by the child; and this latter doubt shakes discipline at its very foundation. So the teacher must, in the face of an infraction, attest in a thoroughly unequivocal way that his feelings have not changed, that his commitment is as strong as ever, that in his view the rule is still the rule, that it has lost none of its worth, and that it always has the right to claim our respect despite the violation against it. To do this he must clearly and forcefully censure the act that has been committed; this vigorous disapproval is the essence of punishment.

Thus, the essential function of punishment is not to make the guilty expiate his crime through suffering or to intimidate possible imitators through threats, but to buttress those consciences which violations of a rule can and must necessarily disturb in their faith—even though they themselves aren't aware of it; to show them that this faith continues to be justified; and, to speak more particularly of the school situation, that it is always felt by the teacher from whom the children receive it. Thus, discipline plays an important part in the functioning of the morality of the school. Certainly, as we have shown, it is not punishment that gives discipline its authority; but it is punishment that prevents discipline from losing this authority, which infractions, if they went unpunished, would progressively erode. So it is quite true that it compensates, that it corrects the evil resulting from the offense. But we see that what produces reparation is not the pain inflicted on the person. What matters is not that the child suffer, but rather that his behavior be vigorously censured. It is the disapproval leveled against the given conduct that alone makes for reparation. Doubtless it is almost inevitable that the blame must make him upon whom it falls suffer. The censure of an act implies censure of the actor; there is only one way of showing that one disapproves of someone, and that is to treat him less well than the people one esteems. This is why punishment almost necessarily implies severe treatment and, as a result, pain for the person affected.

Pain, however, is only an incidental repercussion of punishment; it is not its essential element. It is an external index of the feeling that must assert itself in the face of a violation. It is the feeling expressed, and not the sign by which it is expressed, that neutralizes the morally disruptive effect of the violation. Thus, severity of treatment is justified only to the extent that it is necessary to make disapproval of the act utterly unequivocal. Suffering, then, which would be the whole of a penalty if its principal function were to intimidate or to compel expiation, is in reality a secondary element, which indeed may be totally lacking. Neither punishment in school nor the penalties, properly speaking, of civil life can make basically rebellious souls really suffer. Nonetheless, punishment retains the whole of its *raison d'être*. To set up a scale of penalties is not to imagine a series of pains sagely constructed in hierarchical order. For the moment, however, it will do to point out the idea whose practical consequences we shall next explore.

Now that we understand the function of punishment, let us see what must be done to achieve its objective.

According to a theory that still has some distinguished adherents, punishment should limit itself to allowing misconduct to bring on its natural consequences. This theory has been attributed to Rousseau; and indeed we find in the second volume of *Émile* some propositions that seem to support this principle. "One ought never to inflict punishment, as such upon children; but it ought always to happen to them as the natural consequence of their misbehaving." Again: "Keep the child dependent on natural events: the result will be a genuine education. . . . Émile breaks the windows in his room; we shall then restrain ourselves from repairing the damage he has done and the cold of the night will give him a cold which will be completely his own punishment." However, Rousseau recommends this method only during the first period of childhood, up to twelve years of age. He finds it applicable up to age twelve because, according to him, the moral life only starts after this age. Up to this time, the child, like early man, is a stranger to any conception of morality and lives a purely physical life, like an animal. Animals are not subjected to a system of artificial sanctions; they develop under the influence of natural things. Their lessons are only those of experience. Insofar as the child leads a purely animal-like life he has no need for any other discipline. To subject him to any coercive influence would be to violate the order of nature. Beginning at age twelve, however, a new life begins for him; henceforth discipline, properly speaking, becomes necessary. "We gradually develop moral ideas which distinguish good from bad. Up to this point we have known no law save that of necessity; now we pay attention to what is useful (from twelve to fifteen years of age); and we will presently be concerned with that which is proper and good (beyond fifteen years of age)."

Thus, according to Rousseau, punishment in terms of natural consequences applies only to strictly physical education. As soon as a genuinely moral education begins, the system has to change and the educator must intervene directly.

It is only with Spencer that the theory has been extended to the whole of education. Here is the basic idea of his doctrine:

Whatever one's point of departure, all moral theory will grant that an action whose immediate and long run results are in sum beneficial, is a good action; while an act whose short term and remote results are in sum maleficent is a bad action. The criterion which men use in the last analysis in judging conduct is the happiness or sorrow it produces. We deem drunkenness as bad because it entails physical deterioration and the associated evils affecting both the drunkard and his family. If theft yielded as much pleasure to him who was robbed as to him who stole it would not be on our list of crimes.

Admitting this, it is no longer necessary to resort to an artificial system of punishment for the moral development of the child. One has only to permit things to operate naturally. When conduct is evil, there will be a painful outcome for the actor, which will signal the offense and the memory of which will prevent recurrences. The teacher's role in the matter of punishment then becomes very simple: it is sufficient that he watch lest some artificial factor intervene to prevent the child from experiencing the natural consequences of his conduct.

Such a method, says Spencer, enjoys a double advantage over the systems customarily followed. First, it provides a solid foundation for the moral temperament of the child. One is much more certain of acting as he must in life when he understands the good and bad consequences of his behavior than when his action is based only on the authority of others. When the child acts or refrains from acting to avoid an artificial punishment he does so without really evaluating his conduct—acts only out of respect for authority. Therefore, there is reason to fear that when he arrives at an age when he no longer feels the influence of authority, the child, now an adult, is in no condition to behave properly on his own. In the second place, because this punishment derives from the nature of things, because it follows naturally and necessarily from his behavior, the child cannot attribute it to any individual. He has no one to blame but himself. Thus, one avoids those bursts of anger, the bitterness that too often characterizes and alters the relationship of parent and child, teacher and student. Impersonal punishment doesn't admit of such undesirable outcomes. Rather than interfering, one has only to be sure that the ill-advised behavior produces its effects. Is the child never ready on time for his walk? Then one will leave without him. If he is too careless in wearing out his playthings, then they won't be replaced. Should he refuse to put his playthings in order; then we will put them in place; but when he wants to use them he will no longer be able to find them, etc.

Such is the system. Before looking at the principle on which it is based, it is interesting to observe that the advantages attributed to it are quite uncertain, if not illusory. It is contended that the child will be able to blame neither parents nor teacher for punishments not of their doing. But this is to suppose that the child is in a position to interpret correctly the experience from which he has suffered. This is only possible if he has achieved a certain measure of intellectual sophistication. In reality, there is no such apparent connection—so palpably apparent that even the inexperienced eyes of a child can see it at a glance—between a phenomenon and its cause. A child who has overeaten has indigestion. He suffers; that he knows. But what is responsible for his suffering? This is a problem that the adult himself, in similar cases, cannot always resolve on the spot and in an instant. Too many different explanations are possible; which is all the more reason why it should be so with the child and why his inexperience will readily enable him to explain something in a way which justifies him.

The primitive does not dream of attributing untoward things that befall him to the requirements of natural law, for the very good reason that he knows nothing of natural law. He imputes the ill he suffers or the death of a neighbor, not to some objective and impersonal cause, but to some person who he believes hates him—to a sorcerer, or an enemy. The child is only too easily inclined to reason in the same way. We see him endlessly imputing to those about him the trivial unpleasantnesses for which he alone is responsible. By such a method one must surely tend to perpetuate harmful sentiments better avoided. On the other hand, by virtue of this same fact that there is nothing easy about the interpretation of experience, because it leaves so much room for arbitrariness, it is impossible to rely on it alone to teach the child how he should conduct himself in life. In fact, Spencer himself could not be satisfied with this theory, and, contrary to the rule he himself set up, had the parents surreptitiously intervene and resort to what were, properly speaking, punishments only thinly disguised. When the child left his playthings in disorder and the parents took them away under pretext of putting them in order, did not the deprivation

thus imposed on the child constitute a genuine but completely artificial punishment? If they had allowed the things
to produce their own natural consequences, the playthings
would not by themselves have gone out of circulation; they
would have remained in disorder as the child left them—a
situation to which he would very easily accommodate himself.

Let us return to the principle of the theory itself. An evil
act, says Spencer, is one that has bad consequences for the
child, or for those about him, or for both simultaneously.
There are consequences that explain the penalties. The child
who has experienced these outcomes knows then why he
must avoid certain actions. If it is he himself who has been
directly affected, he is admonished forthwith by the discomfort he feels; if it is those about him, he perceives the repercussions that are no less significant. Not to prolong the
discussion uselessly, let us admit the principle although it
calls for important reservations. At least in a general sense,
one can certainly say that an evil act always has evil repercussions. However, these repercussions must always be of
such a nature as to enable the child to perceive them. Very
often their impact is beyond his view, outside of the small
circle or the little world where he lives and within which
his perceptions are confined. How, then, can such consequences be brought home to him? For example, he should
respect his father. Why? Because the respect for paternal
authority, within well understood limits where it is legitimate,
is indispensable to the maintenance of discipline and to
family morale; and because, on the other hand, a serious
weakening of the familial spirit would have catastrophic consequences for the survival of the whole group. Therefore,
society makes filial devotion a strict obligation and imposes
it on the child. But how can the child perceive the remote
consequences of his behavior? How can he understand that
through his disobedience he contributes his share to shatter-
ing one of the principles of the social order? The adult him-

self is quite often in no position to assess such outcomes. Morality is not so simple as Spencer imagines. Made to regulate social relationships in societies as complex as ours, morality itself is very complex. Behavior condemned by morality is repudiated because of its diverse repercussions that reach throughout the whole extent of the social structure—repercussions that cannot be seen with the naked eye but that science alone discovers step by step, thanks to its special methods and funded knowledge.

Above all, when we are dealing with morality in the school setting Spencer's principle seems inapplicable. In reality, most of the student's obligations are neither ends in themselves nor goals for the near future; they are simple exercises aimed at preparing the child for his life as an adult. If he is asked to apply himself, not to yield as he would naturally to distractions and indolence, it is not simply in order that he perform well those duties that are the pride of the teacher and the class; rather, it is in order that he acquire the culture that he will use later, the habit of exerting himself, which a worker needs to take his place in society. It is only when he will have left school and when he will be involved in serious matters that the natural consequences of his habitual student conduct will emerge. Is it necessary to say that if he waits until then to evaluate his behavior it will be too late? On the contrary, if he is to take account of such matters in time, it is necessary to anticipate the natural course of events. The educator must intervene and link to the rules of discipline sanctions that anticipate those of later life. The method proposed by Spencer is therefore only useful in very special cases and cannot provide us with a basic principle of punishment in the school.

# CHAPTER TWELVE

# THE USE OF PUNISHMENT

# IN THE SCHOOL (*Continued*)

HAVING DETERMINED THE NATURE AND FUNCTION OF SCHOOL discipline, we asked how it might best be used to convey to children a sense of the authority inherent in the rule, so that they yield spontaneously to it; and we have seen that this feeling can and should be communicated to them, not indirectly by threat of punishments that repress acts not informed by such feeling of deference to the rule, but directly and in itself. Respect for the rule is an altogether different thing than the fear of punishment and the wish to avoid it; it is the feeling that the precepts of school conduct involve something making them intangible and ascendant forces, which they dare not challenge. It is the teacher from whom children receive this sense of the authority of the rule. The teacher communciates it to them, and he does so because he himself feels it, that is to say, because he takes account of the importance of his task, because he sees in the numerous rules of school discipline the necessary means for achieving the lofty ideal that he pursues. He suggests this feeling, which he himself experiences, to the students by word, gesture, and example.

What, then, is the function of punishment? Is it not a

kind of parasitic and unwholesome supererogation? Or does it, on the contrary, have a normal part to play in the normal life of the classroom? This is the question we explored in the last chapter. We saw that if it was not punishment that endowed the rule with authority, at least it prevented the rule from losing the authority that daily infractions would whittle away if they went unpunished. For what gives the rule its authority is the child's view of it as inviolable; any act that violates it promotes the belief that it is not in fact inviolable. If students submit to it and respect it, it is on the word of the teacher who asserts its right to their respect. But if the teacher permits a lapse in this respect without intervening, such leniency bears witness—or seems to, which amounts to the same thing—that he no longer deems it so worthy of respect. The hesitation, the doubts, the weakening of conviction which betray his attitude are necessarily communicated to the children.

Confronted with a misdeed, then, the teacher must prevent this weakening of the class's moral convictions by demonstrating in an unequivocal way that his feelings have not changed, that the rule is always sacred in his view, that it merits the same respect despite the offense committed. He must certainly show that he is in no way sympathetic with the offense, that he rejects it and repudiates it, which is to say, in sum, that he disapproves of it with a disapproval consonant with the importance of the misdeed. Such is the principal function of punishment. To punish is to reproach, to disapprove. Furthermore, the principal form of punishment has always consisted in putting the guilty on the *index*, holding him at a distance, ostracizing him, making a void around him, and separating him from decent people. Since one cannot reproach anyone without treating him less well than those whom one esteems, since there is no other way of translating the feeling that the repudiated behavior inspires, all such repudiation generally ends in inflicting some suffering on the delinquent. But this is only a more or less incidental repercussion of the penalty; it is not the essential thing. Punishment retains its *raison d'être* even when it is not felt to be painful by him who submits to it. To punish is not to make others suffer in body or soul; it is to affirm, in the face of an offense, the rule that the offense would deny. This is the great difference between the function of punishment in the education of children and the training of an animal. Punishments inflicted on an animal, in order to train it, cannot produce their effects unless they involve suffering that is actually felt. For the child, on the contrary, punishment is only the palpable symbol through which an inner state is represented; it is a notation, a language, through which either the general social conscience or that of the school teacher expresses the feeling inspired by the disapproved behavior.

The chief function of punishment being thus determined, we were ready to inquire what it ought to be and how it ought to be administered, in order to achieve that end which is its reason for being. On this point, we first of all encountered a theory that would make punishment consist exclusively in the natural consequences spontaneously produced by the culpable act. This is the theory of natural reaction, such as Spencer, notably, has formulated. There is no point in reviewing the difficulties raised by this doctrine. It would seem more useful to emphasize the interesting and correct idea that is its point of departure—an idea that we can retain, although applying it altogether differently than do the teachers whose system we are discussing.

There is an education of the mind and will that takes place directly under the influence of things, without any artificial intervention by man; this spontaneous—as it were, automatic —education is the normal type which every teaching system should approximate. Thus, quite independently, the child learns to speak and to direct himself through his involvement in all those things surrounding him. It is not his parents who can teach him how he should move his limbs or how much effort is required to enable him to move toward or away from external objects depending on their proximity. All this knowledge, in reality so complex, he picks up spontaneously through personal experience, through trial and error in contact with these realities. Through the suffering that follows inadequate or ill-adapted movements, he is warned of failures and of the need to begin again; just as pleasure is the sign of success at the same time that it constitutes a natural reward. In the same way he learns his language—the vocabulary and the grammar that characterizes it as well as the logic implicit in this grammar. So it is by himself, that the child tries to reproduce our way of talking, of pronouncing, combining words, putting phrases together; and what teaching, properly speaking, comes to mean to him in the end—a predilection for the amenities, for elegance and quality—all this is a relatively slight thing compared with the fundamental learning that he owes only to himself.

Furthermore, this education through direct experience with things is prolonged well beyond childhood and adolescence. It lasts throughout life. For learning is continuous, and the adult has no teachers except life itself; and the only sanctions for his behaviors are most often simply the consequences of these acts. It is through this tentative, groping procedure, by trying and failing and beginning again, and correcting little by little our ways of doing things, that we learn the techniques of our trades and everything we possess of the practical wisdom that we significantly term "experience." But then if such a method is effective at this point, if humanity owes so much to it, why should it not be applicable to all education? Why cannot the child acquire moral culture in the same way as the adult acquires his technical culture? This being so, it is useless to contrive a judicious system of graduated punishments. One need only allow the child to develop out of his contact with things; they will warn him when he is mistaken, that is to say, when his acts are not what they should be, are not appropriate to the nature of things.

Tolstoy's theory of teaching rests on the same idea. Indeed, according to Tolstoy, the model of ideal education is that which occurs when people go on their own initiative to discover things in museums, libraries, laboratories, meetings, public lectures, or simply talk with wise men. In all these cases, there is no constraint exercised; yet do we not learn in this way? Why can't the child enjoy the same liberty? It is then only a matter of putting at his disposal that knowledge deemed useful to him; but we must simply offer it to him without forcing him to absorb it. If such knowledge is truly useful to him, he will feel its necessity and come to seek it himself. This is why punishment is unknown at the school of Iasnaïa Poliana. Children come when they wish, learn what they wish, work as they wish.

However surprising these extreme consequences of the doctrine may seem to us—and not without reason—the principle on which they are based is itself incontestable and deserves being preserved. It is altogether certain that we learn how to act only under the influence of that milieu to which our behavior aims to adapt us. The wellsprings of our behavior are within us; they can't be set in motion except by ourselves and from within. Nothing from outside ourselves can tell us which motives should be restrained or contained, or how much energy should be devoted to each of them, or how their influence should be combined, etc. It is ours to feel, and we cannot feel except by coming in contact with the milieu, that is to say, with the things at which our action aims, and by trying things out. It is the way in which the milieu reacts to our behavior that warns us; this reaction is pleasant or unpleasant according to whether our behavior is or is not appropriate. So we may say in general terms that the spontaneous reactions of things or beings surrounding us constitute the natural sanctions of our conduct.

However, this principle, once admitted, does not at all imply that punishment, properly speaking—that is to say, the punishment inflicted by parents on the child, or by the teacher on the student—must disappear from our systems of moral education. What is the natural consequence of the immoral act, if not the impulse of disapproval that it arouses in the conscience? Disapproval is the necessary result following the offense. Since, on the other hand, punishment itself is nothing other than the external manifestation of this disapproval, punishment is also the natural outcome of the offense. It is the way in which the milieu reacts spontaneously against the criminal act. Now doubtless one may not clearly perceive, at first, the connection between these two words.

What is there in common between punishment and offense? They seem to be two heterogeneous things coupled artificially. But this is because we do not see the middle term that links them, that makes a bridge from one to the other: the sentiment evoked by the offense and from which the penalty results, the feeling that is the result of the act and the essence of punishment.

Once this is seen, the intimate tie between offending and punishing appears quite clearly. If Spencer misunderstood this continuity, if, consequently, he only saw in punishment an artificial system, it is because he did not see that the evil of the misdeed does not lie entirely in the injurious consequences, however unpleasant they may be, whether for the guilty person himself or for those about him. More evil derives from the fact that the offending act threatens, compromises, and weakens the authority of the rule that it violates and denies. This is the evil that gives rise to and necessitates the penalty.

If the child misbehaves by destroying his playthings, to

take Spencer's own example, the misbehavior is not that he has thoughtlessly and rather stupidly denied himself a way of entertaining himself; rather, it consists in his being insensitive to the general rule that prohibits useless destruction, or destruction merely for the sake of amusement. Furthermore, he will not take account of the whole extent of his misbehavior merely because people will not buy him new playthings. The deprivation thus imposed upon him will make him understand that he has acted thoughtlessly, that he has misunderstood his own interest—not that he has acted badly in the moral sense of the word. He will not feel that he has committed a moral fault, that he is morally culpable. Only disapproval can warn him that not only was the conduct nonsensical but that it was bad conduct violating a rule that should be obeyed. The true sanction, like the true natural consequence, is blame.

Now, it is true that this objection has no bearing on Tolstoy's argument. Everything we have said supposes school rules, a morality of the schoolroom that punishment protects and creates respect for. Because the child has the obligation to work, indolence and negligence are moral shortcomings that should be punished. But according to Tolstoy, this morality, this complex of obligations imposed on the child, is unjustifiable. It constitutes a totally artificial institution, an artifact of man without basis in the nature of things. According to him, there is no reason for making a moral obligation, a sanctioned duty, out of work or education. Man's spontaneous desires will suffice for everything. Knowledge need not be imposed; it is useful enough so that it will be sought in and for itself. Child or man need only take account of what is, in order for him to desire it. However, I shall not stop to discuss a view so obviously contrary to everything we know of history. If men are taught, it is not by themselves, out of love of knowledge or work; but it is because they are obliged to. They have been required to learn

by society, which makes education an increasingly imperative obligation. Because they need more knowledge, societies
demand more in their members. To the extent that they
become more complex, they need greater amounts of energy
to maintain themselves and demand more work of each of
us. It is through a sense of duty that men develop and instruct
themselves; it is through a sense of duty that they develop
habits of work. The Biblical legend only puts in mythical
form the misery and laborious effort involved in the long
struggle humanity had to make to transcend its initial torpor.
What man has done only through a sense of duty from the
beginning of history, the child can do only through a sense
of duty as he enters into life. We shall see, shortly, how duty
began by being harsh and how slowly it has softened bit by
bit.

Everything draws us to the same conclusion: the essence
of the penalty is blame. If we seek through analysis the
function of punishment, we find that its real reason for
being is the disapproval that it implies. Do we begin with
the idea that punishment should be a natural consequence
of the act, and not something artificial, conventionally superimposed on the act? We come to the same conclusion, since
reproach is the way the milieu spontaneously reacts when
confronted with the offense; and laws, whether academic or
civil, have done nothing but codify, organize, and systematize
these spontaneous reactions to deviant behavior. Thus, we
have a reliable principle for determining what punishment
in the school ought to be. Since punishing is reproaching,
the best punishment is that which puts the blame—which is
the essence of punishment—in the most expressive but least
expensive way possible. Doubtless, and for reasons we have
stated, blame ends in severe treatment. But such severe treatment is not an end in itself; it is only a means; and consequently it is only justified to the extent that it is necessary
to attain the end which is its *raison d'être*—the end of giving

the child the most vivid impression possible of the feelings evoked by his behavior. It is not a matter of making him suffer, as if suffering involved some sort of mystical virtue, or as if the essential thing were to intimidate and terrorize. Rather, it is a matter of reaffirming the obligation at the moment when it is violated, in order to strengthen the sense of duty, both for the guilty party and for those witnessing the offense—those whom the offense tends to demoralize. Every element of the penalty that does not promote this end, all severity that does not contribute to this end, is bad and should be prohibited.

The principle thus stated, let us apply it. First of all, it allows us to justify without difficulty the fundamental precept in our school punishment—the absolute prohibition of corporal punishment. Blows and bad treatment systematically inflicted are readily understood if punishment is an expiation, if suffering is the chief objective. But if the objective is above all to reproach, one must demonstrate that this suffering is necessary in order to make the child feel others' disapproval of him. There are many other ways of giving him this feeling. Doubtless in societies still uncivilized where individual sensibilities are hard to affect, reacting only to the influence of quite intense irritants, it may be necessary for blame, if it is to be strongly felt, to be translated into some violent form. This explains in part—but only in part, as we shall presently see—the great use that has been made of physical correctives at certain periods of history. But among peoples who have achieved a certain level of culture, whose more delicate nervous systems respond even to weak irritants, these gross procedures are no longer necessary. Ideas and feelings need not be expressed through such grossly physical procedures, through such untoward manifestations of force, in order to be communicated. As a matter of fact, such punishments constitute today quite a serious moral handicap. They affront a feeling that is at the bottom of all our morality, the religious respect in which the human person is held. By virtue of this respect, all violence exercised on a person seems to us, in principle, like sacrilege. In beating, in brutality of all kinds, there is something we find repugnant, something that revolts our conscience—in a word, something immoral. Now, defending morality through means repudiated by it, is a remarkable way of protecting morality. It weakens on the one hand the sentiments that one wishes to strengthen on the other. One of the chief aims of moral education is to inspire in the child a feeling for the dignity of man. Corporal punishment is a continual offense to this sentiment. In this respect, then, it has a demoralizing effect, which is why it has been disappearing more and more from our laws. But how much stronger the reason that it should disappear from schoolroom punishment. In a sense—although certainly the expression is egregiously inaccurate—one can say that up to a certain point the criminal is no longer a human being, that we are justified in no longer viewing him as a man. But we never have the right, with the just-developing conscience of the child, to give up hope to the point of putting him henceforth outside the human family.

Corporal punishment is justifiable only when the child is still a small animal. It is then a matter of training, not of education. Above all, at school this type of punishment should be prohibited. In the family, the bad effects are easily softened, neutralized by shows of tenderness, by affectionate expressions continually exchanged between parents and children, by the intimacy of life that reduces the ordinary significance of such violence. At school, there is nothing that can soften harshness and brutality; penalties are applied with a certain impersonality. Whatever there is in physical illtreatment that is morally abhorrent finds nothing to moderate it in the classroom; this is why it is proper to prohibit it without qualification.

Having shown why corporal punishment should be entirely

forbidden, it is not without interest to inquire why, in educational systems of the past, it occupied a positively preponderant position. This inquiry, as we shall see, will yield some unanticipated results.

One might think a priori that the harshness of primitive mores, the barbarism of earlier times, must have given rise to this mode of punishment. The facts do not support this hypothesis, however natural it may seem at first glance. An ethnographer, M. Steinmetz, has collected many documents on education among primitive peoples in an article in the *Zeitschrift für Socialwissenschaft*,[1] and in his *Ethnologische Studien zür ersten Entwicklung der Strafe*.[2] He has come to the remarkable conclusion that, in the great majority of cases, discipline is very gentle. Canadian Indians love their children very tenderly, never beat them, and do not even reprimand them. The veteran missionary, Lejeune, who knew his Indians well, said of the Montagnais Indians: "they cannot see children punished or even reproached; they can refuse nothing to a child who cries." According to the same observer, it is likewise with the Algonquins. A Sioux chief thought the whites barbarous for striking their children. One finds this same absence of corporal punishment in a great number of North and South American tribes. But these American groups, for the most part, have already achieved a certain culture, although certainly inferior to ours and even to that of the Middle Ages. Suppose we descend the scale of civilization by a notch. If we cannot see in indigenous people of Australia the perfect type of primitive man, nevertheless they should certainly be classified among the least developed peoples that we know. Here, the child, far from being mistreated, is rather excessively indulged. On the peninsula of Cobourg in

1. Sebald Rudolf Steinmetz, "Das Verhältnis zwischen Eltern und Kindern bei den Naturvolkern," *Zeitschrift für sozialwissenschaft* (Berlin: Georg Reimer, 1898), I, 60.
2. Sebald Rudolf Steinmetz, *Ethnologische Studien zur ersten Entwicklung der Strafe* (Leiden, 1892), II, 179.

northern Australia, "Children are treated very affectionately, they are neither punished nor reproached." In Nouvelle-Norcie, parents refuse nothing to their children, and the most they do is to make some disapproving remark to the child who has misbehaved. Among the indigenous people of Moreton Bay, the idea of striking a child would be really monstrous, etc.

Among one hundred four societies, which have been thus compared, there were only thirteen where education was severe. Furthermore, this severeity was in no sense excessive. The harshest treatment used was simply a blow given either with the hand or with a switch, or some denial of food. Even more interesting, these thirteen groups wherein education had this quality had a relatively advanced culture. They were, on the whole, much more cultivated than those in which the child was treated with the great indulgence we have mentioned. This increase in severity as the level of civilization rises may be seen in other cases.

In Rome, the history of education comprises two distinct periods—before and after Augustus. Before Augustus it seems to have been very gentle. There is a story about a teacher who created an unprecedented scandal in Rome when he roused a sleeping student with a blow of his hand. Obviously, then, such punishment was not customary. According to Cato, it was a veritable sacrilege to strike one's wife or son. These gentle habits were replaced by far more severe ones when the child was reared no longer by his own father, but by tutors called pedagogues or in the schools, *ludimagister*. From then on, blows became the rule. Horace tells us something of his schoolteacher, Orbilius, who qualified for the very significant epithet, *plagosus* (giver of blows). A mural discovered at Pompeii[3] gives us a picture of school life at that time: a schoolboy, stripped of his clothes, is hoisted on the back of a companion who holds his hands, while another

3. Gaston Boissier, *Revue de Deux Mondes*, March 15, 1884.

holds his feet and a third lifts the rod in preparation for beating him. The gentlest punishment was inflicted by means of the *ferula* (rod), which was used to strike a certain number of times on the hands. The most serious offenses were punished with the *flagellum*, a sort of lash used on slaves. Certainly Cicero, Seneca, and above all Quintilian raised many protests, but without effect on such practices. Furthermore, these practices had their apologists, such as the stoic Chryssipus, who thought it legitimate to use corporal punishment on educational grounds.

However harsh this regime, it was nothing compared to that which was established and became quite general during the Middle Ages. Probably in the first period of Christianity education within the family was gentle enough. But from the time that monastic schools were set up, the lash, the rod, and fasting became very common punishments. Here, again, the severity was less at the beginning than at the end. It was toward the thirteenth century that such harshness attained its maximum, that is to say, at the time when universities and colleges were established and peopled, when the scholarly life of the Middle Ages itself achieved its highest point of development and organization. Indeed, corporal correction took on such importance that everywhere the need for regulating it was felt. The limits within which it was attempted to confine it give eloquent testimony to its abuse. What was authorized allows us to judge what was in fact practiced. The *Sachsenspiegel* (1215-18) permitted up to twelve blows with a lash. A regulation of the school at Worms formally prohibits only those blows resulting in real wounds or the fracturing of a limb. The chief correctional procedures were slapping, kicking, striking with the fist, the rod, the lash, incarceration, fasting, the *vellicatio* (tickling), and kneeling. The lash, particularly, played such a part that it became a sort of idol. One finds it engraved on certain seals. In certain parts of Germany, there was an annual festival in its honor. Students marched solemnly into the woods to gather the rods that would be used to beat them. Even more curious, these school customs seem to  have reacted on domestic patterns, making them harsher. In the family, also, education became more severe. Luther tells us that he got up to fifteen blows in a morning.

During the Renaissance there was an outburst of protest. Everyone knows of the cries of indignation from Rabelais, Erasmus, and Montaigne. But as in Rome, these eloquent demands had little influence on practice, and the practices of punishment were softened only very slowly. Although the Jesuits had written in their *Ratio studiorum* a prohibition against resort to corporal punishment except in the most serious cases, the lash remained up to the middle of the eighteenth century the preferred instrument of correction. Raumer, in his *Geschichte der Paedogogik*,[4] tells us of a teacher who, in the middle of the eighteenth century, boasted of having administered in the course of his career 2,227,302 beatings. It was only at the end of the century that this evil tapered off. Since then, laws prohibiting corporal punishment have constantly gained ground. Nonetheless, it is important to remember that it is still not absolutely prohibited in England, or in the Duchy of Baden, or in Saxony, or Russia. The chief teachers in Germany, those charged with the systematic codification of a complete system of education, Rein and Baumeister, still judge it appropriate not to forbid this mode of correction completely. And it cannot be doubted that practice goes beyond the limits thus marked out by law or theory. Even in France, and despite all the usual prescriptions, these old mistakes have persisted down to our recent school reform.

Such are the facts. Now let us see what lessons can be drawn from them.

---

4. Karl Georg von Raumer, *Geschichte der Paedogogik* (6th ed.; Stuttgart: S. G. Liesching, 1889), II, 241.

The apologists for corporal punishment have often contended, in support of their position, that such punishment is by right a part of familial education, and that in sending his children to school, the father delegates his right to the teacher who becomes his representative. The short historical review of child punishment that we have just presented shows that in all cases these explanations and this justification of physical punishment in the school are completely without historical foundation. These punishments are not constituent elements of family life, subsequently passed on to the school by a delegation either explicit or implicit. Rather, insofar as they constitute a regularly organized system, they have their origin completely in the school. When education is exclusively a family matter, such punishment occurs only sporadically, as isolated phenomena. The general rule is rather extreme indulgence; ill-treatment is rare. It only becomes regularized as constituting a disciplinary method when the school appears; for several centuries this method of punishment developed as the school itself developed. The arsenal of such punishments expanded, and their application became more frequent to the extent that school life expanded, became more complex and organized. There is something in the nature of the school that strongly inclines it to this type of punishment; once established, it persists for centuries despite all protests against it and even despite the most frequently repeated legal prohibitions. It was only very slowly that such practices receded under pressure of public opinion. Evidently there is something in the life of the school, some powerful forces, which prompt the teacher to practice such violent methods of discipline. What, then, are the causes? How does it happen that the school, this seedbed of humane culture, has been, as if by some built-in necessity, a source of cruelty?

One can easily explain why education is necessarily more severe among civilized than among primitive peoples. The primitive life is simple; its ideas are few and not very complex; its occupations, but little differentiated, recur always the same. It is natural that education, which prepares the child for the life he must one day lead, should have the same simplicity. One might even say that in this kind of society education is almost nonexistent. The child readily learns what he needs to know through direct and personal experience. Life is his instructor, without the need of intervention by his parents. Thus, the principle of laissez faire dominates. Any organized or systematic discipline has no reason for being. True education begins only when the moral and intellectual culture acquired by man has become complex and plays too important a part in the whole of the common life to leave its transmission from one generation to the next to the hazards of circumstance. Hence, the elders feel the need to intervene, to bring about themselves the transmission of culture by epitomizing their experiences and deliberately passing on ideas, sentiments, and knowledge from their minds to those of the young. Rather than permitting the young to instruct themselves independently, spontaneously, under the influences of daily life, they instruct them. Now, there is necessarily something laborious and coercive in such action; it constrains the child to go beyond his nature as a child, since it is a matter of making it mature more rapidly than nature would allow; and from now on, instead of letting his actions drift freely at the mercy of circumstance, the child must willingly and laboriously concentrate on matters assigned him. In a word, civilization has necessarily somewhat darkened the child's life, rather than drawing him spontaneously to instruction as Tolstoy claimed. If, further, one reflects that at this point in history violence was common, that it did not seem to affront anyone's conscience, and that it alone had the necessary efficacy for influencing rougher natures, then one can easily explain how the beginnings of culture were signalized by the appearance of corporal punishment.

This explanation, however, only partially accounts for the observed facts. It helps us to understand how corporal punishment appeared at the dawn of civilization. But if no other cause intervened, one would expect the use of such punishment to lose ground progressively from the moment when it came into general use. For as the moral conscience of a people becomes progressively refined, as manners become milder, such violence becomes increasingly repugnant. But we have seen that this repressive system, far from declining, expanded for several long centuries and in the degree that men became more civilized. It was at the end of the Middle Ages that it attained its zenith; nonetheless it is certain that Christian societies, at the beginning of the sixteenth century, had achieved a higher morality than Roman society at the time of Augustus. Above all, one cannot explain how, up to our own times, such crude practices have resisted all the prohibitions leveled against them. There must, then, be something in the character of the school itself, something that inclines it in this direction. Indeed, we shall see that the persistence of this kind of discipline is only the result of a more general law, an examination of which will throw into relief one of the distinctive characteristics of this social life, *sui generis*, which constitutes school life.

# CHAPTER THIRTEEN

~§　THE USE OF PUNISHMENT

IN THE SCHOOL (*Concluded*);

AND THE MEANING AND

USES OF REWARDS

WE SAW IN THE LAST CHAPTER THAT THE METHOD OF CORPORAL punishment was not born in the family, to pass thence to the school. It was established in the school itself, and for a time, it became increasingly common as formal schooling became more common. We began to investigate the causes of this remarkable connection. Certainly we understand that from the time when man's culture had attained a certain level of development the methods aimed at transmitting it must have been marked with a greater severity. Because it had become more complex, it was no longer possible to entrust its transmission to chance encounter and circumstance; it was necessary to gain time, to move quickly; and human intervention became indispensable. This procedure necessarily resulted in forcing nature since the objective was to accelerate maturation. Thus, we account for the rather more forceful methods necessary to achieve the desired result. Since the public conscience had then only a faint repugnance for such violent procedures, and since they alone were effective in influencing these cruder natures, we understand why they were employed. So it is that the method of corporal punishment was only established once man had outrun his early barbarism, once the school had made its appearance. School and civilization are concurrent things and closely connected.

But we cannot explain in this way why such disciplinary methods grew and were strengthened for several centuries—and, moreover, to the extent that civilization progressed and manners softened. Milder mannerrs would seem to have made the customary cruelties intolerable. Above all, we cannot explain in this way the genuine excess of corporal punishment, the orgy of violence that historians describe in the schools of the fourteenth, fifteenth, and sixteenth centuries, when, according to Montaigne, one could hear "only the cries, both of the beaten children and of the teachers drunk with rage."[1] People have sometimes attributed this excess to monastic morality, to the ascetic conception that makes a virtue out of suffering, imputing to misery all kinds of mystic benefactions. But we have discovered the same follies in the schools of Protestant Germany. Today, the elements of the system have been completely abolished in Catholic countries—France, Spain, Italy, Belgium, and Austria; while still surviving in attenuated form in Prussia and England. Therefore, it does not relate to a particular religion, but to some property peculiar to schools in general.

Indeed, it seems that one is justified in seeing here a special case of a law, which might be stated this way: whenever two populations, two groups of people having unequal cultures,

---

1. Montaigne, *Essais*, I, xxv. If Durkheim's footnotes seem excessively casual, the reader must remember that these were simply references inserted in his lecture manuscript. Here, for example, the edition is not specified—there were a great many; but a likely one is *Essais de Michel de Montaigne* (Bordeaux: R. Dezeimeris and H. Barckhausen, 1870-73).

come into continuous contact with one another, certain feelings develop that prompt the more cultivated group—or that which deems itself such—to do violence to the other. This is currently the case in colonies and countries of all kinds where representatives of European civilization find themselves involved with underdeveloped peoples. Although it is useless and involves grave dangers for those who abandon themselves to it, exposing them to formidable reprisals, this violence almost inevitably breaks out. Hence that kind of bloody foolhardiness that seizes the explorer in connection with races he deems inferior. The superiority that he arrogates tends, as though independently, to assert itself brutally, without object or reason, for the mere pleasure of asserting itself. It produces a veritable intoxication, an excessive exaltation of self, a sort of megalomania, which goes to the worst extremes, and the source of which is not difficult to fathom. We have seen, in fact, that the individual controls himself only if he feels himself controlled, only if he confronts moral forces which he respects and on which he dare not encroach. Where this is not the case, he knows no limits and extends himself without measure or bounds. As soon as the only moral forces with which he has anything to do are depreciated in his eyes— from the moment when, because of the inferiority he imputes to them, he sees in them no authority requiring his deference —they cannot perform this moderating function. Consequently, nothing restrains him; he overflows in violence, quite like the tyrant whom nothing can resist. This violence is a game with him, a spectacle in which he indulges himself, a way of demonstrating that superiority he sees in himself.

A phenomenon of the same sort manifests itself in a civilized country whenever elders and young find themselves in continuous contact and associated in the same life. A kind of hostility of a very peculiar sort breaks out between the two groups: it is what we call hazing. Hazing is not simply a sickly fantasy produced by some sort of unreasonable caprice.

Otherwise it would not be so general or so hard to extirpate. In reality, it is the necessary effect of definite causes that cannot fail to produce such an outcome so long as contrary moral forces of at least equal intensity are not opposed to them. The elders feel themselves superior to the newcomers because they are the elders, because they are the guardians of usages and traditions unknown to the newcomers, because they already constitute a cohesive group with esprit de corps —a collective unity; while the newcomers have nothing in common, not even having had the time to establish and organize themselves. Because this superiority has no very solid foundation, because the moral gap between the two generations thus brought together reduces itself basically to relatively few things, because it is altogether temporary and is destined soon to disappear, the violence so produced is not in itself very serious; it has, rather, the air of an inoffensive game. Nonetheless, it remains a special kind of game, characterized by a certain need for violence and harassment. In somewhat different form we discover here the same cause producing the same effect.

Are not the relationships between teachers and students in many respects like the foregoing? There is the same difference between them as that between two populations of unequal culture. Indeed, it is hard to see how there could be between two sets of minds a greater distance, since the ones are strangers to civilization while the others are permeated with it. Furthermore, by its very nature the school brings them closely and continuously together. There is nothing extraordinary in such contact provoking feelings altogether analogous to those we have just described. Is there not at the core of pedantry—that trait so characteristic of our professional makeup—a kind of megalomania? When one is continually in relationship with subjects to whom he is morally and intellectually superior, how can he avoid developing an exaggerated self-conception, expressed in gesture, attitude, and language? Such a feeling readily gives rise to violent expression; for any behavior which offends it easily takes on the character of sacrilege. Patience is much more difficult, demands a much greater effort, vis-à-vis inferiors than between equals. Even unintentional resistance—the mere difficulty in getting desired results—proves irritating, is promptly considered as constituting an offense, and is treated as such without recognizing that the superiority one attributes to himself tends, as we have said, to assert itself for the pleasure of asserting itself. Even in the family we often see phenomena of this sort between brothers and sisters of different ages. There is something like a sort of chronic impatience on the part of the older ones—a tendency to treat the very young as inferior beings. But here familial feelings suffice in general to prevent excesses. In school, this useful countercheck does not exist. There is then, in the situation of school life itself, a predisposition to violent discipline. And *so long as a contrary force does not intervene,* we can readily imagine that this cause becomes increasingly influential to the degree that the school develops and is organized. For as the teacher's role takes on greater social importance and its professional character is emphasized, the force of professional sentiment cannot fail to grow in parallel fashion. The unassuming bard who, during the early Middle ages, carried out the functions of teacher in the parish schools had much less authority than the form masters of the great fourteenth- and fifteenth-century colleges who, as members of a powerful guild, felt sustained by their faith in themselves and their lofty dignity through the common faith of their peers. Perhaps never had this academic megalomania been carried to such extremes; one can thus begin to understand the disciplinary pattern of the times.

There is, however, a force that is—or was, from that time on—in a position to check this kind of thinking: the prevailing climate of moral opinion. It is the force of moral opinion that is chiefly responsible for protecting the child, signalizing his nascent moral character and making him worthy of respect. Thus it is that the abuses into which the civilized so easily fall in their dealings with inferior societies are beginning to be checked, since a better-informed public opinion is in a better position to keep a watch on, and to judge what is going on in, distant countries. The medieval schools were organized in such a way that there was scarcely an echo of public opinion in them. Like all the other guilds, that of the teachers was a sort of closed society, sealed from the outside world, turning in upon itself, almost a secret society. The state itself could not, in principle, intervene. Thus the student was completely separated from the external milieu; and communication between him and his parents was infrequent, sometimes forbidden. Under these conditions, the development of public conscience could scarcely have any influence on the practice of discipline, which is why it persisted so long in its old follies. Despite the eloquent protests (and there were many of them in the Middle Ages), despite the attempts at reform originating with civil authorities, the old patterns persisted, as in other guilds, up to the day when the school finally began to leave the shadows in which it had been hidden from view.

Thus, the make-up of the school is the source of the evil. If I have judged it useful to treat this question, it is not merely because of its historical interest, but also because it provides the occasion for specifying more clearly a particular property of the social system of the school and the special kind of life that develops there. Because this society naturally has a monarchical form, it readily degenerates into despotism. This is a danger of which we must always be aware in order to guard against it; and the danger is all the greater as the gulf between students and teacher is greater—that is to say, as the students are younger. The real way to prevent this danger is to ensure that the school does not shut itself up

within itself, does not live too exclusively its own peculiar
life, and does not have a too narrowly professional character.
By itself, as with all established groups, it tends toward autonomy; it does not readily accept control. But such control is
indispensable, not only from an intellectual but from a moral
point of view.

Not only must we eschew corporal punishment, but all
kinds of punishment that might injure the child's health
must be forbidden. Therefore, depriving him of his playtime
should only take place with the greatest discretion, and it
should never be completely cut off. But denying him participation in a game during the play period is not subject to the
same objections. One might set down as a principle that the
child who has just misbehaved and been reproached hasn't
much heart for playing. A game, with the joy and effusion
accompanying it, should be viewed as the external manifestation of an inner feeling of satisfaction not experienced
when one has failed in his duty. Here, then, there is a legitimate and effective punishment, readily applied and very likely
to promote or sustain that feeling of contrition in the child
which should follow a misdeed.

It is not enough to exclude harmful punishment; we must
seek out and prefer those punishments that are useful to him
who is punished. In a general way, the penal discipline of the
adult tends increasingly to be informed with humanitarian
feelings; it becomes increasingly a kind of educational re-
habilitation. Nor can education, properly speaking, fail to
concern itself with similar problems. This is why the unin-
telligent, dull, copy-work punishment of other times, the
only outcome of which was to bore the child by forcing him
to perform some tedious chores, has finally disappeared.
Furthermore such punishment completely lacked any moral
efficacy. For any penalty to have an educational influence it
must seem worthy of respect to the person on whom it is inflicted. Extra school busy-work (pensum) is an absurd busi-

ness—altogether senseless—and we scorn that which is absurd. Any supplementary tasks required of the child who has misbehaved should have the same character as ordinary duties, and they should be treated and corrected as such.

It sometimes happens that in order to carry out the punishment under the supervision of the teacher, all the delinquent students from one or several classes are brought together to perform the extra work required of them. I take a dim view of the usefulness of this practice, which, although authorized and in common use in school systems of almost all countries, nevertheless presents some serious disadvantages. It is always bad to bring together, to put intimately in contact with one another, persons of middling morality. They can't help doing mutual damage to one another. The indiscriminate mixture of such artificial groups composed entirely of little delinquents is no less dangerous than similar practices in prisons. There always prevails a latent spirit of disorder and rebellion. Furthermore, the students are not generally—at least not all of them—under the supervision of their own teacher. Hence, these extra tasks run the risk of not being directed with the same interest that is true of their ordinary duties, and by that fact alone come close to the old system of after-school busy-work.

Denying participation in games, extra tasks, as well as reproaches and reprimands are the chief elements of school punishment. Whatever the nature of the penalty, there is one principle which completely dominates this business. The system of punishment should be set up with the utmost care as a graduated scale, commencing with the greatest possible leniency; and one should not move from one degree to another except with the greatest discretion.

All punishment, once applied, loses a part of its influence by the very fact of its application. What lends it authority, what makes it formidable, is not so much the misery that it causes as the moral discredit implied in the blame that it expresses. This feeling of moral sensitivity that stands guard against misdeeds is one of the most delicate of sentiments. It is not strong, it is not completely itself, it lacks its full power of influence except among those for whom it has lost nothing of its original purity. We often say that the first offense always leads to others. This is because, once we have felt it, we are less sensitive to this shame. Punishment has this very great limitation of clashing with one of the chief resources of the moral life, and thus reducing its own efficacy in the future. It retains all of its force only when it simply constitutes a threat. This is why the experienced teacher hesitates to punish a good student even should he deserve it. Punishment cannot but contribute to future lapses.

Nothing, then, is so dangerous as having too brief a scale of punishment. Since one runs the risk of going through it too quickly, the threat-value of the penalty which retains its full force only so long as one has not been subjected to it—may be rapidly exhausted. This is the weakness of Draconian laws. Since they move immediately to extremes of harshness, they are soon driven to repeat themselves; and the influence of punishment declines with frequency of repetition. Thus, this is a very important principle: but for rare exceptions, punishment should not be administered in massive doses; its influence is increased as it is wisely diluted. This is why we must contrive to multiply the degrees and stages of the scale of punishment. We can accomplish this by resorting to punishment, properly speaking, only after having tried all the forms of reproach and disapproval—and they are in-finitely numerous. There is the individual reproach—almost secret, so to speak—with which one should always begin; then there is public disapproval before the class, disapproval communicated to the parents, and suspended punishment. Before disapproval itself, what a host of ways to warn the child, making him feel that he is at fault and stopping him! A glance, a gesture, silence—these, when one knows how to use them, are very meaningful procedures, and the child knows what they mean. Even before coming to genuine punishments, there are a thousand ways for the teacher to act, which he can shade and vary infinitely.

There is another reason for going through the scale of punishment at a judiciously measured pace. Punishment produces, proportionately, a slighter effect as it goes up the scale of severity. Indeed, it is a general psychological law that the sensations caused by a stimulus do not increase indefinitely as the intensity of the stimulus increases. There is a limit, beyond which additional increments are not perceived. Thus, beyond a certain degree of suffering, additional suffering is no longer felt. Beyond a certain range, sounds cease to be perceptible. Furthermore, as one approaches the limit, the gap between intensity of impression and intensity of stimulus grows increasingly greater; that is to say, an increasingly greater part of the stimulus is without effect on the consciousness—as though it did not exist. A man of modest resources enjoys the least increase of wealth. But the same addition of wealth would leave a man of considerable fortune completely unmoved. It would take an altogether exceptional windfall to give him any pleasure—and a pleasure not equal to that which an infinitely smaller gain would yield for a man of moderate means. The same law applies naturally to penalties. As one goes up the scale of punishments, an always increasing part of the energy required to effect them is lost. They must be more and more re-enforced to achieve some effect, and this effect is less and less in relation to the increased severity of the penalty. As a result, the higher in the scale punishments are, the less economical they are: their usefulness is increasingly out of line with the loss of force they entail. Therefore, we must somehow leave ourselves room by not resorting too readily to such costly and ineffective punishments.

However, it is not enough to choose well among a carefully graduated scale of punishments. Beyond this, there is an art of applying them in order to produce all their useful effects. The manner of punishing is more important than the punishment itself.

We often say that we must not strike a child in anger. Now, certainly the child should not be given reason to believe that he is beaten under the impulse of thoughtless rage, or out of irritable impatience. This would be enough to discredit the punishment and deprive it of all moral significance. He must feel that it has been thought through, and results from a judgment cooly made. Thus, it is a good idea to let a little time pass, however short, between the time of the misdeed and that of the punishment—a time of silence reserved for reflection. This pause is not simply a deception calculated to give the child the illusion of deliberation; it is a way for the teacher to guard against precipitous decisions, which are quite as hard to reverse later as to enforce. The whole judicial process, with all its slowness and complications, has precisely the function of requiring the judge to forearm himself against the momentary impulse and to render his judgment only in full knowledge of his reasons for doing so. The teacher must take similar precautioins. It is always something of a problem to know whether one should punish and above all how to do it. Unless it is an extremely simple case, the teacher should take some time to resolve the problem. This time can be used to explain the judgment given and to help the students in the class understand it. For it is above all on this matter that he must reflect.

If we must not punish in anger, it is nonetheless necessary to guard against dispassionate punishment. Excessive coldness or impassivity has no better effect than does a transport of rage. In reality, as we have said, punishment is disapproval and disapproval is protest. Ultimately, punishing is disassociating one's self from the disapproved act; punishment bears witness to the revulsion that it inspires. If punishment is

what it ought to be, it is carried through with a certain indignation or, if the word seems too strong, with a more or
less reproachful displeasure. Should all emotion be drained
from it, then it is emptied of all moral content. It is then reduced to the sheer physical act; but there is nothing that
lends the act the significance that is its *raison d'être*. What
use has a rite observed to the letter if the spirit of it is no
longer felt? Everything goes along automatically. A list of
charges is set up: the child knows what he must pay for each
offense. He pays passively on receipt of the order; once his
account is balanced, he considers himself as even, both with
himself and others, since he sees nothing but the punishment
itself. So understood, discipline can train mechanically
(*dresser*); but it cannot educate, since it produces no inner
effects. Furthermore, it runs the risk of creating more rebels.
For it is difficult for the child to accept a punishment that
has no sense for him and that does not speak to his spirit.
The teacher must not allow his professional sensitivity to be
dulled by habituation. He must be sufficiently concerned with
his students not to view their misdeeds apathetically, with
indifference; he must suffer from them, he must complain
of them, and he must show his feelings overtly.

It is so important that punishment not be administered
in cold blood that, although it is useful to allow a moment of
reflection before fixing it, it is nonetheless necessary that the
interval not be too great. The feeling at the root of punishment, which makes a living thing of it, cools with time, and
after that there is something artificial in expressing it. In
our secondary school system, there has recently been established a kind of academic tribunal, charged with passing
judgment on school offenses of some gravity. This set-up may
be useful when it is a matter of imposing a higher penalty,
such as expulsion; but I doubt that in ordinary cases it will
be as useful as expected. Can a solemn sentence, rendered
long after the act has been committed, rendered in official

style and through a kind of impersonal magistracy—can this have as much effect on the child as some words from his own teacher, pronounced just at the time of his offense under the impact of the painful emotion that they cause—if, at least, the student is fond of the teacher and esteems him? Although it may be true that a class is a society, that academic institutions are like the corresponding social institutions, they nevertheless should not be a complete and simple reproduction of the latter. A society of children cannot be organized like one of adults. Schoolroom offenses are peculiar in that they all fall under the heading of *flagrante delicto*. Hence, there are no complicated trial procedures. Furthermore, there is moral value in repressing the misdeed as soon as possible after the wrongdoing itself, in order to neutralize the bad effects of the latter. The child lives in his feelings. The feelings caused by the infraction must be countered without delay.

But whatever the punishment and in whatever way one decides to handle it, once decided it must be irrevocable. This can be said without reservation, except for those instances in which the child atones for his fault in a striking way through some spontaneous act. This is a pedagogical rule that we cannot observe too closely. It means, in effect, that the child feels in the rule all the necessity of a natural law. For it is on this condition that he develops the habit of seeing duty as something that imposes itself irresistibly on our wills, something neither disputed nor evaded, something as inflexible as physical forces, although in a different way. If, on the contrary, he sees the rule yielding to all kinds of contingencies, if he sees it always applied hesitantly if he feels it to be soft, indecisive, plastic, he will so conceive it and treat it. Furthermore, since it seems quite flexible to him, he will not fear bending it to fit the occasion; since it allows of accommodations, he will accommodate it to the circumstances. The weaknesses and uncertainties of enforcement cannot but contribute to making consciences themselves weak and uncertain. The property of resolution is a condition of moral rectitude, and it must be put into practice to be communicated to the child.

We have just seen, step by step, the moral function of punishment—what it ought to be and how it should be applied in order to attain its goal. But punishment is not the only sanction connected with rules of school morality, no more so than with rules of adult morality. In addition there are rewards. Although rewards are, in effect, the opposite and the logical counterpart of punishment, we shall dwell much more briefly on them, for they have a considerably slighter part to play in moral education.

Indeed, it is clear that they are used primarily in the school as a means of stimulating the qualities of intelligence, rather than those of the heart and the character. They have to do with success rather than with moral merit. Good grades, ranks, prizes, and class honors are actually reserved for the most intelligent students rather than for the most upright and sensitive consciences. Reward is an instrument of intellectual culture rather than of moral culture. Some have pointed out as a fatal anomaly the meager part played by virtue in educational rewards:

> What is the character of our current educational system? The part played by punishment is much greater than that of rewards; while the first encompasses all the misdeeds the child can commit, the second is far from extending to everything he can do that is good and praiseworthy. Furthermore, everything seems calculated to promote intellectual emulation; almost nothing is planned to create moral emulation.[2]

First of all, it may be noted that the same disparity between rewards and punishment is found in adult life. Social rewards

---

2. M. Vessiot, *De l'éducation à l'école* (1885), p. 144. The correct citation is probably as follows:

Alexandre Vessiot, *De l'enseignement à l'école et dans les classes élémentaires des lycées et collèges* (Paris: H. Lecene and H. Oudin, 1886).

are much more linked to intellectual, artistic, and industrial achievement than to virtue, properly speaking. Acts contrary to basic obligations are punished; but only very exceptionally are those that go beyond minimum requirements definitely rewarded. What a contrast between the laws, with their manifold prescriptions, with their carefully specified sanctions, and the few prizes, titles, and honorific insignia, which from time to time may reward some act of devotion! It even seems that the number of social rewards may be diminishing and that their prestige is dropping. Most generally, the reward consists exclusively in public approbation, eulogies, in the respect and confidence shown for him who has done especially well. The sanctions bearing on the positive practice of duty do not, then, equal either in number, importance, or in the extent to which they are systematically organized the repressive sanctions connected with the violation of the rule. Since the aim of the school is to prepare for life it would fail in its task if it made the child develop habits that the conditions of life would someday contradict. If the patterns of school life accustom the child to count on a reward for every good thing he does, what great disenchantment he will experience when he discovers that society itself does not reward virtuous behavior with such punctuality and precision! He will have to reconstruct a part of his moral self and learn a disinterestedness that the school will not have taught him.

Shall we say that this underplaying of reward in adult life is abnormal? There is no society where we do not see the same phenomenon, and it is very hard to consider such a universal practice abnormal. In fact, it is not without some *raison d'être*. For if it is important that behavior absolutely indispensable for the moral life be rigorously required and if, as a result, any breach of the rules must have a specific sanction, conversely, anything that goes beyond the strictly necessary minimum of morality resists all regulation. For this is the domain of liberty, of personal endeavor and free initiative, which cannot be foreseen—much less regulated. It is impossible to have a system of rewards parallel to the penal code. Moreover, such behaviors have their full worth only insofar as they are performed without the actor anticipating any regular reward. It is this uncertainty, this indeterminacy of the sanction, its insignificance from a material point of view, which makes for its value. Were there a price tag on such behaviors, they would promptly acquire a degrading commercial air. Therefore it is normal that offenses have more precise, certain, and regular sanctions than genuinely meritorious behavior; and on this point the discipline of the school must resemble that of life.

This is not to say, however, that there is nothing of merit in the criticisms we have discussed. Certainly it is not a question of making the students compete in honesty, veracity, etc. The idea of a prize for virtue makes us smile, not because we hate innovation, but because the ideas thus paired contradict each other. We feel an aversion to recompensing moral merit in the same way as we do talent. There is an opposition here which not unreasonably shocks us. The true reward of virtue is found in a state of inner tranquillity, in the feeling of esteem and sympathy that it brings us, and in the resulting comfort. But there is reason to believe that prestige may attach too exclusively, in school life, to intellectual merit, and that a greater share should be accorded moral value. To do this it is not necessary to add new tests and papers to those we already have, or to add new prizes to our list of honors. It would be enough for the teacher to attach more importance to those qualities that in current practice, evidently are too often treated as a secondary thing. The affection and friendship that he evidences for the hard-working student, whose efforts do not bring the same success as do those of his better-endowed fellow students, would be by itself the best of rewards and would re-establish a balance that, today, is wrongly twisted and disturbed.

# CHAPTER FOURTEEN

# ATTACHMENT TO SOCIAL

# GROUPS: ALTRUISM IN THE CHILD

NOW WE ARE READY TO INQUIRE INTO METHODS OF DEVELOPING the second element of morality in the child. This second element consists, as we have pointed out, in attachment to a social group generally speaking; but more particularly in attachment to one's country, providing that the country is conceived not as a narrowly selfish and aggressive personality but as one of the agencies through which the idea of humanity is realized.

The source of this part of moral life is of course in our faculty of empathy. This is another way of saying that the source of this aspect of moral life resides in the sum of those tendencies that we call altruistic and disinterested. Consequently, the first question we must pose is whether such tendencies do exist in the child, and if so, in what form. Our methods will necessarily be quite different depending upon whether we find support in the innate disposition of the child—whether we find here a lever that we can use and what the nature of this lever indicates. Our attack will vary, according to whether we consider the child either purely selfish or else, on the contrary, already accessible to a nascent altruism, which we simply develop. This initial analysis will determine our basic approach. This is why, before we sought to cultivate in the child the first element of morality, the spirit of discipline, we began by asking about the child's characteristic mental states, so that we might build upon them in order to achieve the desired result. The question we were then dealing with is exactly parallel to the one we must now examine.

We must first know what we are to understand by "altruistic" or "disinterested" tendencies and therefore what we mean when we speak of selfish tendencies. Precisely because they are opposed to each other, they can hardly be defined without each other; the two notions are interconnected. On the other hand, depending on our definition, we will be impelled to resolve the question of selfishness or altruism in the child in quite different ways.

Ordinarily, we define egoistic tendencies as those whose object is the pleasure of the agent; altruistic, as those aiming to secure the pleasure of a human being other than the agent. Seen in this way, the antithesis is as sharp as possible: for my pleasure and the pleasure of a being foreign to me are radically opposed, and it would seem there is nothing intermediate between the two. As a matter of fact, the spread is so considerable that it seems impossible to assign one and the same origin to these sentiments. This is the reason that we tend to base the first, i.e., egoism, in the natural constitution of man; while we make of the latter, altruism, a relatively belated product of culture and education. Instinctively, it is said, man like other animals knows and seeks only pleasure; he is altogether selfish. It has now become commonplace to attribute to the primitive a certain ferocious selfishness, which supposedly is softened only very slowly under the influence of civilization. Now, the child starting in life is evidently very much like a man entering upon the stage of history. Thus, he must also be a purely selfish being; the business of education must, then, be to develop *ab initio* those altruistic dispositions that he lacks to begin with.

One might protest by asking how it is possible to effect a transformation that involves a veritable creation out of nothing. For the fact is that historical evolution cannot draw out of man, and education cannot extract from a child, anything that was not in him, at least in embryo; and it is very hard to see by what means an entirely selfish being could become capable of disinterestedness. But it is not necessary to examine here the theories concocted by moralists and psychologists to render this miracle intelligible. It is much better to attack immediately the very conception that has made the hypothesis necessary—that definition of selfishness and altruism which makes of them two unconnected and antagonistic states of mind. We shall see that however obvious it may be from the commonsense point of view, it raises numerous difficulties.

First of all, it is not accurate to say that all disinterested tendencies have for their object the pleasure of some concrete being other than the agent. There are, in fact, some such tendencies concerning things not concrete but purely ideal —for example, the scholar who loves knowledge, loves it in itself and for itself, and not only in proportion to the beneficent influence that his labors might have on others' fate. No doubt the anticipation of service to humanity way well serve as a secondary stimulus in the quest and might orient it in one direction rather than another; but many other elements enter into the love of knowledge. The desire to know and understand, pure curiosity—there is the true initial motive. The desire to bring great relief to human suffering might have determined Pasteur and his assistants to apply the principle of vaccination to serious diseases like rabies and diphtheria. But the parent idea of the doctrine and its applications is altogether theoretical; it is a view concerning the nature of life, and perhaps even an initial curiosity—altogether speculative—concerning micro-organisms. The historian, the erudite man, and the philosopher cannot even imagine in any specific sense the practical import of their labors. The most they can do is to enable their fellow human beings to understand themselves better. One could even set down as a methodological rule that, as a matter of principle, the scholar should try to know for the sake of knowing without concerning himself with the practical consequences that might ensue from his discoveries. What we say about the love of science can also be repeated about the love of art. Beyond this, among the tendencies of human beings, there are some which are manifestly disinterested and which nevertheless have as their object the causing of pain rather than pleasure to others. There are hatreds so unegotistical that the hater often sacrifices his life to the sentiment driving him on; and yet the end of this sentiment is to harm others. Such are those hatreds between kin groups so frequent in all those regions in which the family vendetta still prevails. Such also are the hatreds of crime and of the criminal. No doubt one could question whether we are dealing here with very praiseworthy forms of disinterestedness; but they do exist, and their unselfishness is unquestionable.

Just as altruistic tendencies do not necessarily aim at pleasing others, selfish tendencies do not necessarily have pleasure as their object. Thus, the dypsomaniac or the kleptomaniac, who yield to the need to drink and to steal, know very well that only trouble and suffering will result from their actions; yet they cannot resist their compulsions. It is therefore not the prospect of expected pleasure that determines their conduct; rather, the drink or the coveted object in itself attracts them as a magnet draws iron, with a necessity that is truly physical, despite the painful consequences to which they expose themselves. One might say that these are morbid states, but we know that illness only exemplifies in exaggerated form the characteristics of the state of health. Indeed, it is not hard to find things of the same sort in normal people. The miser is an egoist; but the true miser loves and seeks gold itself and not for the pleasure that gold commands. In order to conserve the gold he will deprive himself of all satisfactions. He will die by the side of his treasure rather than touch it. Can it be said that he experiences pleasure in the sensation of his own riches although he makes no use of it? Certainly there is no tendency that when satisfied, is not accompanied by pleasure. In this respect, altruistic tendencies are not distinguished from selfish tendencies. The mother sacrifices herself for her child with joy. Still it is quite clear that what she seeks in the sacrifice is the health of the child and not the joy of sacrifice. The joy comes as an addition. It facilitates the sacrifice, makes it a blissful experience. It is neither the determining cause nor the object of it. This is exactly what we have in the case of the miser who sacrifices himself for his gold. It is to his gold that he is attached, as the mother is attached to her child. If passion had no other object than the pleasure that it affords him it would be unintelligible.

We may say the same thing about the love of power. Power often brings misery and bitterness to those who possess it. Yet regardless of the hardship it may bring, once a man has become used to power he loves it, strives for it, cannot do without it. We find the same characteristic in the most elementary urges. In hunger it is the food we seek, not the pleasure accompanying ingestion. Food is the object of that drive: pleasure may come with it, but it is only the condiment of the action, not the goal.

In general, the prototype of selfish drives is what we call, improperly enough, the instinct of preservation—in other words, the tendency of every living creature to keep alive. That tendency makes its action felt without our thinking of the pleasures that life might have for us. It is felt even when life has only pain in store for us, and when we know it.

Thus, a suicide who jumps into the water makes every effort to save himself, although the fact of his immersion has not changed his situation nor the way in which he evaluated it. The fact is that he clung to life more than he knew himself, no matter how miserable that life had been. It is therefore clear that we love life in and for itself, even when it is a source of suffering for us. Now I do not mean to say that pain can never triumpth over this urge. But since it is strong, since the love of life is deeply rooted, one must have endured much suffering to end it. We all remember the verse of La Fontaine: *"Pourvu qu'en somme je vive, c'est assez."* (Let me only stay alive and that is enough.) That line illustrates this fact of experience.

Finally, there are even selfish urges that have as their object not pleasure but suffering. A famous man of the Renaissance, Jerome Cardan, says in his autobiography that he "could not do without suffering"; and that when it happened to him he felt such inner turbulence that any other pain seemed like a relief." In such situations he would torture his body to the point of tears. A very great number of habits of the same sort have been observed in neurotics; but such facts can also be observed in normal subjects. The taste for melancholy has nothing morbid in it; what is it if not a certain love of sadness?

Thus, it is not possible to classify these tendencies by the different kinds of pleasures that our urges give us; selfish tendencies, exactly like other urges, have objectives other than the pleasure that might result from them either for ourselves or for someone else. Normally, what we like, what we seek, are the very things for which we strive—health, fortune, the person of another, pain itself. Without doubt, when an urge is satisfied we experience satisfaction. But that satisfaction is a simple accompaniment of the urge; it is a sign that it functions with ease, that it is developed without resistance, that it reaches its object; but it is neither the object of the urge nor its reason for being. This pleasure accompanies the functioning of all urges, whatever they be—altruistic urges like other ones. Therefore, there is nothing in the degree of pleasure or satisfaction which permits us to differentiate them from each other.

There is, it is true, an inclination whose object is pleasure. It is what one calls the love of pleasure, or better still, of pleasures—the need of experiencing agreeable states; just as there is an inclination whose object is pain. But we have here a particular inclination, unevenly developed among individuals. It is not the prototype of all inclinations. Indeed, excepting the love of pain, there are few inclinations that so easily become morbid. There is a moral danger in the love of pleasure, a moral danger which all moralists have pointed out. We feel that there is something morbid in setting pleasure as an end in itself, to seek it out for itself, when it should only be a consequence, a corollary, or concomitant state. What we need in order to live are those things intimately bound up with our lives, not the agreeable impressions that their pursuit might procure us. Pleasure is not the only thing which is valuable and deserves to be sought.

We must therefore reject the definition and the distinction of urges as they relate to pleasure resulting from them. We must instead consider in themselves the objects of all kinds to which our urges tie us, and seek to classify them once we have abstracted them from their particular contexts. Now, all those objects fall into two major categories, distinguishing which will furnish us with the definition we are seeking. At times, the object of our urge is an element of our individuality; it is our body, our health, our fortune, our social condition, our reputation, together with everything that might indirectly help us to reach our personal ends. Hence, the love of life, riches, honors, etc. All these urges attach us only to different aspects of ourselves and consequently can truly be called selfish.

There are other tendencies whose subjects are outside our individuality; they are not ours by nature. Such objects are first of all those which touch our personality—places where we spend our lives, things of all sorts that are familiar to us. Then there are other objects beyond us, the person of our fellow beings and everything connected with them. Finally, still more remote, there are social groups of which we are members—family, associations, country, humanity, and everything that helps to sustain collective life, such as science, art, profession, morality. All these objects have their own existence distinct from ours, whatever the bonds attaching them to us. In cherishing them and seeking them out, we cherish and seek something other than ourselves. We can only attach ourselves to them by getting out of ourselves, by alienating ourselves, by disinteresting ourselves in things narrowly or essentially personal. It is proper, therefore, to reserve the designation of altruistic for these inclinations. Thus, what differentiates altruism and egotism is not the nature of the pleasure that accompanies these two sorts of our observable behavior. It is the different direction that this activity follows in the two cases. When it is egotistical, it does not go beyond the acting subject; it is centripetal. When it is altruistic, it overflows from its subject. The centers around which it gravitates are outside of him; it is centrifugal.

Once we admit this distinction, the unbridgeable gulf that at first seemed to separate selfish tendencies from altruistic ones disappears. These tendencies seemed at first to be so unlike that it appeared impossible to trace them to one and the same origin. Indeed, my pleasure is entirely within me. Someone else's pleasure is entirely within him. Consequently, between the two forms of activity whose objects are so distant there could not be anything in common; one was even justified in asking how they could ever come together in one and the same being. But this is no longer the case if the difference separating these two sorts of in-

clinations is reduced to that which is between the notion of
an object outside the individual and the notion of an object
that is immanent. There is nothing absolute in this difference.
We have altruism, as was pointed out, when we are attached
to something outside ourselves. But we cannot become attached to an external thing, whatever its nature, without representing it to ourselves, without having an idea of it, a
sentiment about it, no matter how confused. By virtue of this
fact alone—that we do represent an external object to ourselves
—it becomes in certain respects internal. It exists in us in the
form of the representation that expresses it, reflects it, is
closely related to it. Thus—as with the symbolic representation, without which it would mean nothing to us—the object
becomes an element of ourselves, a state of our consciousness.
In this sense, we have become attached to ourselves. If we
suffer because of the death of someone close to us, it is because our image of the physical and moral person of that
relative as well as the representations of all sorts of associations linked with him cease to function. We can no longer
renew the cherished feeling that his presence evoked in us.
Confidences, familiar conversation, comforting words when
we needed them—none of this can ever take place again.
We suddenly feel a painful void in our consciousness. We
are vitally hurt by everything that diminishes the vitality of
the beings to whom we are attached; being attached to them,
it is to a part of ourselves that we are attached.

   Thus, we have egotism embedded in altruism; conversely,
there is altruism in egoism. Indeed, our individuality is not
an empty form. It consists of elements that come to us from
the outside. Take away from us everything that originates
there; what is left? We love wealth, power, honors; but
wealth, power, and honors are external to us, and to achieve
them we must get out of ourselves, we must make efforts,
spend ourselves, leave a part of ourselves outside of ourselves,
develop centrifugal activity. We feel that in the activity de-

ployed to reach these diverse but internalized objectives, there is something other than pure egotism. There is a certain gift of ourselves, a certain aptitude in giving ourselves and spreading ourselves and not turning in on ourselves. We could cite a great many other examples. We cling to our habits, which are elements of individuality, and this tendency is only one aspect of the love of self. However, as a consequence, we are attached to the setting in which these habits developed and which they reflect, to the things which inhabit this environment and to which they are intimately related. Thus, we have here once more a form of self-love that obliges us to go beyond ourselves.

We were saying some time ago that it is very difficult to live a purely self-centered existence. One might even say that it is impossible, because our personality is not a metaphysical entity, a sort of absolute that begins exactly at one determinate point and finishes at another and that, like the monad of Leibniz, has neither windows nor doors open upon the universe. On the contrary, the external world echoes inside of us; it is prolonged in us in the same way that we overflow into it. Things, beings from the outside, penetrate into our consciousness, mingle intimately in our inner lives, become entwined in our existence, and, conversely, we merge our existence with theirs. Our ideas, our sentiments, pass from our minds to others and vice versa. There is in us something other than ourselves, and we are not entire in ourselves; there is also something of us in the objects that become assimilated, or that we assimilate, into our lives.

Our individuality is, therefore, altogether relative. There are certain elements of ourselves that are more simple, in a manner of speaking; more eminently constitutive of our self, our strictly individual self; elements that bear more particularly our imprint; that single us out as ourselves and not someone else—the form of our body, our social status, our character, etc. There are other things in some way more eccentric, not as close to the central core of our personality which, while they are a part of us in some respects, are nevertheless more particularly related to beings distinct from us and which for that reason are common to us and to other people—for example, our images symbolizing our friends, relatives, family, and country. Insofar as we are attached to the first of these elements, it is to ourselves that we are attached, since they have a more personal character; insofar as we are attached to the second, it is rather to something else in ourselves, since they have a more impersonal character than the first. Hence, two sorts of tendencies. But there is only a difference of degree between one kind and the other kind.

At bottom, egotism and altruism are two concurrent and intimately intertwining aspects of all conscious life. As soon as there is consciousness, there is a subject who thinks of himself as distinct from everything that is not he—a subject who says "I." When he thinks of himself in that manner and concentrates his activity on himself, thus represented, he acts like an egotist. To the degree that he represents to himself external beings as external and takes them as the objects of his activity, there is altruism. One form of activity cannot exist without the other. Never does the sense of self, the German *Selbstgefühl*, vanish completely in the sentiment we have of the external object; and, on the other hand, the sentiment of self is never sufficient; it always implies the sensing of an object, which it represents to itself and to which it is opposed. Consequently, egoism and altruism are two abstractions that do not exist in a pure state; one always implies the other, at least to some degree; although in a given, concrete situation they are never developed in the same degree. We can therefore rest assured that the child is not the purely selfish person often described to us. By the very fact that he is a conscious being, no matter how rudimentary his consciousness may be, he is capable of some altruism; and he is capable of it at the very threshold of his life.

We know how readily and intensely a child becomes attached to objects of all kinds that fill his familiar environment. We have already reported some examples of that. He would sooner not drink than drink from a cup other than the one to which he is accustomed; he would rather not sleep than sleep in an unfamiliar room. He is attached to these different things to the point that he suffers when deprived of them. To be sure, such an attachment is of an inferior type. It implies, nevertheless, at least an aptitude in the child to develop solidarity with something other than himself. Between this sentiment and local patriotism, love of birthplace, of the paternal hearth—the moral and altruistic character of which nobody denies—there is only a difference of degree. The child thus becomes attached not only to things but also to people. It is a common fact that a change of nurses at times brings on painful and disquieting crises. The child refuses the breast of a stranger and resists her attentions. Evidently he  was attached to the person who left him although he could only have a very confused image of her. Parents also, and very early in life, are the object of analogous sentiments.

According to Sully:

A little girl 13 months old had been separated from her mother for six weeks. When she came back the girl became mute through joy and could not, for some time, leave her mother even for a minute. At the age of 17 months little M. received her father after five days of absence with every manifestation of great tenderness. She ran to meet him, gently caressed his face and brought him all the toys which were in the room.[1]

In all these cases, the child clearly experiences a need of joining his existence to that of others and suffers when the bond is broken.

In this form, the altruism of the child is related to a

---

1. James Sully, *Etudes sur l'enfance*, French translation (1899), p. 334. The English edition is entitled *Studies of Childhood* (London: Longmans, Green and Co., 1896).

characteristic of the child's nature of which we have already spoken. This is the traditionalism of the child, his attachment to the habits he has developed. Once accustomed to a certain way of feeling and acting, he departs from it with difficulty; he clings to it and, by extension, to the things conditioning it. Because he seeks obstinately the same impressions, he seeks the same objects which awaken these impressions in him.

Another source of altruistic sentiments in the child is the extreme facility, the eagerness, with which he reproduces everything which happens under his eyes. He imitates the facial expressions that he notices on the faces of people around him. He weeps when they weep; he laughs when they laugh. He repeats the same word, the same gestures; when these gestures and words become for him the symbols of definite ideas and sentiments, he reproduces the ideas and sentiments that he thinks he reads in the faces of those around him or understands through the words he hears. Thus, everything that occurs in the part of the external world within his purview echoes in his consciousness.

The internal life of the child is very poor; it comprises only a small number of elements, which are rather fugitive; consequently, his internal life is in no condition to resist the intrusion of strange elements. A more strongly developed personality, an adult's personality—especially an adult who has received a certain culture—is invaded less easily. Strange influences work upon us only if they are in harmony with our internal disposition, if they are in the direction in which we naturally lean. An emotional state that we observe will not be communicated to us simply because we are witnessing it; beyond this, it must be consonant with our temper, with our personal feelings. Otherwise it will not touch us, or will only touch us superficially. An idea will not become ours through the simple fact that it is expressed in our presence. If it is not in harmony with our mentality, we will reject it; or, if finally imposed upon us, it will be due to very strong moral pressure, convincing argument, or a captivating and persuasive ardor.

But the child is much more open to adventitious actions, because he has not yet a solid and determined mental constitution. He hasn't many strong habits, which a momentary impression cannot cut into. Without any doubt—as we pointed out a while ago—he has obviously some habits, very powerful ones, but they are few in number. His consciousness is made up more than anything else of fluid, inconstant states, which continually displace each other, passing too rapidly to crystallize. Such a frame of mind cannot stave off strong suggestions from the outside.

We have here the origin of what is so improperly called the "instinct of imitation." There is nothing instinctive here in the precise meaning of the word. There is no need to imitate, which is inscribed, in some way, in the child's organic makeup. The child imitates because his budding consciousness does not yet have a very strongly marked capacity for choice. Consequently, his consciousness assimilates readily and without resistance all the stronger impressions coming to him from the outside.

Now, that aptitude to reproduce and therefore to share other peoples' sentiments—what can it be if not an aptitude for sympathizing with them, a first form of an eminently altruistic and social tendency? Indeed, this is how a bond of constant communication is established between the consciousness of the child and others' consciousnesses. What happens in the latter reverberates in the former. He lives their lives, enjoys their pleasures, suffers their sorrows. He is thus naturally induced to act so as to prevent or soften others' sorrows.

A baby of fourteen months was crawling on the floor. His sister Catherine, six years old, who was trying with little success to knit, began to cry. The baby looked at her and began to grunt all the while rubbing his fingers downward on his own cheeks. His aunt called Catherine's attention to the baby and that provoked a new outburst of tears. Whereupon the baby succeeded in moving jerkily

across the room until he got to Catherine, all the while uttering his
sounds and making his expressive gestures. Catherine, overcome with
so much solicitude, took the baby in her arms and smiled. Immediately the baby began to clap its hands, to chatter excitedly and to
trace the tears on his sister's cheeks.[2]

Just as he seeks to console others in the sorrow that he sees
and shares, the child makes an effort to give them pleasure.
But very likely the positive acts, which he thus performs to
make himself useful, appear only at a more advanced stage;
for they presuppose a mentality which is already developed.
The pain that one tries to assuage is real. It is a given fact,
immediately perceived, which in itself elicits the action destined to vanquish or attenuate that sorrow. The pleasure that
one causes is a phenomenon yet to come, which one must
anticipate, represent to one's self in advance. The mental
development of the child must therefore be such as to permit
him to see the future consequences of the action. Observation
shows that from the third year on, and sometimes even before
that, the child is capable of anticipatory sympathy:

A little boy two years and one month old heard his nurse say, "If
only Anne would remember to fill the kettle in the playroom!" The
attention of the child being aroused he went and found Anne who
was cleaning a fireplace in a room some distance away. He began to
pull her by her apron, took her to the playroom and pointed to the
kettle all the while saying, "There, there." The girl understood and
did what he asked her.[3]

In summary, altruism, the attachment to something other
than one's self, is not, as has at times been said, a sort of
mysterious, extraordinary, almost inexplicable faculty, through
which man does violence to his initial nature and contradicts
it. Renan, in a speech about *prix de vertu*, thought he could
speak of devotion, of the spirit of sacrifice and solidarity, as
if that spirit were a beautiful absurdity and a praiseworthy
illogicality. In reality there is nothing less mysterious or more

2. *Ibid.,* p. 336.
3. *Ibid.,* p. 338.

natural. In order to dissipate this so-called mystery, we need not—as did La Rochefoucauld and the utilitarians—reduce altruism to a degenerate form of egotism, which amounts to stripping it of all its distinctive characteristics. These two sentiments do not derive at all from each other, but are both rooted in our nature—a nature of which they only express two aspects implying and mutually complementing one another.

Thus, we have been able to find altruism in the child beginning with the first years of his life. Without a doubt, the altruism of the child is neither very extensive nor very complicated, for the excellent reason that his intellectual horizon is very limited. Beyond what touches him immediately, the unknown begins for him. However, we must take into account the fact that, in certain respects, the circle of beings with whom he sympathizes is more extensive than that of the adult; for as the child endows even inanimate things with sensibility, he participates in their lives, he suffers their imaginary sufferings and exults in their pleasures: he commiserates with his wounded doll, the paper that is torn and crumpled, the stones that cannot move from a given spot. Moreover, his egotism is related to his altruism because his individuality is not at all complex. It offers only a small number of points of contact for selfish sentiments. The only ones that he experiences are those concerning the material aspects of his life. The egotism of the adult is more complicated. Still, we must not lose sight of the fact that the effect of culture is to develop, proportionally, much more the altruistic aspect of our nature than its opposite. It is no less true that we have found in the child the lever that we need in order to influence him. It remains to be seen how to make use of it.

# CHAPTER FIFTEEN

# ✑ THE INFLUENCE OF THE

# SCHOOL ENVIRONMENT

ALTRUISM, THE ATTACHMENT TO SOMETHING OUTSIDE THE SELF, has often been presented as a sort of mysterious, extraordinary, almost inexplicable faculty, by reason of which man does violence to his original nature and contradicts it. We saw in the last chapter that nothing is less mysterious or more natural than altruism. And to dissipate this so-called mystery, it is not at all necessary to reduce altruism, as did La Rochefoucald and the utilitarians, to a disguised form of selfishness, which amounts to denying altriusm under the pretext of making it intelligible. In truth, altruism is as deeply rooted as is its contrary in the psychological nature of man. The two types of sentiments only express two different but inseparable aspects of our entire psychological make-up. Insofar as our activity is concentrated on ourselves, on that which comprises our individuality and differentiates us from beings and from things outside ourselves, we are selfish. On the other hand, there is altruism when our activity pursues objects outside of ourselves, objects that do not enter into the characteristics of our personality. However, as we cannot become attached to these external objects unless we imagine them in some way, they are central elements of ourselves; they exist and live in us in the form of the representation expressing them. Indeed, we are attached to the representation itself and directly: that symbol or image frustrates us when the thing represented is no longer there or is no longer itself; and consequently there is some egotism in all altruism. Conversely, since the self is made up of elements that we perforce borrow from the outside, since the mind cannot feed exclusively on itself, since it cannot think in a vacuum, so there must necessarily be something palpable that comes from the outside world. There is in ourselves something other than ourselves; therefore, there is altruism in egotism itself. More particularly, we saw how selfishness—active, aggressive, and having as its objective the extension of our being—implies a certain expansion, a certain deployment in external activity, a veritable aptitude to give ourselves and spend ourselves. To put it briefly, by the very requirements of man's nature, consciousness is simultaneously oriented in those two directions conventionally opposed to each other—the inward and the outward; it cannot be self-contained, and it cannot be entirely outside of itself. In either state, conscious life is suspended. In pure ecstasy, as in the self-absorption of the fakir, thinking stops simultaneously with activity. These are two forms of mental death.

Although selfishness and altruism are thus brought together to the point of interpenetration, they are definitely distinct. The fact that they are no longer opposed to each other does not mean that they are indistinguishable. For there is always a difference between the objects to which we are attached in these two cases; although that difference is only one of degree, it is most assuredly real. It might be said that since altruistic drives, when they are satisfied, give us satisfaction, they are selfish like any other drives. But there is always this considerable difference: that in the one case we find our satisfaction in the pursuit of objects personal to ourselves; whereas in the other case we find satisfaction in the pursuit of objects that, although they penetrate our consciousness symbolically, are nevertheless not distinctive elements of our personality. So put, we may be assured that the consciousness of the child, by the very fact that it is a consciousness, is necessarily open to these two kinds of feeling. Indeed, we find in the child a double source of altruism. First, by dint of habit, the child becomes attached to objects and to beings in his familiar environment. A bond develops between them and the child, solely by virtue of repetition and its effect upon the nature of the child. Second, the child's great receptivity to external influences causes the sentiments expressed before him to be easily internalized. He reproduces them and afterwards shares them. He suffers because of the suffering whose expression he witnesses. He shares in the joys of others; in short, he sympathizes with others. That sympathy is not simply passive; it suggests positive actions to the child.

What, then, is the meaning of the facts adduced so often that seem to establish the child as constitutionally refractory to altruism? In the first place, he has often been accused of manifesting an inborn cruelty toward animals. As the classical writers say: "This is a pitiless age." Not only does the child not suffer because of the suffering that he inflicts, but it even seems to amuse him. Does this not prove that there is an instinct of malice in the child? If we want to judge the child thus severely, we must establish that the actions of which he is guilty have their root in a genuine desire to inflict suffering. There is nothing to justify us in attributing to the child a natural bent toward cruelty. He is led to such behavior by urges that in themselves are not at all immoral. Very often it is nothing more than curiosity, a sentiment that in itself is not mean. He wants to know how the body is put together, where the blood is, the blood he hears people talk about; how wings are attached to the body, and so on.

It has also been conjectured, and not altogether implausibly, that the child has a certain need to show his domination over the animal, to assert his superior rights. "The fact that he tramples on kittens," says Sully, "is perhaps in his eyes only the assertion of pure possession."[1] Indeed, how often do we see destructive impulses with no aim of any kind. The child seems to have a sort of cumulative activity potential, which is in a perpetual state of tension. That activity is not spent in small discharges, evenly spaced. It explodes suddenly, and these explosions are necessarily violent and destructive. The child smashes just as he jumps, just as he makes noise, to satisfy his need of motion. On the other hand, it is only confusedly, uncertainly, that he visualizes the suffering that he causes. He has no clear idea of what goes on in the consciousness of the animal, for it does not articulate its feelings as do human beings. To the child, these feelings are so obscure and doubtful that they are in no position to restrain him in his cruel play. The child does not intend cruelty. If, therefore, he does not sympathize with the animal it is not because of his alleged native perversity, because he has an instinctive bent to hurt. It is because he does not realize what he is doing.

The same reasoning holds with regard to the child's insensitivity to calamities that hit the family. The child, until he reaches a certain age, is not in any condition to conceive of the consequences which the disappearance of a member of the family entails. A certain amount of thought is necessary in order to realize what dying can mean. A change as radical as a sudden cessation of being, complete annihilation, is not easily conceived of, even by an adult. If you say to the child that he will never again see the deceased person, you cannot touch him very deeply; the word "never," like the word "always," conveys nothing precise to his mind. Thus, he cannot distinguish that definitive separation from a temporary one. Moreover, he does not have a very distinct notion of the different personalities with whom he deals, unless they be people very close to him, with whom he has imme-

---

1. James Sully, *op. cit.*, p. 329.

diate contact, as with his nurse or mother. As for the others, substitutions are easy; substitutions that permit him to fill in the void that is now a fact of his existence. One of the faces familiar to him will quite readily displace that of the person who has just disappeared. After the slight disturbance produced by this little change, life will resume its course. Let us add that his natural instability will make him more accessible to distractions; his mobile thinking has no trouble in turning aside from a depressing subject. It is a well known fact that children are the sooner sensitive to the death of their relatives and friends in proportion to their intelligence and to the vividness of their imagination, unless bad influences stimulate their egotism and deaden their faculties for sympathy.

Thus, there is nothing in the facts we have observed to indicate the unqualified egotism so often attributed to the child. No doubt his altruism is still rudimentary. We can see the principal reason for that. His mentality, generally speaking, is likewise rudimentary. Because his mind is in the process of formation, it does not reach far beyond his most immediate surroundings and consequently beyond a small number of human beings who are outside of himself: his family, his friends, objects familiar to him—they are all he knows. As a matter of fact, he conceives of everything else, because of its remoteness, only in uncertain and ephemeral fashion, in which the individuality of things is more or less attenuated. He feels most vividly his own organism and its condition. Therefore, during the first years of his life, personal sensations—and none present themselves in that guise more than do organic sensations—play the preponderant part; they have the greatest bearing on his behavior; they are the center of gravity of child life, although from that moment on there are already urges of another type. One can therefore really say that there is in the child more egotism than altruism, but not that he is a stranger to the latter sentiment. The fact is, that even here one can notice the close connection binding these two urges. If altruism is less developed in the child than in the adult, that is no less true of egotism. For the very reason that the field of child consciousness is so narrow, that a very small part of the external world reverberates in it and does so without evoking very distinct impressions, the personality of the child is low in nourishment, and thus offers only slight leverage for egotistic sentiment. The circle of personal interests in the child is very restricted. It does not extend beyond what feeds and entertains it. The egotism of the adult is infinitely more complex. Love of money, power, honors, reputation, elegant clothes, comfort in living—all of that takes shape only in proportion as man extends his horizon and comes into contact with many beings and things. These two aspects of our nature develop in parallel ways, not necessarily at an even pace but under the influence of the same causes.

While we are quite sure that we can find in the child a type of altruism, which education has only to develop, what has been said so far permits us to determine the means by which this development can be effected. Since the weakness of altruistic sentiments at the beginning of life derives from the limitations of the child's consciousness, we must extend it gradually beyond the bounds of the organism. It is only with difficulty, and to a slight degree, that he transcends these boundaries. We must acquaint him with things that he perceives at first only confusedly.

Above all we must give the child the clearest possible idea of the social groups to which he belongs. It is here that the role of the educator is most important. If the child were left to himself he would conceive of the groups in which he is implicated only imperfectly and very late. They are too vast and complex for him to see with his eyes—except, of course, the family, since it is so small he can have face to face contact with it. Now, in order to attach the child to these groups, which is the final goal of moral education, it is not enough to give him an image of them. Beyond this, the image must be repeated with such persistence that it becomes, through the sole fact of repetition, an integrating element in himself, such that he can no longer do without it. Once again, we can only become attached to things through the impressions or images we have of them. To say that the idea we acquire of these social groups is a part of our consciousness is really to say that it cannot disappear without creating a painful void. Not only must we repeat this representation, but in repeating it, give the idea enough color, form, and life to stimulate action. It must warm the heart and set the will in motion. The point here is not to enrich the mind with some theoretical notion, a speculative conception; but to give it a principle of action, which we must make as effective as necessary and possible. In other words, the representation must have something emotional; it must have the characteristic of a sentiment more than of a conception. Since, in the long run, one only learns to do by doing, we must multiply the opportunities in which the sentiments thus communicated to the child can manifest themselves in actions. To learn the love of collective life we must live it, not only in our minds and imaginations, but in reality. It is not enough to form in a child the potential for attaching himself to the group. We must stimulate this power by effective exercise; for only thus can it take shape and become strengthened.

In sum, by broadening gradually the consciousness of the child so as to infuse it with the idea of the social groups to which he belongs and will belong; by linking, through repetition, these ideas intimately with the greatest possible number of other ideas and feelings, so that the former are constantly called to mind and come to occupy such an important place in the child's mind that he will resist any diminution or weakening of them; by communicating them with such warmth and sincerity that their emotive power becomes an active force; by developing that power of action through exercise—such is the general method we must follow to commit the child to the collective goals that he must pursue. There is nothing in this method beyond the power of the educator since it is simply a matter of giving the child an impression, as vivid and as forceful as possible, of things as they actually exist. The problem, then, at this stage, is to find out how this method is applicable in the school. There are two vehicles at our disposal: first, the school environment itself; secondly, that which is taught. Let us examine how these instruments of action should be used to achieve the desired end.

## General Influence
## of the School Environment

To understand clearly the important role that the school environment can and should play in moral education we must first realize what the child faces when he comes to school. Up to that point he has only been acquainted with two kinds of groups. In the family the sentiment of solidarity is derived from blood relationships; and the moral bonds that result from such relationships are further re-enforced by intimate and constant contact of all the associated minds and by a mutual interpenetration of their lives. Then there are little groups of friends and companions—groups that have taken shape outside the family through free selection. Now, political society presents neither of these two characteristics. The bonds uniting the citizens of a given country have nothing to do with relationships or personal inclinations. There is therefore a great distance between the moral state in which the child finds himself as he leaves the family and the one toward which he must strive. This road cannot be traveled in a single stage. Intermediaries are necessary. The school environment is the most desirable. It is a more extensive association than the family or the little societies of friends. It results neither from blood relationships nor from free choice, but from a fortuitous and inevitable meeting among subjects brought together on the basis of similar age and social conditions. In that respect it resembles political society. On the other hand, it is limited enough so that personal relations can crystallize. The horizon is not too vast; the consciousness of the child can easily embrace it. The habit of common life in the class and attachment to the class and even to the school constitute an altogether natural preparation for the more elevated sentiments that we wish to develop in the child. We have here a precious instrument, which is used all too little and which can be of the greatest service.

It is the more natural to use the school to this end since it is precisely groups of young persons, more or less like those constituting the social system of the school, which have enabled the formation of societies larger than the family. With respect to animals, M. Espinas has already demonstrated that groupings of birds and mammals could not have taken shape if, at a certain moment in their lives, the young had not been induced to separate from their parents and formed societies of a new type, which no longer have domestic characteristics. Indeed, wherever the family keeps its members to itself it is easily self-sufficient; each particular family tends to live its own life, an autonomous life—tends to isolate itself from other families so as to provide more easily for itself; under these conditions, it is clearly impossible for another society to be formed. The small group appears only where the new generation, once it has been brought up, is induced to free itself from the family setting to lead a collective life of a new sort. Similarly, if, from the very beginning, inferior human societies are not limited to one household, if they comprise even in their humblest form a number of families, it is largely because the moral education of children is not undertaken by their parents, but by the elders of the clan. The elders would assemble the young, after they had reached a given age, to initiate them collectively into the religious beliefs, rites, traditions—in a word, to everything constituting the intellectual and moral patrimony of the group. Because of this gathering of the young into special groups, determined by age and not by blood, extrafamilial societies have been able to come into being and perpetuate themselves. The school is precisely a group of this kind; it is recruited according to the same principle. The gatherings of young neophytes, directed and taught by the elders, which we can observe in primitive societies, are already actual school societies and may be considered as the first form of the school. In asking the school to prepare children for a higher social life than that of the family, we are only asking something that is quite in accord with its character.

Furthermore, if there is a country in which the role of the school is particularly important and necessary, it is ours. In this respect, we are living under quite special conditions. Indeed, with the exception of the school, there is no longer in this country any society intermediate between the family and the state—that is to say, a society that is not merely artificial or superficial. All the groups of this kind, which at one time ranged between domestic society and political society—provinces, communes, guilds—have been totally abolished or at least survive only in very attenuated form. The province and the guild are only memories; communal life is very impoverished and now holds a very secondary place in our consciousness.

The causes of this situation are well known. In order to achieve political and moral unity, the monarchy fought all forms of local particularism; it strove to reduce the autonomy of towns and provinces, to weaken their moral individuality so as to fuse the more easily and completely into the great collective personality of France. In this regard, the Revolution continued and completed the work of the monarchy. All

groupings that were opposed to this great movement of national consolidation—which was the essence of the revolu·
tionary movement—anything that was an obstacle to the
unity and to indivisibility of the Republic, was broken. Moreover, the spirit that animated the men of the Revolution
became quite hostile toward intermediate groupings. This is
the reason why until very recently our laws were frankly
hostile to societies of this kind.

Now, this state of affairs constitutes a serious crisis. For
morality to have a sound basis, the citizen must have an
inclination toward collective life. It is only on this condition
that he can become attached, as he should, to collective aims
that are moral aims par excellence. This does not happen automatically; above all, this inclination toward collective life can
only become strong enough to shape behavior by the most
continuous practice. To appreciate social life to the point
where one cannot do without it, one must have developed
the habit of acting and thinking in common. We must learn
to cherish these social bonds that for the unsocial being are
heavy chains. We must learn through experience how cold
and pale the pleasures of solitary life are in comparison. The
development of such a temperament, such a mental outlook,
can only be formed through repeated practice, through perpetual conditioning. If, on the contrary, we are invited only
infrequently to act like social beings, it is impossible to be
very interested in an existence to which we can only adapt
ourselves imperfectly.

The nature of political life is such that we take part in it
only intermittently. The State is far away. We are not directly
involved in its activity. Among events at the national level,
only the most considerable have repercussions that reach us.
We do not constantly encounter those great political causes
that can excite us, to which we can give ourselves entirely.

If then, with the exception of the family, there is no collective life in which we participate, if in all the forms of

human activity—scientific, artistic, professional, and so on—
in other words, in all that constitutes the core of our existence,
we are in the habit of acting like lone wolves, our social
temperament has only rare opportunities to strengthen and
develop itself. Consequently, we are inevitably inclined to
a more or less suspicious isolation, at least in regard to everything concerning life outside the family. Indeed, the weakness
of the spirit of association is one of the characteristics of our
national temperament. We have a marked inclination toward
a fierce individualism, which makes the obligations of social
life appear intolerable to us and which prevents us from
experiencing its joys.

We seem to think that we cannot participate in a society
without losing our freedom and reducing our stature. Therefore, we join associations only reluctantly, and as seldom as
possible. There is nothing more instructive in this respect
than a comparison of the life of the German and the French
student. In Germany, everything is done in a group. People
sing together. They take walks together. They play together.
They philosophize together, or talk about science and literature. All kinds of associations, corresponding to every kind
of human activity, function in parallel ways; thus, the young
man is constantly involved in group life. He engages in
serious occupations in a group, and he relaxes in a group.
In France, on the other hand, until very recently, the principle was that of isolation; and if the appreciation of life
in common is beginning to revive, it is far from being very
deep. This is true of the adult as well as the young man. The
only social relations for which we show any inclination are
those sufficiently external so that we commit only the most
superficial part of ourselves. That is why *salon* life has taken
on such importance and attained such a great development
in this country. It is because it is a way of satisfying to some
extent—or rather a way of pretending to satisfy—that need
of sociability, which, in spite of everything, still survives in

us. Need we demonstrate how illusory that satisfaction is, since that form of life in common is only a game without any connection with the serious aspects of life?

No matter how necessary it is to remedy the situation, there can be no question of reviving the groupings of the past or of allotting them their erstwhile functions; if they disappeared, it is because they were no longer consonant with the new conditions of collective existence. What we must do is to try to bring to life new groupings, which are in harmony with the present-day social order and with the principles on which it reposes. But the only way of succeeding in this is to breathe life into the spirit of association. These groups cannot be created by force. If they are to have any real life they must be created by public opinion. Men must feel the need for them and be inclined to form groups of their own accord. Thus, we seem to be caught in a vicious circle. For these associations can only be reborn if the spirit of association and the sense of the group are aroused. On the other hand, we have seen that this sense can only be acquired through practice in the context of already existing associations. We can only reanimate collective life, revive it from this torpor, if we love it; we cannot learn to love it unless we live it, and in order to do so it must exist.

It is precisely at this point that the role of the school can be considerable. It is the means, perhaps the only one, by which we can leave this vicious circle. The school is a real group, of which the child is naturally and necessarily a part. It is a group other than the family. Its principal function is not, as in the case of the family, that of emotional release and the sharing of affections. Every form of intellectual activity finds scope in it, in embryonic form. Consequently, we have through the school the means of training the child in a collective life different from home life. We can give him habits that, once developed, will survive beyond school years and demand the satisfaction that is their due. We have here a unique and irreplacable opportunity to take hold of the child at a time when the gaps in our social organization have not yet been able to alter his nature profoundly, or to arouse in him feelings that make him partially rebellious to common life. This is virgin territory in which we can sow seeds that, once taken root, will grow by themselves. Of course, I do not mean that education alone can remedy the evil—that institutions are not necessary demanding legislative action. But that action can only be fruitful if it is rooted in a state of opinion, if it is an answer to needs that are really felt. Thus, although we could not at any time do without the school to instill in the child a social sense, although we have here a natural function from which the school should never withdraw, today because of the critical situation in which we find ourselves, the services that the school can render are of incomparable importance.

# CHAPTER SIXTEEN

~§  THE SCHOOL ENVIRONMENT

(Concluded); AND TEACHING

THE SCIENCES

IN THE LAST CHAPTER, I POINTED OUT THAT ONE OF THE PECU-liarities of our national temperament was the weakening of the spirit of association in this country. Collective life is not very attractive to us; on the contrary, we feel keenly the obligations and restrictions it imposes on us. As a result, we are only willing to commit the most superficial aspects of ourselves to group life. In fact, we engage in it as little as possible. The best proof of the aversion to groups intermediate between family and state is the multitude of obstacles that, until very recently, French law has placed in their way. This trait of our national character is the more deeply rooted in us as it stems from profound and distant historical sources. It results, indeed, from that entire movement of moral consolidation and unification begun by the French monarchy as soon as it became conscious of itself and its role, and which the French Revolution continued and completed. In order to impart the moral unity that characterizes France, it was necessary to combat all forms of particularism—communal,

provincial, and corporative. Recognizing the fact that societies, like living beings in general, are the more highly developed
in proportion as they are unified, one cannot regret the historical movement that made of our country the first and most
completely unified in Europe. Nonetheless, it is true that the
radical disappearance of intermediate groups has impaired
public morality at one of its most vital points. Under these
conditions, the principal forms of human activity are developed outside any group; man has fewer opportunities to share
in the common life. Having less experience of life in common,
he will have less liking for it. He will have a diminished
appreciation of its charms and will feel the disadvantages
more vividly and more painfully.

In order to commit ourselves to collective ends, we must
have above all a feeling and affection for the collectivity.
Before one gives one's self to a group, he must be fond of
life in a group setting. We are beginning to appreciate the
gravity of our deficiency in this respect. In the last several
years, we have had a new burgeoning of intermediate associations. Hence, we have all sorts of commercial and industrial
organizations, scientific societies and congresses in intellectual
life, and groups of students in university life. Some persons
are even trying to revive, more or less in vain, the vanishing
life of local communities. There is more and more talk of
town decentralization and of provincial decentralization.
Without passing judgment on these very uneven attempts,
we are compelled to say that most of them are legal artifacts;
they are not an integral part of our way of life. They are most
often external arrangements that reveal a felt need for such
organizations; but they are not very vital. The central fact
is that they cannot become living realities unless they are
willed, desired, demanded by grass-roots sentiment—in other
words, unless the spirit of association comes alive, not only
in a few educated circles, but in the deep mass of the
population.

It is here, as we indicated previously, that we seem to be

caught in a vicious circle. On the one hand, associations can only spring up again when the feeling for association awakens; and, on the other hand, it cannot awaken except within already existing associations. The only way of getting out of this circle is to get hold of the child when he leaves his family and enters school. It is at that moment that we can instill in him the inclination for collective life. For the school is a society, a natural group capable of branching out in derivative groupings and in all sorts of ramifications. If the child, at this decisive time, is carried along in the current of social life, the chances are strong that he will remain oriented in this way throughout his life. If he develops the habit of expressing his interests and activities in various groups, he will keep the habit in his post-school life; and then the action of the lawmaker will really be fruitful, for it will emerge from soil that education will have prepared. This is what accounts for the tremendous social significance of the school today. And this is why the nation hopes for so much in the teacher. It is not simply because of the intellectual training that he can give. What many people feel strongly is that we have here an unexcelled opportunity to exert a kind of influence on the child which nothing else can replace.

What should the school be, what should the class be, to fulfill this expectation? The entire problem consists of how to take advantage of that association in which children of the same class perforce find themselves. How to make them acquire a liking for a collective life both more extensive and impersonal than the one to which they are accustomed? There is nothing insurmountable in this problem. As a matter of fact, there is nothing more agreeable than collective life if one has had a little experience with it at an early age. It has the effect of enhancing the vitality of each individual. The child feels himself stronger, more confident, when he feels that he is not alone. There is something in all common activities that warms the heart and fortifies the will.

Religious minorities are an interesting example of the tempering of character, of the training in life that a strongly cohesive group communicates to its members. Wherever a church is in the minority it is obliged to fall back on itself, to fight against hostility or ill will from outside. There are much tighter bonds of solidarity among the faithful than when external resistance is no longer a factor and the church can function freely—a condition that brings about a loosening of the social bonds. With the religious minority, there is a backlog of solidarity, of mutual aid and comfort; there is something unifying, which sustains the faithful against the difficulties of life. That is why the tendency to suicide in given religions varies according to its minority status. There is pleasure in saying "we," rather than "I," because anyone in a position to say "we" feels behind him a support, a force on which he can count, a force that is much more intense than that upon which isolated individuals can rely. The pleasure grows in proportion as we can say "we" with more assurance and conviction.

The whole point is to give the child a taste for this pleasure and to instill in him the need for it. We will succeed the more easily because in certain respects he is much more amenable than the adult. For the greatest obstacle to this fusion, this joining of minds in a common consciousness, is the individual personality. The more decided that personality is, the more clearly its contours are outlined, the more difficult for it to merge into something other than itself. To experience the pleasure of saying "we," it is important not to enjoy saying "I" too much. At least to the extent that the idiosyncratic is emphasized, only a very complex solidarity is possible; and it implies an organization skilled enough to connect the different parts of the whole all the while leaving to each his autonomy. We do not have to inquire here how these contrasting requirements can be reconciled. We do have to realize that the problem is difficult. But for the child, there is no such problem; today, as in the past, he is suggestible and

malleable. The characteristic traits of the individual have not
yet asserted themselves to the point of masking the general
traits of the species. Life in common requires no sacrifice
of his individuality. It gives him more than it takes from
him; consequently, it has much greater attractions for him.
The observer has only to note the moral transformation that
takes place in the child who, after a solitary upbringing in
his family, enters a lively and well-organized class for the
first time. He comes out of it entirely changed. He is alert,
his face is expressive, he talks with animation; for the first
time the child has had a tonic experience—he has known
a new life far more intense than the one he knew before;
he is happy with it. He is no longer supported by his own
energy alone: to his own strength that of others is added.
He participates in the collective life, and his whole being is
enhanced. (I assume that he has not run afoul of a teacher
who thinks it is his duty to make a somber business of school
life. But I will come back to this point.)

To achieve this tonic effect on the child, the class must
really share in a collective life. The instructor must therefore
exert every effort to bring that about. Such phrases as *the
class*, the *spirit of the class*, and the *honor of the class* must
become something more than abstract expressions in the
student's mind. Everybody knows that almost spontaneously,
without anyone's intervention, every class has its own characteristic features, its ways of being, of feeling and thinking
—its temperament—which persist from year to year. A class
is a personal being, a genuine "individual," whose identity
may be recognized several years later. When one says of a
class that it is good or bad, that it has a good or bad spirit,
that it has warmth or life, or that on the contrary it is dull
and dead, it is the collective individuality that is being judged
and qualified. What gives it this character are the conditions
under which it is recruited and the extent to which it is
morally and intellectually homogeneous; a class is altogether

different depending on whether its members have a common background or, on the contrary, quite different ones—e.g., classes in elementary mathematics. The collective life, which comes into being by itself and which results from the exchange of ideas and sentiments among associated children, takes shape haphazardly. Such a community could arise just as easily on the basis of undesirable sentiments as on the basis of precise ideas and good habits. It is the teacher's responsibility to direct it into normal channels. How should he go about it?

It is a fact, and one resulting from what we have just said, that we must be on our guard in thinking that the class can be molded and fashioned at will. A teacher can no more make the temper of a class than a king can fashion that of a nation. As we have just shown, the composition of a class partly determines its character. Although each of the classes that passes through the hands of the same teacher reflects his influence, they nevertheless differ from each other. There is an entirely spontaneous collective life that cannot be created out of whole cloth and that nothing can replace.

The role of the teacher, although thus limited, is very important: he directs the class. His task is above all to multiply the circumstances in which a free elaboration of common ideas and sentiments can take place, to bring out the positive results, to co-ordinate them, and give them stable shape. Preventing the spread of destructive sentiments; discouraging their expression; re-enforcing wholesome ones with the full weight of his authority, by taking advantage of all the incidents of school life; awakening them in such a manner that they become crystallized and durable—these are the procedures he may use. In a word, he must lie in wait for everything that causes the children of a given class to sense their unity in a common enterprise. The opportunities to achieve this goal are abundantly present if we watch for them. It may be a common emotion that grips the class upon reading a touching piece. It may be a judgment passed on some historical character or event after general discussion of its moral value and social bearing. It may be a common impulse of esteem or blame, which any of a thousand events in everyday life may suggest—reprehensible or praiseworthy behavior. It has been suggested that the class itself could become a sort of court, which would judge the conduct of its members with the tearcher acting only as the chief justice. The idea is not compatible with the dominant role that the teacher must play in the moral life of the school. On the other hand, a class in which justice is dispensed by the teacher alone, without securing the support of the group, would be like a society in which the judges render sentence against actions that the public does not condemn. Such judgments would lack both influence and authority. The teacher must gain the support of the class when he punishes or rewards.

Clearly, there are many sources of the collective life of a class. But if the emotions of all sorts that thus pervade this small group disappear as fast as they are felt, the collective life would immediately be too chaotic and unstable to have any impact on the child. Therefore, it is well for the collective sentiments of the class not to remain at the level of fugitive impressions, producing no ties between the students and lacking any sequel. Something of them must remain, something durable, something that recalls them. In the ideas evoked by a historical narration or an event in the life of the school, there is always something that transcends the particular case. There is a general conclusion to draw. It must be drawn, and it must be impressed on the group. If this is done, the child will have the feeling that he sees here, not a series of unconnected incidents, but a consistent and unified life. At the same time, he will acquire the eminently social habit of emulating in the future types of conduct or ways of thinking worked out collectively. It is thus that in adult society collective sentiments are crystallized in the form of popular proverbs, apothegms, and moral or legal maxims. Similarly, each class should have its little code of precepts, worked out in the course of everyday life—a sort of condensed summary of its collective experiences. In the turn of these maxims, quite naturally, the spirit of the teacher and the spirit of the class would stand revealed, as the spirit of a people is revealed by its laws, its familiar precepts, its proverbs, and so on.

Another means that could awaken in the child the feeling of solidarity is the very discreet and deliberate use of collective punishments and rewards. Such a proposition, it is true, encounters certain prejudices. It seems to be agreed that all responsibility must necessarily be individual. However, strictly individual responsibility is only justified as long as the individual is completely and solely the author of his action. In fact, it is nearly impossible that the community of which we are a part should not have a smaller or greater share in what we do. Thus, it is impossible that it be free of responsibility for the actions of the individual. Neither our temperament nor the ideas and habits that our education have inculcated in us are strictly our own. It cannot be said, then, that collective responsibility is a thing of the past, an archaic conception never to be revived. On the contrary, it is important that the group be conscious of its responsibility for the morality of its members. What is true of civil society is equally applicable to the classroom. It would even seem that, because of the smaller scale of the school society and the resulting closeness of each person to every other, phenomena of social contagion should be more intense here than in other situations. There are many actions in the school that result from the general situation and are not attributable to any one person in particular. There are times when a class is particularly restive, showing a general impatience of all discipline. That impatience often shows most markedly in those least responsible for initiating it. The excitement reverberates through the students and is amplified and exaggerated through them, although they did nothing to start it. They are the prime targets of punishment, although they are not the most guilty. Conversely, there is such a thing as a general atmosphere of moral health, which contributes to the development of good students although they themselves do not personally deserve the entire credit. Everybody contributes to the whole. Normally, therefore, collective sanctions play a very important part in the life of the classroom. What is the most powerful means to instill in children the feeling of solidarity that binds them to their companions, a sense of sharing in a common life? Nothing can draw them out of their narrow individualism as much as making them feel that the value of each is a function of the worth of all; and that our actions are at the same time causes and consequences, which transcend the sphere of our individual personalities. There is no better way of instilling the feeling that we are not self-sufficient, but a part of a whole that envelops, penetrates, and supports us.

Once acknowledged, this principle demands that we apply it with restraint and judgment. We cannot, of course, discriminate between individual and collective responsibility for every misdeed. Collective responsibility is reduced to very little in each particular act isolated from all the others. In reality it is felt only in the whole pattern of actions performed by everybody during a given period of time—in the general temper of the class. To evaluate it one must set up, as it were, a moral balance sheet at regular intervals, not for such and such an individual, but for the class taken collectively. We mst judge it as a whole and impose appropriate sanctions. For example, the teacher might make an inventory of everything accomplished—good and bad—during the week, sum up notes and observations made from day to day; and, on the general impression that emerges from this summary he could grant or withhold certain rewards from the entire class—a game everyone enjoys, an exceptional type of recreation or reading, a desirable trip, etc. A reward would go to everyone without any distinction between individuals since everyone had earned it. I am not here inquiring into the detailed rules that apply to this evaluation—how to assess the seriousness or the frequency of good or bad behavior. Experience will easily take care of that. The important thing is for the child to realize clearly that to a certain extent he is working for everybody and everybody is working for him. The availability of collective rewards helps us in the solution of a problem of schoolroom casuistry that often plagues the conscience of the teacher: namely, whether to punish an entire class for the misdeed of a single person when that person is unknown. To allow that misdeed to go unpunished is a serious thing; to punish innocent people is cruelty. Nothing is more natural than to withhold a gratification that is justified only when things go well. The denial of collective rewards is the best sanction against anonymous offenses.

Common ideas, common feeling, common responsibilities —we have enough here to nurture the collective life of the class. But a class is a group of young people of the same age and generation. Society, on the contrary, comprises a plurality of generations superimposed on each other and connected with each other. When we start life we find already established and all around us a complex of ideas, beliefs, and behaviors, which others have acknowledged and practiced before us. These are the legacy of our forebears and will not change very much in the course of our lives. In this matter we are bound, not only to our contemporaries, but to those who came before us; and we have the feeling that there is an impersonal force beyond us, one which took shape before we were born, which will outlast us, and which dominates us; and that force is society. Without this feeling of the bond thus joining generation to generation—sense of continuity that makes of each generation a phase in the development of the collective being—social solidarity would be singularly precarious, since its life would not, perforce, outlast that of a single man, and since it would have to be renewed with each generation. Therefore, it would be well for the child if, upon entering the class, he realized that the group of which he is a member is not a mere improvisation just sprung into being from the time of his arrival. He should be made aware of the legacy of those who preceded him. Collections of the best work done in the class by students in past years would be one of the best ways of giving each class an identification with the past and some sense of continuity. In the same manner it would be well to record and collect all the unusual awards, all the exceptional actions, and all the special celebrations that have taken place in the past. In short, each class would have its history, would learn that it has a past and the meaning of that past. For the same reason, each teacher would have to know the history of the class he is taking over—the students and the events that marked its past. Thus, the child would not feel at the end of each year that a bond is severed and, at the beginning of each year, that an altogether new one is being created, which will itself only last for a time. He would feel that the entire school, the succession of classes through which he passes, forms a continuous whole and a coherent moral environment, enveloping and sustaining him and re-enforcing his sense of solidarity.

It is true that, to forestall discontinuity in school life, it has been suggested that a given teacher should continue with the same class. Indeed, this practice is followed in a number of places. We have gone over its disadvantages and dangers. The authority of the teacher is too great to allow children to be exposed to the influence of one and the same teacher throughout the course of their studies. It is important that the diversity of teachers succeeding each other prevent the influence of any one from being too exclusive and therefore too restricting to the individuality of the child.

But it is also important that these successive influences do not cancel each other. To some degree, it is necessary to establish a bond between them, to instill in the child a sense of the continuity of that influence, diverse though it is, to which he is exposed. It is especially the principal of the school who must insure this continuity. Not that he must do the entire job himself, in an authoritarian manner—just as the teacher does not have the entire job of fashioning the spirit of the classroom. However, he must put the teachers in contact with each other to prevent them from acting autonomously rather than in concert. In brief, the principal is responsible for the spirit and the moral unity of the school, as the teacher is responsible for the spirit and moral unity of the class.

Thus, the school possesses everything it needs to awaken in the child the feeling of solidarity, of group life. If this collective life were to end abruptly upon leaving the closely knit school society, the person's sense of social solidarity would be jeopardized in the context of the larger society. Fortunately, in recent times school groups have felt a need to carry on beyond school life itself, to continue into the life of adult groups. We now have alumni activities of all sorts, in which recent and former graduates get together and take part in a common life. Not only are they wholesome civic organizations, but they are invaluable in providing for the child encouragement, stimulation, and protection from the depressing influence of moral isolation. Generally speaking, everything that can multiply contacts between successive generations—which is what alumni organizations do—is of the greatest social service. Indeed, every generation has its own spirit, its own way of thinking and feeling, its own needs, and its special aspirations. We have a fact here whose causes are as yet not well known, but an indisputable fact, nonetheless. There are linguistic changes in each generation, changes in fashion, in aesthetic appreciation, and in philosophical views. A cosmopolitan generation is succeeded by a very nationalistic generation, or vice versa. Optimism follows pessimism. Anarchism follows religious dogmatism, and so on. Such moral discontinuity between generations runs the risk of giving social evolution a jerky and erratic character, promoting chaotic impulses, if precautions are not taken to bring differing generations together as soon and as completely as possible, so as to encourage their interpenetration and so closing the moral gaps between them.

## The General Influence
## of Teaching

We have just seen how the school, because it is constituted as a group, is capable of inducing in the child the habits of group life, the need to tie into collective forces. Outside that very general influence there is still another, which the school can exert in the same direction through the intermediation of the teaching process.

Doubtless it would seem surprising at first that mere classroom education could possibly promote moral education. Classroom education runs along the lines of theory and speculation; whereas morals command action and practice. However, our conduct is touched by the way in which we conceive action. Our morality, by the very fact that we are intelligent, has its roots in intelligence. Particularly according to our conception of social reality, we will be more or less disposed to tie into it. We are more or less inclined toward something depending on the idea we have of it. Now, this conception of social reality is theoretical, built up out of the various things we have learned. The teaching of physical and natural sciences plays an enormous role in determining the way in which we see things.

The fact is that there is a turn of mind which is an extremely serious obstacle in the formation of the feeling of solidarity and which scientific teaching is particularly adapted to combat: it is something we might call oversimplified rationalism. This state of mind is characterized by the fundamental tendency to consider as real in this world only that which is perfectly simple and so poor and denuded in qualities and properties that reason can grasp it at a glance and conceive of it in a luminous representation, analogous to that which we have in grasping mathematical matters. From this point of view, one cannot be sure that he is dealing with a genuine element of reality unless it can be embraced in an immediate and self-evident intuition in which there is nothing obscure or murky. Thus, it is said of matter that the only thing truly real is the atom, the simple atom, the indivisible atom without color, savor, or sound; without form or dimension—a simple determination of abstract space. What, then, are these complex qualities of sound, smell and shape, which are never given to us except as confused perceptions? The answer, of course, would be that they are simple and superficial impressions, caused by the fact that we are poorly situated to see things. As we perceive them from afar and outside themselves through the mediation of our senses, they appear to us at first as nebula in which we see nothing definite. However, if we admit them to the probings of reason this disturbing veil is rent apart; this cloud, which cloaks reality and which is only a product of our special optics, will be dissipated. What we saw up to that moment as an undifferentiated mass will be perceived as a cluster of elements distinct from each other and altogether simple. Instead of tangled complexes of properties that interpenetrate each other we will only have, in a manner of speaking, a system of mathematical points. In modern times, Descartes has been the most illustrious and distinguished exponent of this attitude. Indeed, we know that for Descartes there is nothing real unless it can be clearly conceptualized, made transparent to the mind; and that for him nothing can fulfill this function if it cannot be reduced to mathematical simplicity.

If that turn of mind were peculiar to the circle of scholars and philosophers there would be no reason to speak of it here. But, for various reasons, this oversimplification has become an integral element of the French mind. Although this manner of conceiving things is in principle a theoretical matter, it has had tremendous repercussions in practice— particularly regarding moral practices. Society is indeed an enormously complex whole. If we apply to it the principle of oversimplified rationalism, we must say that this complexity is nothing in itself, that it has no reality, that the only thing real in society is that which is simple, clear, and easily grasped. Now, the only thing that satisfies all these conditions is the individual. The individual would then be the only real thing in society. Which is to say that society is nothing in itself, that it does not constitute a reality *sui generis*. It is only a collective term designating the sum of individuals. According to this kind of reasoning, our moral behavior finds itself stripped of any objective. In order to cherish society, to de-vote one's self to it, and to take it as the objective of conduct, it must be something more than a word, an abstract term. A living reality is needed, animated by a special exist-ence distinct from the individuals composing it Only such a reality can draw us out of ourselves and so perform the function of providing a moral goal. We can see how this dangerous view of reality can influence behavior, and why, therefore, it is important to correct it. The teaching of science can help us in this; and we shall see in what manner.

# ᴄᔖ TEACHING THE SCIENCES

## (*Concluded*)

IN THE LAST CHAPTER I TRIED TO SHOW HOW CERTAIN INTELLEC-
tual conceptions could affect the moral orientation of nations
and individuals. In particular, we were considering that special
turn of mind which I called oversimplified rationalism. In
general, it may be said that we understand things in proportion as they are simple. If we can gain a perfect understanding of mathematical things it is because they are extremely
simple. The complex, on the other hand, for the very reason
that it is complex, can be conceptualized only in a murky
and confused way. There follows, then, a tendency to deny
all reality to the complex, to convert it into a simple thing,
and to view the complex as an illusion whose sole cause is
the weakness of our intellectual faculties. The complex appears as such to us only because we are unable to distinguish
the very simple elements of which it is compounded. In fact,
however, this attitude would only make of the complex a
composite of simple things thus evading the question of
knowing how it can even be translated in intelligible language. Thus, for Descartes, e.g., all secondary qualities of
matter—form, color, and sound—are without any foundation
in reality; there is therefore nothing real, so it is alleged, ex-

cept mathematical extension, and bodies are made up only of parts of extension.

If this way of conceiving the subject were only confined to a few philosophers, there would be no point in mentioning it here. But it is deeply rooted in our national thinking; it has become one of the characteristic traits of the French mind, at least until reecnt times. Indeed, we have just seen that it leans most heavily on Cartesian thinking. Now, it might be said that in general a Frenchman is to some degree a conscious or unconscious Cartesian. The need to distinguish and clarify, which characterizes our national temper, inclines us to turn away from anything too complex to be easily and clearly conceptualized; and that which we are inclined not to see and not to look at is something we are naturally inclined to deny. Our language itself is not suited to translate the obscure substructure of things that we may glimpse but do not clearly understand. Precisely because our language is analytical it expresses well only those things that are analyzed—in other words, reduced to their elements. It denotes every one of them by means of a precise word whose sense is clearly outlined. But the complex and living unity that these elements form when they are joined together, when they interpenetrate or fuse—all of that escapes because it escapes analysis. Our language seeks the simple. The ideal thing for it would be to have one single word for each indivisible part of reality, and to express the totality formed by everything through a simple, mechanical combination of these elementary notions. As for the aspect that the totality takes on as a totality; as for that which makes its unity, continuity, and life—it is in large measure uninterested. This is the origin of the abstract character of our literature. For a long time, our poets, novelists, and moralists confined themselves to depicting man in general—in other words, to the most abstract faculties of a human being. The hero conceived by a dramatic poet was not a given individual whose characteristics were multiple, fluctuating, contradictory, interpenetrating, and so numerous that any analytical breakdown of them would be impossible. Not at all. It was such and such a sentiment incarnated in an historical or fictional character. The point is that the real individual is complexity itself. In each of us, there is an infinity of aptitudes and properties —some of them overt, others latent, others in process of formation and intermediary between these two states of being. The general, on the contrary, is very simple and stripped of qualities, since in order to arrive at the general, one must methodically strip away elements of reality. Behind these simple and abstract notions, which our writers contrive for us, we very rarely have the impression of those unlimited depths, glimpsed but unexplored, which we perceive in Goethe's Faust or Shakespeare's Hamlet. Everything is under the floodlight of consciousness. Everything is blindingly clear. Moreover, even in science we find evidence of this tendency. It is not without reason that our nation is distinguished among all others by the number and quality of our men of mathematical talent and genius.

Now, nobody proposes to renounce the rationalistic postulate at the very root of this conception, since we ourselves have laid that down as the cornerstone of our philosophy of education. We must maintain that there is no reason to admit anything in the nature of things that is irreducibly irrational. However, rationalism does not imply the radical oversimplification we have just described. Because the complex is difficult to handle intellectually, because an intelligible presentation can only be achieved laboriously, because it is always imperfect, it does not at all follow that one is entitled to deny its reality. Such a conception is, as a matter of fact, contradictory. After all, the complex exists, and no one can assert that things that are, are not.

We say that complexity is an appearance; let us accept that world provisionally. But an appearance is not an unreality. It is a real phenomenon like any other. The reflection of an object as seen in a mirror is not as real as the object; but it has another kind of reality. It is said that there are no colors, no tastes, no sounds, and no heat in the atoms of which the body is made. Granted, but the colors, tastes, odors, and heat that I perceive in my contact with these bodies are certainly real. I live through these realities. They are far more interesting and important to me than the impersonal and abstract behavior of physical elements. Supposing, then, that they are not based on the invisible elements of matter, we would have to conclude that they are based elsewhere and otherwise. It is said that, objectively speaking, heat is only motion; and it seems that something extremely complex, fugitive, and multiform has been reduced to the simplest phenomenon: motion. But whatever one may say, heat is not motion. Whatever factors may be involved in the production of the phenomenon, heat, it is impossible to identify two realities as different as that. We can say as much of all the complex properties whose complexities, it is claimed, are dissolved through the methods of analysis. In a word, if we perceive things as complex, it is because there is complexity somewhere. It is said that it is our point of view, the nature of our consciousness, that alters things and invests them with qualities that are in fact spurious. What of it? Whether the cause of complexity be here or there, within ourselves or in the thing perceived, there is always a real cause for the apparent complexity; and the effects of the cause are themselves real.

Moreover, why would the complex exist only in us and through us? Why would it be found only in our physical and mental organization? Let us admit that the world is entirely reducible to simple elements. But because these elements—instead of remaining isolated—are brought together, combined, and act on each other, they might, through these actions and reactions, release new properties, which each of the component elements by itself would not present. Combine two homogenous forces by applying both of them to a given variable and you will have, as a result, one single force altogether different than either of the components, both as to intensity and as to direction. Combine copper and tin—both flexible metals—and you will have one of the hardest bodies in existence: bronze. Thus, even though at the base of reality there are only very simple elements, in combination they give rise to altogether new properties, which no longer have the same simplicity and whose representation already is much more complex and difficult.

I would go further and add that the very hypothesis that there are perfectly simple elements is altogether arbitrary. Never, under direct observation, have we been able to perceive any, and we cannot even form an adequate notion of them. The most perfect simplicity imaginable is always relative. We say that the atom is indivisible, but we cannot conceive of a portion of space that is indivisible. We say it is without shape, but we cannot conceive of a material element without form. Moreover, in every atom the action of other atoms is felt; the entire world reverberates in each of its elements, and there is thus an infinity in each infinitely small unit. The simple is an ideal limit, to which thought aspires without ever encountering it in reality.

If I have insisted on showing in some detail what is wrong in this way of conceiving things, it is not because of the theoretical interest that the question presents; it is in order to enable the reader to trace the serious practical objections to this viewpoint, and the better to appreciate these objections. Man, we have said, acts morally only when he takes the collectivity as the goal of his conduct. This being so, there must be a collectivity. If society is considered only from a naively simplified point of view, nothing remains that may be called by this name. Indeed, one would then have to postulate as certain that society, this complex whole, as

such, is merely an appearance; while that which truly constitutes the reality of the collectivity—that which we must
apprehend—is something simple, definite, and clear.

Now, the simple element of society is the individual. We
must therefore say that there is nothing real in society except the individuals composing it, that it is nothing in itself,
and that it does not have a special personality, sentiments,
and interests peculiar to it. We wind up with a veritable
social atomism. Society becomes only a collective noun, a
spurious name given to a sum of individuals externally juxta-
posed. It is a mental construct.

One doesn't cherish a mental construct. It would be absurd to sacrifice the real, concrete, and living being that we
are to a purely verbal artifact. We can only dedicate ourselves
to society if we see in it a moral power more elevated than
ourselves. But if the individual is the only real thing in
society, whence could it derive that dignity and superiority?
Far from our depending on it, society would then depend
on us, For if we follow this hypothesis, it could not have
any reality except that deriving from us. It can only be what
we want it to be. Even the values of generations past do
not condition ours at all. These people are no longer with us,
and consequently they are no longer active and effective
realities. To be able to conceive of past traditions as committing the future, we must conceive of them as dominating
the individual and so maintaining themselves above the ebb
and flow of generations. But if there are only individuals,
then, at each moment of history, it is the living individuals
and they alone who constitute the being of society by willing
it, as the God of Descartes creates the world at each moment
of its duration by willing it perpetually.

Let our will suddenly turn, for one reason or another, in
a different direction, and the entire social edifice depending
on that will crumbles or is transformed. Here is what makes
and keeps alive the prejudice still so current concerning the

omnipotence of the legislator. Since society has no existence except that which individual wills lend it, is it not enough that these wills reach an understanding and decide by a common accord that society should change its nature and accomplish its metamorphosis? No one today thinks that we can get together and alter the laws of physical nature. Yet there are few among us who realize that the citizens of a country, even if they are unanimously agreed in promoting an economic or political revolution, can only fail miserably in this enterprise if the revolution is not implied in the nature, in the conditions of existence, of that society.

Few people understand that to give France a social organization—one which is only possible centuries hence—is just as unthinkable as to re-establish the social system of the Middle Ages—even should the majority of the French desire one or the other of these revolutions. How can we doubt that we are confronted with something like a physical force, against which our wills would founder; and that, even if we could destroy the existing social order, we could not construct another that is impossible by definition? This being the case, how could anyone become attached and subordinate to an organization that is nothing in itself and that is perpetually subject to our own wills?

The danger that I am indicating is by no means imaginary, witness what has happened in France. The *esprit simpliste* of the seventeenth century applied at first only to the physical world. People at that time did not speculate on the social and moral order, which was considered too sacred to be subjected to the profanation of lay thought—in other words, to science. With the eighteenth century that reservation went by the board. Science dared much more. It became more ambitious because it got stronger as it went along. It attacked social problems. A social and political philosophy took shape.

The science of the eighteenth century was, as is only natural, the daughter of seventeenth-century science. It was animated by the same spirit. It therefore brought to the study of the new problems it attacked, i.e., the study of the social world, the same naive simplicity that was the inspiration of the previous century in the study of the material world. This is why the social philosophy of the period is essentially atomistic. For Rousseau, who can be considered as the theorist par excellence of the period, there is nothing real in society except the individual. In order to find out what society should be, he does not bother to inquire into history, to find out how society was developed and constituted, in what direction it tends to develop, etc. All he wanted to know was what man should want it to be. As he saw it, the social order is not the product of an historical evolution, which can only be directed to the extent that we have ascertained its laws. It is an act of individual wills tied to each other by a contract whose clauses are freely debated—the social contract. Consequently, to know what is to be done, one has only to be self-aware and firm in his resolution.

This tendency was in part held in check by an opposing tendency. French society had even then a lively self-awareness, a sense of its unity, and that is why we were able to say that the revolutionary movement was in large part a great movement of national consolidation, as is proven by the abhorrence of the men of The Revolution for all moral and political particularism. Never did we have a more vivid feeling for the supremacy of collective interests over individual interests; and of the sovereignty of the law, dominating in its majesty the multitude of individuals. These sentiments are expressed by the theorists as well as the statesmen of the period.

Rousseau dreams of a law imposed upon all citizens with the same nececessity as physical laws, of an impersonal law armed with such strength that it can bend individual wills as do the laws of nature.

Only the simplistic prejudice that imposed itself at the

same time upon all minds made it impossible for the theorists to resolve the problems which they stated as they did; the problems were self-contradictory in their very terms. They began by acknowledging as self-evident that there is nothing real in society except individuals; it is from them that society derives its being; it is what they want to be. But then how can one derive from the individual a social order that transcends the individual? How can one extract from individual wills a law that dominates individual wills? If the law is the work of men, how could it bind them, why should it not be perpetually dependent on them? It is not for us to expose or examine here the artifices people have used to reconcile these irreconcilable views. But this fundamental contradiction is certainly one of the causes that have partially paralyzed the work of the Revolution and prevented it from achieving the results that might have been expected from it.

Thus, history shows what serious practical difficulties this French turn of mind can raise. From our lay point of view, the danger is great and the need to combat it is pressing. Let us not forget that we cannot institute lay education unless we assign to the individual an end that transcends him, unless we can provide some objective for the need for devotion and sacrifice that lies at the root of all moral life. If society is only an appearance and moral reality ends with the individual, to what can he become devoted? To what can he sacrifice himself?

In order to feel that society is something other than a simple appearance; that although it is exclusively composed of individuals, it is nevertheless an independent reality; that it is a being worthy of love and service; one must shake this simplistic prejudice. One must have come to understand, at least to have the impression, that the degree of reality in things is not measured by the degree of simplicity. We are therefore dealing with a state of mind that we must resolutely combat. We must give the child a sense of the real complexity of things. This sense must finally become organic to him—natural, as it were—and constitute a category in his mind. To achieve that goal a complete intellectual education is necessary as a matter of practical interest, and it is to that education that the elementary teaching of science can and must contribute; certainly not mathematical sciences, which on the contrary are simplistic by principle and by method, but physical and natural sciences. No doubt they can only give a feeling for the complexity of things in those matters bearing on the physical world; for this perception to be extended to the social realm, it must first of all be elaborated and gain ground and force with respect to the other realms of nature. We have here an essential phase of preliminary education. This is the function of the sciences in moral education.

Let us examine somewhat more precisely what that function ought to be.

When we believe that complexity is merely superficial, that at bottom things are simple, we tend to admit also that the systematic analysis of these phenomena is likewise simple. For anything that is simple is easily intelligible. We can achieve a clear notion of it—adequate, clear-cut, and altogether analogous to those principles at the basis of mathematics; and once we have this notion, all we have to do if we want to develop a body of scientific truths is to extract, through reasoning, those things implicit in it, as does the mathematician. Simplicism, therefore, is an act of faith in abstract reasoning. The belief at the basis of it is that the mind can draw knowledge out of itself, if only it has constructed the initial concepts that contain that knowledge implicitly. There is no need for any laborious and complicated methods, in order to get at the secrets of nature. There is nothing so mysterious in nature, nothing to disconcert our understanding, since it is as simple as that understanding itself. Once we rend the veil that masks this simplicity,

everything stands brightly revealed. This tendency is so inherent in the simplistic mind that Cartesianism is, in essence,
nothing but the attempt to reduce knowledge of the world
to universal mathematics; when the philosophers of the
eighteenth century applied Cartesian principles to social
phenomena they imagined that the new science could be
conceived and constructed at a single stroke, by way of definitions and deductions, with no need to resort to observation—in other words, to history.

To forestall simplistic thinking, it is therefore necessary
first to give the child a defense against these constructions
and deductions. The child must be brought to see how science is studied; how the labor, time, and trouble that study
entails contrasts with such deductive improvisations. Suppose
we are discussing a given discovery, say the laws governing
light. Instead of merely summarizing the results, we must
tell the child how we arrived at these laws after long and
patient experiments, gropings, and failures of all sorts. We
must indicate the hypotheses that successively followed and
displaced one another, the investment in thought and labor
that they entailed. We must explain to him that the knowledge we now have is itself provisional and that tomorrow,
perhaps, a new fact may be discovered that may put everything into question again, or may require us to modify these
conclusions, at least in part. We are far from being able to
discover truth at a single stroke, far from shaping it to fit
our abstract understanding. In short, we must convey the
need for experimentation, for observation, and the necessity
of getting out of ourselves and submitting to the teachings
of experience, if we really want to know and to understand.
These are the only conditions under which the child will
acquire a feeling for the lack of articulation between the
simplistic workings of our minds and the complexity of
things; for it is exactly in proportion as men take account of
this difference that they realize the importance of the experi-

mental method. With the experimental method, abstract simplicism acknowledges its limitations and abdicates the absolute dominion it at first enjoyed.

Another way of inculcating that sentiment is to make the child realize that very often the result of scientific inquiry is quite different from what one would expect, relying only on reasoning. D'Alembert amused himself by formulating a certain number of physical laws that reasoning alone should a priori have proven to be true, but that experience demonstrated to be false. For example, the barometer should rise to herald rain. Reasoning: before rain, the atmosphere is loaded with vapors and therefore heavier. Hence, it must cause the column of mercury in the barometer to rise. Proposition: hail is to be expected chiefly in the winter. Reasoning: raindrops should congeal at that time as they drop through cold air.[1] There are, of course, a thousand other examples: the shape of the earth, its motion around the sun, the conception of the celestial vault, and so on. In all of these cases, sheer abstract reasoning learns to suspect itself as it sees what errors it entails. How often it could prompt us to deny incontestable realities! We should not hesitate to teach the child that there are observed facts whose existence is unquestionable but which nevertheless sharply contradict our customary logic—so much so that our first inclination is to deny them purely and simply. The way in which hypnotism was at first appraised is an excellent example of the opposition between abstract reasoning and actual experience.

The biological sciences are especially useful in making the child understand the complexity of things and the vital importance of that complexity. Any organism is made up of cells. The cell, then, would seem to be something perfectly simple. But the cell is a perfect demonstration of the fact that this simplicity is only apparent. Nothing is more

---

1. The reference here is apparently to Joseph Bertrand, *L'Académie des sciences et les Académiciens de 1666 à 1793* (Paris: J. Hetzel, 1869), pp. 272-84, which have to do with D'Alembert.

complicated than the cell. All of life is resumed in it. Indeed, the cell works, reacts to external stimuli, assimilates, and excretes—in a word, feeds and grows and reproduces just like the most highly developed organisms. The complexity of function and of closely related activities operating in so constricted a space, in which the locus of a function is everywhere and nowhere—such complexity may well be calculated to strike the imagination more vividly than the complexity we observe in higher animals. One could even go further and broaden the scope of this observation. That small living mass is of course made up of inorganic elements—atoms of hydrogen, oxygen, nitrogen, and carbon. We have here inorganic elements, which in combination and association suddenly manifest completely new properties characterizing life. Here is one thing that will make the child understand —and the child can understand all this—that in one sense a whole is not identical with the sum of its parts. This can lead him on the road to understanding that society is not simply the sum of individuals who compose it.

If such teaching is to have the best effect on thought and action, it must be done with the utmost care. If it is important to put the child on guard against too facile a rationalism, he must also be forearmed with as much vigilance against mysticism. We must certainly tell him that everything is not as simple as our mind, so enamored of simplicity, would have us believe; but certainly not that things are forever beyond understanding, that there is in them a fundamental obscurity forever inaccessible to reason. It has happened, and it still happens all too often, that, in emphasizing the obscurity of things and beings, we promote obscurantism. When we stress the inadequacies of unsupported reasoning, we abdicate in favor of some unknown superior principle outside of ourselves.

Thus, there are two pitfalls against which we must protect the child: he must understand that things are not suddenly self-evident, that man perhaps will never achieve complete clarity of understanding, that there may always remain an obscure residue in things; but, at the same time, it is very important to show him through history that such areas of ignorance are progressively reduced, that there is no unsurpassable limit to this process that began with human history and seems destined to continue indefinitely. Rationalism does not necessarily imply the completion of knowledge in a day or a given time. The only thing rationalism postulates, the only thing it asserts, is that there is no reason to set a limit to the progress of science, to say: "thus far shall you go and no further." To be a rationalist it is not necessary to believe that science will be completely mastered in the near future. It is enough to recognize that there is no precise point at which the domain of the mysterious, of the irrational, begins, a definite point at which scientific thought is impotent and cannot pass. The point here is not to cast aside completely the Cartesianism that is in our blood. We must remain impenitent rationalists, but our rationalism must be rid of its simplicism. It must learn to suspect facile and formal explanations. It must be increasingly imbued with a sense of the complexity of things.

In recent times, science has often been accused of amorality. It is not, so people say, by learning how bodies fall or how the stomach digests that we will learn how to behave toward other men. The preceding discussion shows that such reproaches are not merited. Without mentioning the moral sciences, which can also be understood positively and guide men's actions, we have just shown that even the physical and biological sciences can play an important part in the formation of moral character. Indeed they could only be useless if moral life were separated by some abyss from the rest of nature. If moral life were exclusively oriented toward the transcendental, beyond the realm of experience, and in no way connected with the temporal world, then the sciences studying that world would of course be no help in understanding and carrying out our duties. But we have rejected that duality. The universe is one. Moral behavior has as its end entities that are superior to the individual, but that are also empirical and natural—as are minerals and organisms. These entities are societies. Societies are part of nature. They are only one separate and special compartment of it, a particularly complicated form; therefore, natural sciences can indeed help us better understand the human realm, and equip us with precise ideas, good intellectual habits which can help us in directing our behavior.

# ᵉᵍ TEACHING AESTHETICS

# AND HISTORY

IN THE LAST CHAPTER I DISCUSSED THE ROLE OF THE TEACHING OF science in moral education, suggesting that it is much more important than the teaching of art or literature. This proposition, formulated in passing, will not, I hope, be considered frivolous. Although aesthetic education is not particularly stressed in the primary years, I can hardly waive discussion of it. There is a widespread belief that it plays a very considerable part in the formation of moral character; and so I cannot simply pass it by. I must at least explain why I would assign it only a secondary and accessory role in moral education.

To be sure, there is an aspect under which art—and I include in this expression both *beaux arts* and literature—can rightfully appear as an instrument of moral education. Art is indeed essentially idealistic. It is true that this assertion could, at first blush, seem to imply partisanship in the continual controversy between idealism, on the one hand, and realism or naturalism, on the other. But this is not the point here; naturalists are also idealists after their fashion. In the first place, nature can never be slavishly copied. Along with the beautiful in nature there is also the ugly and the banal;

267

consequently, the imagination of the artist must transform nature. Furthermore, that which constitutes the beauty of nature—when it is beautiful—is the impressions, the emotions *sui generis* that it evokes in us; and the object of art is precisely to translate, by means other than nature affords, those completely idealistic states. Every work of art, then, is the expression of an ideal; the only difference is that for realists the ideal is immediately provoked by the spectacle of the real, whereas for the others it is to a greater extent the product of an internal elaboration. These are only differences of degree.

The ideal is, by definition, something that cannot be contained within reality, something that overflows it, that goes beyond it and consequently beyond ourselves. Thus, no matter how we conceive of it, it is endowed with a sort of superiority over us. It exceeds the natural forces at our command. One cannot be attached to an ideal, whatever it may be, without being connected at the same time with something other than one's self. Thus, the love of art, the predilection for artistic joys, is accompanied by a certain aptitude for getting oustide of ourselves, a certain detachment or disinterestedness. When we are under the influence of a strong aesthetic impression, we give ourselves completely to the work that evokes the impression. We cannot tear ourselves away from it, we forget ourselves. We lose sight of our surroundings, our ordinary cares, our immediate interests. Indeed, this is the essence of the healing power of art. Art consoles us because it turns us away from ourselves. In the artist, that self-forgetfulness induces states of ecstasy. So absorbed is the poet, the painter, or musician in the idea or the sentiment he is trying to express, that he becomes engulfed in it. He finally becomes so involved with the character he is trying to represent that he becomes that character; witness Flaubert, who, when he was depicting a poisoning, actually felt all the symptoms.

The artist's mental processes, or, for that matter, those of a person experiencing aesthetic pleasure, are in their internal make-up identical at every point to the process that gives rise to great acts of devotion and sacrifice. The man who gives himself wholly to the beauty that he contemplates is at one with it, as the man who gives himself to a group of which he is a part, wholly identifying himself with it, is at one with that group. When we awaken a taste for the beautiful, we open the avenues of the mind to disinterestedness and sacrifice. Anything that prompts man to lose sight of himself, to look beyond and around him, not to consider himself as the center of the world, everything that attaches him to some transcendent objective, cannot but develop in him those habits and tendencies found at the root of morality. We have here, in both cases, the same needs and capacity for getting away from self-centeredness, for opening one's self fully to the outside, for a hospitality to external stimuli and complete absorption in them. In one sense, aesthetic education shapes the will to moral ends and can therefore prepare the student for his moral education.

However, looking at the reverse side of the coin, we find that aesthetic education diverges radically from moral education.

The domain of art is not that of reality. Although the images that the artist presents us are based upon reality, their beauty does not reside in reality. It matters little whether a landscape exists here or there, or whether a dramatic character actually existed historically. It is not because it is historical that we admire the character on the stage; it is because the role is beautifully executed; our emotion would not be diminished in any way if that character were entirely a product of poetic fiction. In fact, the remark has been made with some accuracy that at the very point when illusion is too complete, when the scene portrayed before us has the impact of reality, the sense of beauty vanishes. To be sure, if the men and the things we are looking at were palpably improbable we could not be interested in them, and therefore aesthetic emotion would die stillborn. But all that we require is that the unreality not be too blatant, that it not be altogether implausible. Even so, one cannot determine at what point or at what moment the implausible becomes intolerable. How often the poets make us accept themes which are scientifically absurd and which we know to be such! We lend ourselves as accomplices to error, because we do not want to spoil our aesthetic pleasure. For the artist, there are no laws of nature or history that must always be respected.

The character of a work of art is explained by the fact that it conveys neither percepts nor concepts, but images. The impact of art derives not from our senses or understanding but from our imagination. The artist does not portray things as does the scholar, objectively and impersonally, nor as we ourselves might feel them in the direct experiences of daily life. His business is to arouse in us feelings that, abstracted from reality and through their internal interplay and combination, give us that specific pleasure we call aesthetic. These are images; and images constitute the most plastic of mental phenomena. There is nothing less resistant. Sensation is immediately caused in us by an external stimulus; it is the extension of it in our inner selves. It must therefore reproduce the object of which it is only an aspect. Objective reality being what it is, our sensory apparatus must record whatever aspects of that reality we experience. The concept elaboratetd by science also has as its function the expression of reality —although in a different way than sensation; therefore, the concept must also pattern itself on reality. The image, on the contrary, is a thing apart, altogether privileged. It is not caused by the external impact of an object, of which it is only the internal extension. It is no longer the product of a severely regulated scientific elaboration. It is free. Although subordinate to an external reality, which it would represent, it is malleable almost at will. It depends above all on our whim and internal disposition. Depending on how we handle it, it changes—becomes brighter or darker, more vivid or dull. Images are not compelled to express the real inter-relations of things. They may combine in the most capricious manner, depending on our conscious or unconscious desires. They are, therefore, not bound by the hard necessities govern-ing nature. That is why, in a manner of speaking, natural laws do not exist for the artist, and why, generally speaking, the domain of art is not reality. The artist's world is the world of images, and the world of images is the world of dreams, of untrammeled mental play.

From this point of view, there is genuine opposition be-tween art and ethics. Art, we maintain, makes us live in an imaginary environment. By this very fact it detaches us from reality, from the concrete beings—individual and collective—that compose it. People say, do they not, that the real service that art performs is to make us forget life as it is and men as they are? Quite to the contrary, the world of morals is precisely the world of the real. Morality demands that we love the group of which we are a part, the men who compose this group, the land they live on—all concrete and real things, which we must see as they are, even though we are trying to perfect them as much as possible. Morals are in the do-main of action, and there is no action divorced from specific objects of reality. To do one's duty is always to serve some other actual living being. The realm of art diverges from that of moral life since it departs from reality. Thus, it is only in part and in limited ways that the habits developed by aes-thetic education can be compared to moral habits properly speaking. The two spheres of aesthetics and morals are alike in their internal organization: both tend to draw the individ-ual out of himself. The one links us only to images, purely mental creations; while the other relates us to the world of the living. We must see people as they are—their ugliness and wretchedness—if we want to help them. Art faces the other way; its orientation is very different. Wherever morality is rooted simply in aesthetic principles it dissipates itself and vanishes, in a manner of speaking, in pure imaginative play. It takes refuge in vague if lofty daydreams, instead of resting upon definite and effective actions aimed at maintaining or transforming reality. The impact of a wholly artistic education is all too often to induce some men to elaborate ideas and ideals, which they contemplate with affection and indolence, instead of energetically participating in the common life.

This antagonism could be expressed in the following manner: Art has often been compared to a game; indeed, these two kinds of activities are closely related. When we play, just as when we contemplate a work of art, we experience an imaginary life, which as a matter of fact would lose its entire charm if it were indistinguishable from real life. If we like to play cards or roll dice, it is because the contest implied in these games is not without a certain similarity to the contests that pit us against each other in everyday life. But let that resemblance be too complete, e.g., when the stakes are too high and therefore too close to the regular income we receive from our work, the pleasure of the game disappears. We become serious, we once more become earnestly engaged in what we are doing. We are no longer playing. Thus, it is imagination that lends interest to the game, an imagination that does not fool us. That interest is the product of an illusion, but an illusion of which we are aware, an illusion of which we must be aware lest it become too complete.

Similarly, a work of art would not interest us if it had no connection with reality. But, on the other hand, it would cease to be a work of art for us if we mistook the beings and events represented by it for reality and if we evinced the same feelings for them that we have for real things and beings. Games and art allow us to live in a world of images, which we know to be precisely that; these combinations of images constitute the pleasure of the game, as they constitute the pleasure of art. In a sense, we might say that art is a game. Morality, on the contrary, is life in earnest. It is in fact the most serious part of real living. It is easy to see at a glance the distance separating art and morality; it is the very distance that separates play from work. Not therefore by learning to play that special game, art, will we learn to do our duty.

However, this is not to say that art has nothing to do with moral education. Quite the contrary. What we have just said permits us to determine its appropriate function and what we may expect of it. Art, we suggest, is a game; but games are a part of life. We cannot work all the time. We cannot always make that effort. The concentration of energy implied by single-minded striving toward a given end is something almost abnormal and cannot last. Relaxation must succeed effort, and activity must sometimes take the form of play. But there are many kinds of play. Some are gross and material; they appeal to gross and selfish and sometimes even brutal instincts, like certain sports; and these are too like our daily battles. Others appeal to sentiments that, although not moral in themselves, are in some respects very close to moral impulses. The game presenting that character in the highest degree is art. As a matter of fact, we have seen how art implies a certain disinterestedness, a certain detachment, a certain remoteness from the coarsest material interests, and how it imparts a certain spiritual tinge to our feelings and will. Art is relevant, because we must have leisure; we must use it worthily, as morally as possible. Art alone gives us the means of doing that. Art is a noble form of play; it is morality extending its action into our hours of leisure and marking it with its own character. This is why it would be well to give all children an aesthetic education. In itself, leisure is always dangerous. In serious life, man is sustained against temptation by the obligation of work. Once his regular work is done he must be able to resist these lapses; and keep busy without debasing himself. When man has acquired artistic capacities he is sheltered against such dangers. However, it is evident at the same time that if art has a part to play in moral education, it is an entirely negative role. Art does not contribute to the formation of moral character. It does not commit one to activities moral in themselves. It is not a positive factor in morality. It is a means of preserving us against certain evil influences once the moral character is formed. This is why I have assigned to aesthetics a secondary and incidental position in this discussion. As we analyze the factors that contribute to the moral education of the child, we are led to the conclusion that aesthetics is not of central significance.

This discussion also helps us to understand why, on the contrary, we attach so much importance to the teaching of science. Morality, we suggest, is life in earnest. It focuses on reality. The actions it demands of us concern beings and things that actually exist around us. Consequently, the better we know these beings and things, the better we are able to do what we ought. The clearer our notion of reality, the more apt we are to behave as we should. It is science that teaches us what is. Therefore, from science, and from it alone, must we demand the ideas that guide action, moral action as well as any other. This is what constitutes the moral bearing of the teaching of science.

We have seen how the physical sciences can and must serve this end: they allow the child to acquire wholesome intellectual habits, which will strengthen his moral conduct. However, there is one reality that above all we must understand and teach since it is the chief object of moral conduct. This is social reality.

It is certain that, since the social world is not separated

by an abyss from the natural world but reproduces its fundamental traits, the physical sciences provide an indisputably useful preparation for morality. Nevertheless, society has its own character, its special constitution; it is therefore important to make known its intrinsic character, to give the child first-hand contact with it. The science of social phenomena is still too undeveloped to be taught in the lower grades. But in the curriculum there is a subject closely akin to sociology that can give the student a very adequate idea of society and the way in which it is linked with the individual. This is history.

To become attached to society, the child must feel in it something that is real, alive, and powerful, which dominates the person and to which he also owes the best of himself. To be sure, if we fall into the trap of obsolete historical teachings and tell the child that modern law was created by Napoleon, that the literature of the seventeenth century was caused by the personal influence of Louis XIV, and that Luther made Protestantism, we will simply maintain that old prejudice we were discussing a while back. This doctrine strengthens old prejudices by attributing history to the making of a few *individuals* instead of recognizing in society a definite nature of its own which imposes itself on men. Worse than that, this prejudice may lead people to identify their country with one man. Today, we no longer need dwell on this naively oversimplified theory of history. For a century now, historians have emphasized the action of the collective and anonymous forces, which move nations because they are the work of nations, because they emanate not from such and such an individual, but from society as a whole. The history of France alone furnishes a thousand examples which give the child an idea of the reality of this impersonal life—feudalism, the crusades, the Renaissance.

There is one thing that may have an even more forceful impact on the student's mind. It is when he is shown, not only how at every moment each of us is affected by the collective action of our contemporaries, but also how each generation depends upon previous generations, how each century continues the work of its predecessors and advances in that path that they have traced for it—even when it thinks it is proceeding in an exactly opposite direction. What more instructive spectacle than to see social life inexorably moving in its own direction despite the endlessly changing composition of its personnel. Now then, there is no need at all to engage students in abstract philosophical considerations concerning the necessity of social evolution. Nothing would be more out of place. The point is simply to give them a strong impression of what historical development is. The point is, above all, to prevent false ideas, still only too current, from taking hold; and the history of this country lends itself admirably to the type of teaching we are proposing. That history, at bottom, has a remarkable unity. Few things are easier to demonstrate than the marvelous continuity with which it develops, from the moment monarchy consolidates itself and subordinates feudalism to it, when the towns appeared, to the French Revolution. The most diverse and contrasting regimes were the unwitting instruments of this achievement, so compelling were the convergent circumstances pushing them in that direction. Absolute monarchy and revolutionary democracy are mutually exclusive; yet the former cleared the way for the latter. I have previously shown how the moral unity of this country, wrought by men of the Revolution, was prepared by the Ancien Régime. The connection between the struggle of the communes, the towns, to assert themselves on the one hand, and the French Revolution on the other is recognized today by everybody. It is also well known that the emancipation of the communes was favored by the kings. We must nevertheless be wary of facile notions about continuity. The teaching of history would be false to its goal if it did not leave the impression that, as a well-known aphorism puts it, history neither begins nor ends anywhere. In order to secure loyalty to the ideas that found their expression at the end of the last century, we need not present them as a sort of unintelligible improvisation. Are they not, on the contrary, clothed with more authority if we show that they were actually the natural product of everything that went on before? Indeed, the glory of the men of the Revolution would not be diminished in this way; true merit is to have drawn out of the historic situation the consequences that it logically implied. Thus, the child and later the adult will understand that rights accorded him today, the liberties he enjoys, the moral dignity he feels —all this is the work not of such and such an individual or of such and such a generation but of that being, personal and impersonal at the same time, we call France. In other words, it is all of society, going back to its most remote reaches, that prepared his emancipation.

To bind the child to the social group of which he is a part, it is not enough to make him feel the reality of it. He must be attached to it with his whole being. There is only one effective way of doing this, and that is by making his society an integral part of him, so that he can no more separate himself from it than from himself. Society is not the work of the individuals that compose it at a given stage of history, nor is it a given place. It is a complex of ideas and sentiments, of ways of seeing and of feeling, a certain intellectual and moral framework distinctive of the entire group. Society is above all a consciousness of the whole. It is, therefore, this collective consciousness that we must instill in the child.

Of course, this penetration of the child's consciousness is effected in part by the mere fact of living, by the autonomous play of human relations. These ideas and sentiments are all around the child, and he is immersed in them by living. But there is another operation much too important to leave to chance. It is the business of the school to organize it methodically. An enlightened mind must select from among the welter of confused and often contradictory states of mind that constitute the social consciousness; it must set off what is essential and vital; and play down the trivial and the secondary. The teacher must bring this about and here again history will furnish him the means to this end.

The point is that to imbue children with the collective spirit it is useless to analyze it abstractly. On the contrary, they must be put in direct contact with this collective spirit. Now, what is the history of a people if not the genius of that people developing through time? By making the history of their country come alive for the children, we can at the same time make them live in close intimacy with the collective consciousness. Is it not through intimate and prolonged contact with a man that we finally get to know him? In this respect, a history lesson is the lesson of experience. But since our national character is immanent in historical events, the child would neither see nor feel them if the teacher did not try to set them off in bold relief, especially highlighting those events that merit it. Once again, the point is not to give a course on the French character. All that is needed is a knowledge of what it is and how to disentangle it from the welter of facts.

Such teaching evidently presupposes that the teacher is not proceeding haphazardly, that he has a clear idea of what the French character is. He must have this if his influence is not to be dissipated, but concentrated on a small number of well-defined points. This is not the time to determine the principal traits of our national character. But there is at least one that I would like to stress, for it seems to me to be a focal point around which others naturally cluster. It is the universalist and therefore cosmopolitan tendency of all our conceptions and productions. This, of course, is one of the characteristics of the mathematical and Cartesian intellect, which I discussed in the last chapter and which is embedded in French thought. Our simplistic thinking and our thirst for rationalism incline us to strip things of their individual and concrete elements and to represent them to ourselves in the most general and abstract form. Precisely because notions of this type are general, because they are denuded of everything that particularizes them, every mind can share them. This is why people have suggested that we think for humanity. When we try to work out a constitution, we set out to construct it, not just for our own exclusive use or with the idea of making it work under the specific conditions prevailing in this country; we want it for all mankind. Hence the declarations of rights valid for all of humanity, for which we have been upbraided in the name of the so-called historical method. The universalist way of seeing things is so fundamentally inherent in our character that our language itself bears the imprint of it. Because it is essentially analytical, it is marvelously suited to expressing this way of thinking. This is what made for its remarkable power of expansion.

Now, as I have shown, it is desirable, even necessary, to go beyond that stage of geometrical simplicity that has so long held us back. But it is possible to do so while conserving that inclination to conceive of things in their impersonal form, which is the very essence of the scientific spirit. We can learn to be no longer content with excessively simplified notions, while at the same time we continue to seek general and intelligible notions. To think scientifically will always be to think in clearcut and definite terms. Of course, as I have shown, we must come to realize that the most elementary concepts are not the most objective; that reality is infinitely complex; and that therefore we can succeed in expressing it only slowly, laboriously, and by using complex systems of distinct concepts; that, as a matter of fact, we will never arrive at anything but an imperfect expression of reality. But a renunciation of distinct and clear-cut ideas would be a renunciation of reason—a fall into mysticism. There can be no question of that. Once again, we are not wrong in seeking clarity in trying to see things reasonably; but we are wrong in having stopped at a level of rationalism that is too elementary, facile, and simple. We can, therefore, develop a keener sense of the complexity of things without losing what is most excellent in an essential tendency of our national character.

If I insist on this aspect of our collective character, it is because here our national consciousness merges with human consciousness, and, in consequence, patriotism and cosmopolitanism also merge. What is our greatest national glory, that to which we should be more devoted than anything else, if not these universal ideas that have spread throughout the world? Of course, in referring thus to cosmopolitanism as a trait of the French mind, I do not mean that among all the nations we have a monopoly, and the exclusive franchise for it. Our cosmopolitanism itself has, in a manner of speaking, its own special, national characteristics and leaves plenty of room for others. What distinguishes it is its intellectualism. We are universalists more in the realm of ideas, so to speak, than in our actions. We think for humanity, perhaps, more often than we act for it. Indeed, not without reason have we been taxed with chauvinism. Because of these contradictory traits—by no means inexplicable—and although in our moral and political conceptions we tend to disregard national differences, we are often excessively sensitive and all too readily shut out foreign ideas, exclude foreigners from our intimate life, and feel very little need, at least until recently, to reach beyond our own lives.

Alongside this intellectual cosmopolitanism, or cosmopolitanism of intellectuals, there may be other kinds that complete it. There may, for example, be economic cosmopolitanism— less personal in its temper, less exclusive, more receptive to people and things from abroad. In a word, each nation conceives of human ideals in its own fashion; among these ideals, there is none that enjoys a sort of supremacy and excellence. Each ideal corresponds to the temperament of the given society. To make people appreciate our society, it is altogether vain to praise it as if it alone were good. A civilized man may love his family without thinking his relatives and children superior to others in intelligence and morality. The only thing we have to make people understand is our own way of contributing to the common good of humanity; we need not fear, on occasion, to show what is necessarily incomplete in our way of life.

Printed in the United States
By Bookmasters